'This is a book filled with surprising insights, humour, and deep wisdom. Ladson Hinton is an unusually bold and creative Jungian psychoanalyst whose genius for original and provocative thinking shines through brightly in these fabulous essays. What a gift that these contributions to the field of psychoanalysis have now been collected and published. I recommend a deep reading of them to all who have been called to bear the burden of working in this soulful tradition.'

Murray Stein, *PhD, author of* Four Pillars of Jungian Psychoanalysis

'This collection of writings by Ladson Hinton invites the reader into a captivating and extended fireside conversation that delightfully ignores the stodgy boundaries that would keep philosophy and psychology apart. With a unique flare for vivid examples, a deep sense of appreciation for history, a vivid capacity to describe meaning in art, and incredibly insightful readings of texts, Hinton draws readers into a deeper and more profound understanding of our shared world. These pieces were not originally written to constitute a coherent whole, but they hold together remarkably well as a series of delightful thought experiments and investigations. To read this book is to make a friend – the kind of friend that gently invites one to think more astutely, to care more effectively, and to live with authenticity and intentionality.'

Eric R. Severson, *Associate Teaching Professor of Philosophy, Seattle University*

'A debt of gratitude is owed Dr. Hessel Willemsen for compiling this remarkable tour of a full, rich, complex analytic life of an esteemed friend and colleague, Dr. Ladson Hinton. The selection of articles retains their vibrancy and relevance in an almost timeless manner. The weaving of Dr. Hinton's personal narrative into the text creates a warm relatedness that invites deeper exploration of the topics offered. Taken as a whole the reader is offered a mosaic of individuation, to be savored repeatedly.'

Joseph Cambray, *PhD, IAAP, Past-president IAAP, Past-President/CEO Pacifica Graduate Institute*

'One of the pleasures of my decades of friendship and collegial discussions with Ladson has been the gift of his wide-ranging perspective on life in general as well as the life of the mind. That view is well represented in this compilation of his writings. A glance at the richness and variety of topics is reminiscent of the many conversations that I had the privilege to partake of with him. While Ladson's leadership and scholarship in the Jungian psychoanalytic perspective are noteworthy, his generosity and wisdom are a gift to all of us.'

Maxine Anderson, *MD, teaches and writes in Seattle, Washington*

'These collected works of Ladson Hinton reflect a deep passion and curiosity about being human – in all its wide-ranging permutations. He has never been content to follow one luminaries' voice, but rather the interdisciplinary thought from diverse and creative scholars. His opus is an intertextual and dialogical montage, originating from early philosophical interests in existence, phenomena and temporality, over pre-existing, hierarchical and essential ideals that lie beyond knowing (Kant).

He illustrates these developing themes throughout his work: *shame as a teacher* (von Eschenbach); seeking *lowly wisdom over the heights of Heaven* (Milton); the medieval Court *Fool*, invoking the fertility of the unconscious, who breaks his King's egoic certainty, sterility and lifelessness; the *decentered subject* (LaPlanche); *the Pharmakon* identifying the *cure in the poison and the poison in the cure* (Plato, Stiegler); societies' *Ominous Transitions* wrought by the *shadow of Enlightenment and modernity*.

These are reflective of the values at his moral core. He's told me often, "We're all just clumps of dirt." Just humus (earth)-human-humble. . . . These dialogical ideas deconstruct the narcissistic, all-knowing subject/self/author/authority-*sameness* that is privileged over the dialogical *otherness* and the multitudinous voices who claim no final answer or end (Dostoevsky, Bakhtin, Levinas). The temporal human experience of being in the messiness and suffering of life calls into question Eternal, Transcendent and pre-existing Truths that attempt to remain above the blows of time.

The wonderful case vignettes scattered throughout his writings bring into bold relief this ethos. They break the stiff confines and intransigence of much of traditional psychiatric and psychoanalytical work, through warmth, humor, deep intuitive presence, and his recognition of the meaningfulness of all psychic experience. He accomplishes this without sacrificing his strong ethical barometer.

I am thrilled, without reservation, to recommend this volume reflecting the profound life and work of Ladson Hinton.'

Kenneth Kimmel, *Jungian psychoanalyst,*
co-founder of the New School for Analytical Psychology

Selected Essays of Ladson Hinton

This volume introduces readers to the work of Jungian psychoanalyst Ladson Hinton and his development of thought in the fields of psychoanalysis and existential philosophy throughout his career.

Working as an analyst for nearly 50 years, strongly emphasizing humility with a central focus on shame and temporality, this new volume edited by friend and colleague Hessel Willemsen encompasses reflections and writings dating from his emergence as a young analyst in 1975 through to the present day. Mindful of the deep and considerable changes in contemporary society, his work provides a helpful lens for understanding how aspects of our politics, technologies and social media underlie our contemporary loss of freedom of thought and experience amidst our time of ominous transitions. Chapters cover topics such as death, foolishness and shame, reconnecting with our animal soul, temporality and Jung's theoretical position on existential philosophy, among many others.

Psychoanalysts, psychotherapists, philosophers, anthropologists and academics and students engaged in cultural studies and critical theory will gain valuable insights through this book's rich and engaging variety of perspectives.

Hessel Willemsen, MA, MSc, DClinPsych (UK), is a training and supervising analyst at the Society of Analytical Psychology. He works as a Jungian psychoanalyst with adults and as a clinical psychologist with children and their parents in the field of child protection and custody. The book *Temporality and Shame: Perspectives from Psychoanalysis and Philosophy*, which he edited with Ladson Hinton, is the winner of the '2018 American Board and Academy of Psychoanalysis Prize' for best edited book. He recently edited *Shame, Temporality and Social Change* (Routledge, 2021), also with Ladson Hinton, which won the 2022 International Association of Jungian Studies' Award for best edited book.

Philosophy and Psychoanalysis Book Series
Series Editor: JON MILLS

Philosophy and Psychoanalysis is dedicated to current developments and cutting-edge research in the philosophical sciences, phenomenology, hermeneutics, existentialism, logic, semiotics, cultural studies, social criticism, and the humanities that engage and enrich psychoanalytic thought through philosophical rigor. With the philosophical turn in psychoanalysis comes a new era of theoretical research that revisits past paradigms while invigorating new approaches to theoretical, historical, contemporary, and applied psychoanalysis. No subject or discipline is immune from psychoanalytic reflection within a philosophical context including psychology, sociology, anthropology, politics, the arts, religion, science, culture, physics, and the nature of morality. Philosophical approaches to psychoanalysis may stimulate new areas of knowledge that have conceptual and applied value beyond the consulting room reflective of greater society at large. In the spirit of pluralism, *Philosophy and Psychoanalysis* is open to any theoretical school in philosophy and psychoanalysis that offers novel, scholarly, and important insights in the way we come to understand our world.

Titles in this series:

A Psycho-Political Analysis of Netanyahu's Israel
The Israeli Anxiety
Itzhak Benyamini

Selected Essays of Ladson Hinton
Psychoanalytic and Existential Reflections on Shame and Temporality
Edited by Hessel Willemsen

Selected Essays of Ladson Hinton

Psychoanalytic and Existential Reflections on Shame and Temporality

Edited by Hessel Willemsen

Routledge
Taylor & Francis Group

LONDON AND NEW YORK

Designed cover image: Paul Klee, Swiss, 1879–1940, *Angelus Novus*, 1920, Oil transfer and watercolor on paper, 318 x 242 mm, Gift of Fania and Gershom Scholem, Jerusalem, John Herring, Marlene and Paul Herring, Jo-Carole and Ronald Lauder, New York, Collection The Israel Museum, Jerusalem, B87.0994, Photo ©The Israel Museum, Jerusalem by Elie Posner

First published 2026
by Routledge
4 Park Square, Milton Park, Abingdon, Oxon OX14 4RN

and by Routledge
605 Third Avenue, New York, NY 10158

Routledge is an imprint of the Taylor & Francis Group, an informa business

© 2026 selection and editorial matter, Hessel Willemsen; individual chapters, the contributors

British Library Cataloguing-in-Publication Data
A catalogue record for this book is available from the British Library

ISBN: 978-1-041-07551-6 (hbk)
ISBN: 978-1-041-07550-9 (pbk)
ISBN: 978-1-003-64106-3 (ebk)

DOI: 10.4324/9781003641063

Typeset in Times New Roman
by Apex CoVantage, LLC

In Ladson's Memory
For his colleagues, friends, his family, and his patients

Contents

Acknowledgments

These Collected Essays are the work of a lifetime of a man steeped in the ordinariness of life. Ladson's friendship and warmth have been invaluable, his work inspiring, and his patience enriching. Ladson died on the 4th of September 2025 and had remained involved in the creation of this collection throughout.

I'd like to thank the members of the New School for Analytical Psychology, specifically, Sharon Green, Kenneth Kimmel, and Robin McCoy Brooks. Their hearts are close to Ladson and his work. I also think of Jeffrey Eaton and Eric Severson, who meant much to Ladson.

There are many colleagues and friends who helped and were encouraging. I am grateful to my family for their patience and the time this work has taken me away from them.

Sarah Dadson and Pramila Bennett have studiously worked on editorial tasks, and Manon Berset of Routledge has made the process of production and editing so much easier to cope with.

Front Cover Description (Paperback)

In the ninth thesis of his 1940 essay "Theses on the Philosophy of History", Benjamin describes *Angelus Novus* as an image of the angel of history:

A Klee painting named Angelus Novus *shows an angel looking as though he is about to move away from something he is fixedly contemplating. His eyes are staring, his mouth is open, his wings are spread. This is how one pictures the angel of history. His face is turned toward the past. Where we perceive a chain of events, he sees one single catastrophe which keeps piling wreckage upon wreckage and hurls it in front of his feet. The angel would like to stay, awaken the dead, and make whole what has been smashed. But a storm is blowing from Paradise; it has got caught in his wings with such violence that the angel can no longer close them. The storm irresistibly propels him into the future to which his back is turned, while the pile of debris before him grows skyward. This storm is what we call progress.*

Benjamin, W. (1969), "Theses on the Philosophy of History", *Illuminations*, trans. Harry Zohn, New York: Schocken Books, p. 249.

Foreword

This volume encompasses reflections and writings dating from my emergence as a young analyst, newly graduated from the C. G. Jung Institute of San Francisco in 1975. Viewing the list of my writings immerses me in a flow, a perspective, a core of wellsprings that have fed the core of who I am and the subjects and perspectives that I pursued – and that pursued me – over a lifetime. These threads of reflection stemmed from experiences that were sometimes small vestiges that often grew slowly but were sometimes intrusive and dramatic, some dating from childhood to the present. They were not necessarily 'inner' or 'outer', but took on the particular coloring of the timing and circumstances of my life. These were the factors that drew me, sometimes quietly demanding attention, other times shaking me to my core.

After completing analytic training, I needed to renew a sense of flow of trust in my own ideas and judgment, and the present volume consists of writings after that time. However, open and stimulating an analytic training program may be, every candidate, to some degree, falls into the fantasy of being "the one who knows", of now being one of the *cognoscenti*! Hidden beneath 'knowing' lies the threat of another, deeper knowing: the hidden shame that knowledge is always, to some degree, lacking: what is desired is Being itself, but our knowledge is always incomplete.

The Fool's motley, in its colorful disarray, signifies that experience can never be fully integrated. Indeed, we are all, to some degree, fools. Our lack is humbling and makes us feel like fools. Shame in all its forms reminds us of that fact. However, without that humbling awareness, thought becomes dogmatic and dead, and authority becomes tyrannical and deathlike. This is a crucial lesson for both individuals and nations. Humor is the main assistant to the fool and is an embodiment in words and manner of a truth that is not absolute and needs to be constantly tested by the 'facts of life'. Shame can be a demon, but it is our most useful teacher. Without shame, tyrannies proliferate. The wise Fool and laughter, supported by devoted scholarship, are the best antidotes for cruelties, fears, and pomposities that block the flow of life.

Temporality is a basic thread that recurs throughout my writings. I consider this as lived life, the time that lies at the core of the human. We seem to be the only creature that anticipates death at some unknown time in the future. Faced with this fact, we love one another and – all too often – destroy one another. The shadow of death always lies before us as *homo* temporalis: creatures who are limited, bounded by time, but with the capacity for living lives with a portion of virtue and integrity that is sometimes remarkable.

I am deeply grateful to my friend and editor, Hessel Willemsen, for his talented and persistent efforts to put my writings together as a coherent whole. Without his devotion to the project, it could not have taken place.

In addition, my deepest thanks to family, friends, mentors, and colleagues too numerous to mention, who have supported and fostered my creative perspectives over the decades.

Ladson Hinton

Introduction

This book is the culmination of a lifetime of work – personal, intellectual, and clinical. It gathers essays that reflect Ladson Hinton's evolution as a Jungian analyst and existential thinker, deeply engaged with the complexities of the human condition. Each chapter is written with the clarity and warmth of someone devoted to understanding others not merely as cases or concepts, but as fellow beings navigating the intricacies of life, death, meaning, time, and shame.

Although the volume follows the chronological development of Ladson Hinton's professional work, it opens with his final essay and an accompanying interview. These set the stage for recurring themes that ripple throughout the book: temporality, death, shame, the limits of human understanding, and the importance of imagination and myth. At the heart of Hinton's philosophy is the conviction that the personal and the philosophical, the clinical and the existential, are inseparably intertwined.

In confronting death, Hinton defines temporality as our most fundamental reality – our essential humanity. Death, he argues, is not only a biological event but also a confrontation with the absolute limits of being. It resists intellectual containment, exposes the illusion of control, and forces recognition of our ontological vulnerability. Reflecting on the Holocaust and personal family history, he evokes the "Infernal Machine" – the machinery of hatred and genocide – as a grim counterpoint to our capacity for reflection and care. Against this backdrop, death becomes paradoxically intertwined with freedom, as life is understood as a being-toward-death.

An interview sheds light on Hinton's philosophical lineage. Drawing on Husserl, Heidegger, and the phenomenological tradition more generally, he describes the development of ideas grounded in the lived experience of lack, incompleteness, and suffering. These concepts invite a humble, dialogical stance toward others and the world – one shaped not by mastery, but by shared limitations.

Shame, a central focus of Hinton's work, is explored in "Fools, Foolery and Feeling Foolish", one of Hinton's earlier works. He distinguishes between the unconscious fool, who denies lack, and the conscious fool, who embraces it creatively. Shame emerges as the emotional response to the recognition of limitation – an ontological experience as much as a moral one. Humor,

DOI: 10.4324/9781003641063-1

imagination, and the archetype of the fool become paths to wholeness, offering a way to reconcile with our own imperfection.

In subsequent chapters, Hinton extends his exploration to our relationship with nature. He posits that reconnection with the "animal soul" is vital for human authenticity and ecological survival. Drawing on Jung's *Vision Seminars* and mythological imagery such as the unicorn in medieval tapestries, he calls for a renewed engagement with the mystery and vitality of the mythical world.

The idea of the "black hole" – a metaphor for psychic and cultural void – is examined as a hallmark of modern alienation. These gaps in being, far from purely negative, can serve as generative spaces from which new insight and creativity emerge. The unconscious is not simply a repository of trauma but a dialogue with the enigmatic, a place where the symbolic and the real meet.

In Chapters 8 through 15, Hinton develops his ideas in rich philosophical, literary, and clinical contexts – from critiques of Jung's archetypal theory in light of existential temporality to reflections on Joseph Conrad's *Lord Jim*, consumer culture, and the ethical implications of technological progress. Hinton challenges idealised unity (as in the concept of the *Unus Mundus*), arguing instead for a more fractured, embodied understanding of truth and human experience.

The modern world has witnessed a collapse of faith in the idea of linear, enlightened progress. War, genocide, terrorism, and economic instability have challenged long-held assumptions about human development and the psyche's teleological unfolding. Alongside this, there is increasing skepticism toward the notion of a coherent Self or central agent guiding psychological life. Contemporary thought has shifted toward understanding the subject as *decentered*, developing in response to a pervasive and enigmatic Otherness.

Jean Laplanche offers a profound metapsychology to describe this condition. He foregrounds the infant's primordial vulnerability, immersed from birth in enigmatic messages from the adult world – messages often unconsciously imbued with sexual meaning. This dynamic, which he terms *primal seduction*, leaves the child unable to fully assimilate such content. Instead, through *primal repression*, these experiences form the unconscious core of subjectivity. They persist as internal enigmas – messages that seem to signify something essential but whose meaning is never fully available, like stumbling upon a cryptic hieroglyph in a desert. Human development, culture, and relationships are ongoing efforts to decode these messages. An analytic case study demonstrates how such dynamics emerge in the transference – initially through gaps, monsters, and fragmentation, but ultimately through moments of surprising, transformative laughter. These clinical encounters highlight the centrality of the enigmatic signifier in shaping the subject.

Time itself plays a pivotal role in the birth of consciousness. With the evolution of temporal awareness came the ability to anticipate future dangers – spurring the formation of protective cultures and rich symbolic life through poetry, religion, and art. Psychoanalysis, deeply temporal in nature, seeks to reconnect individuals with their past, helping to metabolise experience and cultivate reflective awareness. Building on Freud's foundations, theorists like Lacan and Laplanche have made temporality central to psychoanalytic theory. Their work suggests a rhythmic, non-linear unfolding of psychic life. A substantial clinical case illustrates how memory and temporality shape the analytic process, while ideas from recent neuroscience on memory and mental "time travel" echo and are drawn upon to enrich these psychoanalytic insights. Importantly, accepting the contradictions of temporal experience can open space for greater freedom and imaginative engagement with the self and others.

This discussion contrasts Jung's archetypal psychology with existential philosophy, particularly the work of Martin Heidegger. In *Being and Time*, Heidegger sought the primordial ground (*arché*) of being but eventually turned toward a hermeneutic approach, emphasizing interpretation over metaphysical certainty. For existentialists, the dictum that "existence precedes essence" captures a foundational truth: human life is defined not by preexisting forms but by contingency, temporality, and radical openness. In this view, freedom emerges from an absence of fixed structure – a position that stands in sharp contrast to Jung's belief in archetypes as timeless, Platonic realities.

Jung's model privileges the "eternal" and often downplays the temporality of personal experience. The personal unconscious, for Jung, primarily serves to usher forth archetypal material from a timeless realm. In doing so, his theory risks minimizing the existential significance of lived time and ethical responsibility. In contrast, existential thought sees awareness of death and the passage of time as central to selfhood. As a Jungian analyst, he argues that Jung's perspective on time stands at odds with existential practice, which emphasises living authentically in the face of mortality.

Shame, temporality, and truth are core concepts for understanding the human condition today. Hinton stays close to his own experiences as a guide to his thinking and describes a vivid encounter on the streets of Seattle that reveals emerging psychological and social undercurrents. This episode, along with other clinical and cultural examples, provides a window into how shame and temporality shape both individual and collective life. Philosophical and psychoanalytic reflections expand upon these observations, all grounded in a concern for the future of human meaning.

From an ethical standpoint, temporality sheds light on C.G. Jung's psychology. A brief historical genealogy shows how temporality and culture are intimately linked. Aristotle contrasted *phronesis* – practical, time-bound wisdom – with *epistêmê*, timeless theoretical knowledge. Jung, influenced by Platonic traditions, often privileged archetypal timelessness over temporal, ethical awareness. His early work, such as *The Seven Sermons to the Dead*, illustrates this emphasis. Later in life, however, Jung's engagement with alchemy and the *prima materia* – the raw material of lived experience – signals a turn toward valuing the temporal and embodied aspects of psyche. Letters from his final years show signs of this evolving view, which begins to integrate the timeless and the everyday.

The idea of *unsilencing* – bringing hidden truths to light – is central to psychoanalysis. It requires acknowledging the buried dramas that shape human lives.

Oedipus, for example, evaded the truth of his origins until memory's return erupted in horror, shame, and insight. Psychoanalytic work involves turning ghosts into ancestors, giving voice to what was once unspeakable. Shame plays a paradoxical role here: it can stall time, freezing development, but it can also interrupt the flow of habit, creating space for reflection. Shame signals disruptions in our sense of self-coherence and often carries profound ontological weight. Primo Levi, reflecting on Auschwitz, described feeling shame not for his own actions but for the fact that such atrocities were humanly possible. Shame, in this light, becomes a compass pointing us toward moral and existential truth – not through conformity, but through creativity, confrontation, and renewal.

Ultimately, this volume is an invitation to live more reflectively and courageously in time – to feel our way through the enigmas of shame, death, and otherness. Hinton proposes that only through this engagement can we rediscover depth in our personal lives, our relationships, and the cultural psyche.

Chapter 1

Love, Death and the Infernal Machine*

Tyger, Tyger burning bright,
In the forests of the night:
What immortal hand or eye
Dare frame thy fearful symmetry?
                    William Blake, 1794

Introduction

Death exceeds all efforts to escape it and defies our capacity to understand. And yet we continually reflect and wonder about it, in fear, or in shame at our vulnerability, peering into that abyss. We are creatures who must live within the parameter of time . . . transient creatures who are time-bound, who die.

Death remains something whose nature is inapparent. Why is human life so transient? We do our thing and are good and foolish and sometimes evil. Then life ends. No religion or mythology or mystical revelation has provided a satisfactory final answer.

However, amidst the failures of our efforts to understand, something draws us back to death, something hidden or inapparent. That is part of its phenomenology. We want to understand, but the subject is endlessly elusive. Death itself is a fact, and that fact invokes a penumbra of uncanniness, invoking an urgent passion to know more, or to flee. A meditation on the penumbra, the experiential surround of death in multiple situations, can perhaps expand our knowledge in a subtle way that has its own kind of truth. Such a phenomenology of death may provide a more nuanced sort of knowledge and have more 'depth' than a gross facticity (Inverso, 2022).

* Hinton, L. (2024). Love, Death, and the Infernal Machine. In: Luis Moris (ed.). *Confronting Death.* Asheville, NC, Chiron Publications. Reprinted with permission.

DOI: 10.4324/9781003641063-2

We human beings endlessly return to questions of life and death. That is part of its phenomenology. Death pulls us, provokes us, seduces us to endlessly fear and wonder about it. Religions all have their deep and thoughtful reflections, mythologies and promises. Tyrants and criminals try to project death into sub-groups of others, declaring them, among other things, 'unworthy life'. Ritual killings – in war or otherwise – seem are all too common in human history. In the 20th century, Nazism and the Cambodian Khmer Rouge provided vivid examples. Cults of death bring forth the most terrible dimensions of human be-ings. It is important to try and understand such phenomena, rather than merely recoil in horror. That is try personal experience of death as well as social vio-lence; death as an 'Infernal Machine' of horror and mystery is always poten-tially present in our personal and social lives.

The interconnection of psychoanalysis and death is so strong that some have suggested that *hauntology* should replace the term *psychoanalysis* (Gunn, 2006). Amidst this gargantuan history, I can only offer my own experiences of death and the torments of being a time-bound creature (Hin-ton, 2015). Such sharing can be deeply gratifying as we go along our paths in the world. There is penumbra around death that often brings us closer to others as well as ourselves. I hope that my own narrative of death will contribute a small amount to that endeavour. I have not indulged in conclu-sions about the subject and will leave that to the imagination and intellect of my readers.

I will begin by describing some early childhood experiences of death, then proceed towards the present.

Death

My first conscious memory of death is viewing the dead body of my great-grandfather on my father's side. Augustus 'Papa' Reichert had died at age 88 of 'old age' when I was 8 years old. His parents were German immigrants from Saxony who had settled in Fort Smith, Arkansas, in the mid-19th century. Papa's father was a shoemaker, and Papa had become a Master Plumber at a time when indoor plumbing was all the rage. The Re-ichert family was prosperous, with a large home near the centre of town – a small city of 34,000 when I was born in 1934.

The Reichert family was Lutheran, and Papa's body was laid out in an open coffin in the large dining room, which was lighted by a colourful Tif-fany chandelier that I liked. I can still recall my sense of boredom and restlessness when visiting there as a child, perhaps echoing the mood of my mother when she was around that side of the family. Mother was a divorcee – a somewhat taboo situation at that time, in that culture. She had felt they were judgmental.

I surveyed the open coffin across the dining room. My younger female cousins were playing on the floor near it. A mood came over me, like I was frozen or suspended. I think I saw some adults come by and kiss Papa on the forehead. That seemed to be the expected behaviour, but I felt totally incapable of even approaching the casket, much less kissing him (Actually, I have no memory of ever kissing him!). The cousins were all younger girls, and they seemed to have no problem with being around dead Papa. My shame was great.

My usual 'escape' from the family gatherings at that old house had been to go to the large glass-fronted bookcase in the living room and look through the books. That's what I did that day. It was a refuge, and I could let my shame subside. The books could be interesting, and I was a precocious reader.

I can still feel my paralysing anxiety regarding the coffin and Papa's dead body, along with the strong sense of shame. As I sit now at the desk in my study, writing this remembrance of death, that same bookcase is at my right hand, full of favourite tomes! The Hinton Coat of Arms is on the wall to my upper right, and a reproduction of Klee's painting, the *Angel of History* – so beloved by Walter Benjamin – is on my upper left. Continuity with the past is quite apparent!

***

World War II began in 1941, and the outbreak of war was very frightening to me. I clearly recall the first news of the Japanese attack on Pearl Harbor and how scary it felt. President Franklin Roosevelt's radio speech announcing a Declaration of War on Germany and Japan impacted me greatly, and I feared the Japanese might bomb our house, although we lived in the middle of the United States, far from both the Atlantic and Pacific Oceans. I recall crying, feeling very fearful of death and destruction, as I played with my toy soldiers on the floor near the large radio. I asked my dad whether 'they' would bomb our house, and he kindly reassured me. Nevertheless, war and death were strongly in the air. The world no longer seemed safe.

When the war ended in 1945, I was eleven and had another memorable experience concerning death. My Uncle Ken, who was married to my favourite aunt, returned home from service in the US Army Medical Corps.

He was a strong early influence on me, a gregarious masculine presence who was a contrast to my more reticent father. After World War II began, he volunteered for military service because he was the youngest physician in the clinic where he practiced internal medicine. He felt it was his duty, and I deeply admired that.

When my uncle left for military service, he gave me his young dog, a fierce Airedale Terrier. 'Frankie – short for Frankenstein – became my faithful companion for the next dozen years of my life. I intermittently sent simple letters to Ken while he was in Europe and faithfully followed the progression of the war in the newspaper. Often, there were maps, including specific units like my uncle's, marking the progress of the American army in Europe.

When he returned after the war, I didn't see much of him at first and heard that he was in a strange state, maybe a bit 'shell-shocked'. A few weeks after his return, my aunt asked me to stop by and say hello, and I was happy to comply. I biked to their home a few blocks from mine, and we sat down in the living room. He gave me a German helmet that he had transported back. Then he offered to show me some photos. I was, of course, extremely curious.

He was an excellent amateur photographer and had managed to get film to photograph a lot of his experiences. There were photos of meeting the advance units of the Russian army coming from the East. He said the Russians were generally friendly towards him but 'uncivilised' towards German civilians. He said he had several times witnessed them 'attacking' German women and then throwing them in the river, where the American soldiers would often try to rescue them.

What struck me most strongly were photos of the concentration camps his units had liberated. There were stacks of skeletal bodies, as well as a few tattered figures in ragged, striped clothed – that looked to me like pyjamas – walking around. I must have looked upset because he gave a little clarification. He told me, 'Laddie, that's what Hitler did to the Jews'. He said very little more. It was a powerful shock. Our family had Jewish friends, and I had Jewish pals. Those photos and that experience with my uncle could have happened yesterday. The impact has never left my mind and has affected me in many ways. The world contains death-makers who might kill anyone for no reason.

Many years later, when I was a young psychiatrist in practice, married with family, my uncle and I had a long conversation that was special and moving. He was probably in his late eighties. I was visiting at his home with my wife and children and saw a brochure from a veterans' organisation lying on a table. I asked him whether he was still active in that group. He said he wasn't, but it set off a long conversation, which led into more memories of World War II. He especially focused on the 'Battle of the Bulge', in the Ardennes Forest in France, a last desperate German attempt to turn back the Allies before they reached the homeland. There was extensive fog for days, and the US and Allies could not use their rule of the air. The German artillery ('88s') had a longer range than the Americans, who had to hunker down and survive until the weather changed. My uncle described the endless shelling and feeling terribly helpless. He had to take care of the many wounded, whom it was difficult to evacuate. Ken broke down in sobs when describing the experience, including a close friend who was blown up, standing just beside him. Death had clearly been his companion throughout the rest of his life. I have never forgotten his stories and those photos . . . further evidence of death and horror in the world.

***

When I was a junior in college, I had a powerful 'inner' experience with death that dramatically changed the course of my life. I was feeling aimless and uncertain about the future. Because of my uncle, I had considered becoming a physician. However, I had never much liked the sciences but enjoyed my studies in literature and history. Graduate studies were mildly appealing, but not engaging. My teachers seemed okay, but not inspiring. In that context, a fateful sequence of inner and outer events disrupted my life.

I was barely 20 and had transferred to Southern Methodist University in Dallas, Texas, to be near an 'older woman' of 24! I was in love! She was an artist, teaching at a private school. I still recall one of her paintings of a beautiful young woman who had a tear coursing down her cheek. We had lively and engrossing conversations, often losing track of time. Erotic feelings were in the air but minimally expressed. Her level of maturity in the relationship was greater than mine, but I was persistent. This pattern continued for several weeks, and then one day she said that we had to talk about something important. It turned out that she had a strong barrier in our relationship because she and her family were traditional Roman Catholics – and I was from a Protestant background. She couldn't consider a deep relationship unless I converted. I was not only totally shocked but also proud and stubborn and angry. I broke off the relationship. In retrospect, I think that her stand was at least partially an excuse because she realised how immature I was. In any case, I felt deeply wounded, dejected and lost.

Soon after that, I was alone during the late afternoon in my little apartment in Dallas, reading *The Brothers Karamazov*. I fell asleep and had a dream/vision of death that changed the course of my life: in the dream, I was lying in the gutter of a golden road in a deep forest, clearly dying. A deep male voice, absolute and powerful, pronounced, *You will go to medical school!* I awakened in a panic, terrified.

A simple dream in structure, but the affective punch was powerful and pervaded my being. Warned of death along the road of life! It is difficult to convey, in writing, the absolute certainty of that voice, that time when I was alone and bereft in my little apartment. I was terrified. The message was simple, and I had no doubt that *the choice was life or death*. It felt like an absolute commandment and radically changed the course of my life.

My immediate sense of urgency was unequivocal. I was quite literally unable to attend classes that didn't relate to a pre-med course of studies and received a lot of incompletes. I couldn't even walk through the entrance to a classroom or lecture hall if it didn't relate to my goal. I meditated a lot and became more ascetic. At times, I feared I was crazy, but I had a profoundly clear sense of what I had to do. It was live or die. I had my orders. No choice at all! I soon told my parents that I was 'changing my major;' and they were emotionally and financially supportive. Recalling now their accepting love and kindness, I feel a deep sense of gratitude.

Once during that time, I saw a sign at the student infirmary about a psychiatrist being available at certain hours and impulsively went back later. However, they were not there at the hour advertised. Years later, my analyst remarked that I was lucky! The likelihood of my experience being misunderstood would have been great, and I could easily have been medicalised.

I didn't share my experience with anyone until 4 years later, when I told the story to my wife-to-be. She was the first person. Her understanding was a part of the early, basic cement for our 60 years of marriage. We sometimes had differences over the years, but whatever the turbulence, a level of deeper trust and bonding was always there.

My experience of death helped ground me, provided discipline and fostered a supply of energy and focus that generally persists to this day. I can feel it as I write. It has often given me at least a grain of confidence, whatever the turbulence. The encounter with death opened many authentic gateways to life and enabled me to be who I am. It provided a standard that has served me well, a sense of what is authentic and what is B.S. Death is a wise but demanding teacher!

*****

To return to the earlier thread of my story: I married and graduated from Washington University (in St. Louis) Medical School in 1961. At that time, the US military was expanding in size due to tensions with the Soviet Union, and I was drafted into the Army Medical Corps in 1962, during my internal medicine internship at Georgetown University Hospital in Washington, D.C. (At that time, a year of clinical/medical internship was required before entering training in psychiatry.) I was offered the option of entering the army in 1962 as a general medical officer, or entering 3 years later, after both the internship and a subsequent three-year residency in psychiatry at Stanford University Hospital. The Medical Corps had a shortage of psychiatrists, so they were willing to wait!

My medical internship itself was demanding, scary and deeply gratifying. We had two small children at the time, and I was on call every other night at the hospital. My wife was extraordinarily hardworking and loving, and I remain eternally grateful to her for that. It was a time of deep initiation for her as well as for me.

Georgetown Hospital was a large general hospital, sharing responsibilities for medical emergencies with District of Columbia General Hospital. The University was administered by the Jesuit Religious Order, and the hospital was administered by Roman Catholic Sisters. It was not sectarian in spirit, and I, with my Protestant background, felt a congenial welcome there. I liked the religious aura in the background and the Jesuit respect for learning.

The maelstrom of emergency care and recovery . . . or death was intense. During most of my rotations, I was on call for 36 hours and off 12 with, as I recall, a two-week vacation. The experience was demanding and sometimes scary. Georgetown was an acute care hospital, and severe illness and death were common. It was a core role of the medical interns to draw blood samples for testing very early each morning, before rounds and daily routines began.

Among the many responsibilities, a core role was to break the news of deaths to families and to request permission for an autopsy. Often, the interns were the ones who pronounced the patient dead. I discovered that it is often difficult to know when someone is dead! Perhaps there is now a more precise measure. I know that most of the interns mentioned a nightmare of having made an error, of corpses arising ghoulishly from their coffins and the like. It was an unforgettable initiation into both the deep grief of families and rituals of death that go back to the origins of human culture. Funeral/burial objects are perhaps the earliest cultural artifacts (Knight et al., 1995). *Homo sapiens* seems to be the creature that most fully knows of its own mortality.

At the graduation banquet at the end of training, I received a small verbal recognition for having had the least deaths on my services during my year at Georgetown. As I recall, the number was 26. It was totally unexpected. I had not been forewarned. It was evidently a customary thing, among other, more major awards that were given with large custom plaques. I was deeply gratified because I had sometimes felt inferior to other interns who were major scientific intellects, many of whom went on to careers in academia. I later joked that my own fear of death had motivated me, and that is clearly part of the truth!

***

After my year at Georgetown, I crossed the country with my young family to begin 3 years of psychiatric training at Stanford University Hospital in Palo Alto, California. I had had a difficult time deciding between a residency at Massachusetts General Hospital in Boston and Stanford. I really enjoyed my interviews at 'Mass General'. The faculty was very open and dynamic, although a bit more on the traditional side. California was at the core of a new horizon in America and a world centre of the 'New Age'.

Indeed, new and exciting things filled the air at Stanford, as well as the whole Bay Area. I quickly caught the scent of the spirit that was beginning to emerge. At Stanford, David Hamburg had just begun as Chair of Psychiatry, and new beginnings were in the air. Hamburg had psychiatry residents designated as 'Fellows of the University', and that appealed to me. We were encouraged to take advantage of the possibilities of the larger University, and not remain ensconced within a narrow medical enclave. Irv Yalom, the Existentialist, soon became one of my clinical supervisors. William Dement, the co-discoverer of REM sleep, arrived and was an active teacher. Karl Pribram, a pioneer in the neuropsychology of brain processing, had his monkey lab not far from my office at Stanford Medical Center. Don Jackson, who had trained under Harry Stack Sullivan, was an early and influential supervisor.

My training group of seven psychiatric residents was lively and diverse. One of them was Tom Kirsch, who added an important part among all the eclectic influences whirling around me.

The informal learning was lively and intense. I recall long discussions of the *Case of Ellen West*, a key chapter in Rollo May's pioneering, early work on Existential Psychotherapy (Binswanger, 1958). It was the story of a young woman who ended her life by choosing death after extensively trying multiple forms of therapy for her disabling symptoms, without success. Ludwig Binswanger, the pioneer of *Daseinanalysis*, was her psychiatrist. Carl Rogers later disagreed with Binswanger's conclusions. I recall many intense discussions about this case. I ended by siding with Rogers! This experience stimulated thoughts and questions about death and hopefully conveys the depth of my psychiatric education at Stanford. I feel grateful for that.

During my last year of residency, we were encouraged to undertake special studies in some area that had stimulated us during training. Tom Kirsch and I chose a year-long period of studies with Kurt Reinhardt, a Professor Emeritus at Stanford who was still actively writing and teaching. He was born and educated in Germany and was the author of *The Existential Revolt*, as well as a monumental study of German history (Reinhardt, 1960). It was a fateful decision for me because I had also seriously considered working in the Dream Lab of William Dement. I went with my heart and took the less conventional course. Perhaps my decision was affected by the earlier death experiences, to take and trust the less-known path. Death and freedom do often seem connected!

Reinhardt had been at the University of Freiburg as a young student and attended Martin Heidegger's lectures. Tom Kirsch and I met with Kurt for two hours every other week, slowly reading and reflecting together. He suggested we begin with *Being and Time*, which had recently been released in its first English translation (Heidegger, 1962). It was a transformative experience to study with this revered teacher and philosopher for a year. Life as being-towards-death was at the centre of my studies!

Is the basic being of the human indeed Temporality? This reversed the ancient tradition that privileged eternal iterations of (Platonic) ideas that were atemporal, beyond time and deathless. In contrast, under the Heideggerian aegis of being-towards-death, temporality is our fundamental reality, and death is the most profound manifestation of our boundedness by temporality. We know that we are creatures who die. Temporality is our core being and our core humanity. This is the insight that Kurt Reinhardt power-fully reinforced in my worldview, and I will always be grateful to him.

***

After finishing my residency, at least 2 years of military service were re-quired. I had originally been drafted into military service as a general prac-titioner while I was at Georgetown but instead agreed to go into military service later, after completing my specialty training in psychiatry. I, like many others at that time, considered it a primal duty to serve the country – and there was often some travel and adventure involved!

The military allowed doctors to state their preferred geographical area for service, and I had chosen Europe. Family housing and transport were to be provided. There was a large contingent of American military forces in Germany, as well as many American families, for whom housing, schooling for children and commissaries for groceries and other general needs were available. Indeed, there was an entire American sub-community in Europe at that time, mainly in Germany.

Especially with the example of my uncle, I saw military service as part of my duty as a citizen and had no resentment about being drafted. To my mind, the Soviet Union was an aggressive threat to Western culture, and Com-munism was an ideology that had gone terribly wrong and was a threat to the freedom of the citizenry. In addition, my uncle had had some significant interactions with Soviet military people at the end of the war and had a very strong reaction to the atrocities that he thought were perpetrated on German civilians. The Russian officers did not seem to control acts of revenge on civilians. He thought this reflected basic cultural differences.

The German civilians largely welcomed the Americans, even as they continued rebuilding their bombed-out cities. There was a strong fear of the Russians and often a sense of shame about being betrayed and misled into horrible crimes by Nazi leaders. This was the cultural surround that greeted me and my family in West Germany. Once we were settled in an apartment in a pleasant, small area of housing for military families near downtown Munich, I could turn towards my military/professional duties.

My unit, the 24th Infantry Division, had small clinics in Munich and Augsburg. As a Captain and physician, I was the chief psychiatric medical officer for all military personnel and their families in Southwest Germany. There were thousands at that time. As my administrator, I had a military-trained psychiatric social worker who was also an officer, as well as ten or so college graduates, enlisted men who had been trained in interviewing, along with a modicum of diagnostic knowledge.

In addition, I discovered that I was responsible for a military stockade (small prison) in Dachau, not far from Munich. The jail had been one part of the infamous concentration camp, where 'people of special interest' to the Nazi regime had been held: political prisoners, Russian officers and the like. After the war, it was administered by the US Army Military Police, and it was used as a prison for members of the military.

This was not the camp that was liberated by my uncle's unit during the war but was the first 'concentration camp', built prior to World War II, originally for political prisoners. Munich, nearby, had been a hotbed of the Nazi movement. After the war, the Dachau prison had become a US Army stockade, administered by the Military Police. Not surprisingly, this assignment immediately aroused my curiosity. One of the experienced enlisted men who worked in one of my clinics volunteered to drive me to Dachau to see the premises and meet the Commanding Officer.

It was an hour or so drive through Munich's suburbia. Then the camp came into view. I caught sight of the famous sign typical of all the camps, an immensely ironic and iconic wrought iron sign over the gate reading *Arbeit Macht Frei*! (Work makes free!) It was notorious, and it was a shock. The Nazi propaganda had framed the camps as a place where 'unworthy' or 'lazy' elements of society could learn how to be honest, hardworking 'real Germans'. What began as a jail soon had become a place of torturous human experimentation and extermination.

We entered the gates and parked, then walked towards the jail building that was the core of the prison compound. My guide pointed out the 'shooting wall' where prisoners were regularly executed, before the later installation of large human gas chambers for more massive killings. We approached the jail building and showed our IDs. We went through one gate, and I shuddered as it clanged shut behind me.[1] Then a second gate and a brief perusal by the MPs, who were friendly and efficient. We met with the Commander of the prison, and he was professional in a friendly way. I think he knew the effect the prison had on people. He was pleased when I proposed that I would try to arrange group therapy for interested prisoners.

There was much to think about when I made my biweekly visits to Dachau. I soon realised that my main job would be to process people out of the army, and only very limited psychotherapy would be possible due to the brief time most of the inmates stayed in the prison. However, the effect of those visits to the prison will stay with me forever.

Then something very shocking occurred. A substantial part of the main Concentration Camp had been preserved as a Museum and Memorial. The prison where I consulted was a smaller, separate entity. A couple that my wife and I had known at Stanford were in Europe and stopped in Munich to visit us. He was Jewish, and they were both eager to visit the Museum at the Dachau Camp. My wife and I had not visited the larger Camp area and its museum.

We went there together. It was a shocking experience. Indeed, beyond shocking! There were photos of prisoners being frozen as 'experiments' to test for 'treatments' to be used 'for the benefit of the troops in cold climates'. I recall another in which the top of the skull of a prisoner was sawed off to expose the brain. Then the medical experimenters could create very careful brain mapping, using electrical stimulation to the exposed brain of the prisoners. Some of these mappings were so accurate that they were used later in medical schools when I was a student.[2]

As we left the camp with our friends, I felt a terrible pain in my right ankle. I could hardly walk! It was red and swollen and exquisitely painful. We drove to the US Army Hospital in Munich, and I was hospitalised for tests. It turned out to be acute gout, a very treatable but extremely painful condition.

I had often thought of the wounded state of the world, especially the Western world, after Nazism and the Holocaust. This was my wound too! Indeed, a deep collective wound.

Being within these remnants of such a gigantic human horror had exceeded my capacity to assimilate. It was clearly and dramatically psychophysiological, the scream of my body or the *Weltschmerz*, a blow of the world that was too much for my psyche.

I quickly responded to medical treatment and remained on preventive medication for many years. Later, I had two very minor attacks in other joints, nothing like the first. Some years ago, my physician took me off all gout medication, and I have not had any further problems. Hopefully, that is a sign of progress!

My family and I had many wonderful experiences in larger Europe, as well as in Germany, touring around in our Volkswagen bus. The German people were very hospitable to us . . . especially considering that we were occupiers.

***

Another notable experience of death and horror came to my door in Germany. I was the only US Army psychiatrist in Bavaria, and military attorneys asked me to evaluate two soldiers who were being tried for the murder of a German woman in Augsburg. The accused men were at the stockade in Dachau. I received a packet of evidence for the trial to come. I vividly recall the many autopsy pictures of the victim, with descriptions by the pathologist. The victim had been brutalised and ravaged, killed by blows to the head. There were large gouges in her body, especially her breasts, made by human teeth. The cause of death, as I recall, was trauma to the brain. It was unbelievably bloody and brutal. It was very difficult to make myself view the reality of the sadistic brutality inflicted upon her.

The next day, I went to the Dachau prison to interview the accused. I was told by the administrator that the defence attorneys knew that guilt was not an issue. There was abundant evidence. However, because of the grisly nature of the murder, they hoped that an insanity defence might be possible. Were the perpetrators insane? They told the accused men to be totally honest with me, to tell all. The evidence was so strong that a plea of 'diminished capacity' seemed to be their only chance.

I interviewed the men, who were in full uniform, in a private room at the prison. The first was a hulking young man from the rural South. His speech was flat and unexpressive, and his powers of description were poor. He seemed almost illiterate and readily admitted the crime. Details were hard to clarify. I was a bit flummoxed. He was able to know what they had done but showed no signs of remorse. The victim was just a 'German whore' to him, who had resisted sex and 'pissed them off'.

Then, I interviewed the other man. He was a somewhat handsome young man whose uniform was embellished by a variety of medals for marksmanship and good conduct. He was verbal and seemed intelligent. It quickly became clear that he wanted to blame the other guy. They had been drinking with the woman in a local pub and intended to rape and rob her, but things went wrong when she strongly resisted. He smiled with a kind of pleasure as he described the other soldier. 'He was really violent and crazy', he said with a strange smile as he recalled the violent murder. After she was unconscious and likely dead, they had taken her money and left the scene. He also told me with a smirk that they had methodically beaten several drunken soldiers in the past, after they had left a pub alone. 'Crazy shit, huh?' the soldier said, obviously hoping that I would support a plea of insanity. He seemed to especially enjoy detailing the violent frenzy of his fellow soldier.

From a traditional psychiatric point of view, they were not psychotic, and their capacity for judgment was not legally impaired. I left the prison, shaken by the tales of cruel, sadistic violence, basically without remorse. Some days later, I felt a bit frightened when I later testified at their trial. They stared at me as I recited my opinion that they were sane in the light of the law. They were found guilty and then were sent back to the United States, where their attorneys, without much hope, planned to appeal.

This was a major experience for me as a young psychiatrist who had just finished his residency training. What was the most shocking, most disturbing, was the sheer pleasure they seemed to take in their sadistic crime. No awareness of morality at all, no sense of what they had done to another human being, no regret. This experience of raw darkness was forever imprinted in my memory. I maintained my professional demeanour and reasoning, but down deep, I hoped that they would never walk the streets again. This event brought me severely down to earth. The look of pleasure on the faces of brutal murderers shattered any remnants of my naive idealism!

***

The nineteen eighties were a time of restless exploration for Darlene and me. The details of that period would require a book of their own! We travelled and wondered and eventually decided to launch a new life in Seattle in 1990. A part of that restless energy was amplified by a monthlong stay in Bali in 1987.

The psychic background of my interest in Bali was partly due to a memorable experience during my residency training, a film that Gregory Bateson showed and discussed in 1963.[3] It was entitled *Trance and Dance in Bali*. He made the film there with Margaret Mead during the 1930s (see *YouTube*). It conveyed the reality of a true dance of life and death. In the ritual, a group of men is put into a trance by the witch, Rangda, who then commands them to kill themselves with their swords. They are entranced and terrified but resist. The ritual music and dance accompanying this enacted struggle between life and death are potent and unforgettable. At last, the helpful dragon, the *Barong*, arrives and drives Rangda away. The families and friends in the surrounding rush to the aid of the exhausted, still half-entranced men. The healing Barong music and energy continue as they revive. I was later told that some men would kill themselves during the ritual in the old days. A dance of death for sure!

With this background, and an underlying desire to deepen my knowledge of the culture that had produced that trance and dance of life and death, my wife and I planned a month's stay in Bali. Coincidentally, I heard from friends about a rental house available near Ubud, the cultural centre of the island. Within a few weeks, we made plans for a three-week stay. I was a bit possessed by the excitement of the trip, and studied the history and culture of the island, learnt some Malay, the national language of Indonesia, as well as a small amount of 'Old Bali', a Sanskrit-based language that was originally the primary language of the island. Those preparations were very important to my later experiences.

After the journey via Garuda Airlines, we settled in a small house that was half Balinese and half California style, in a beautiful setting on a small hill overlooking a valley and a small river, with the outskirts of Ubud town visible on the low hill on the other side of the river. It was quite beautiful. The population of the core city is now about 11,900, and of the larger Ubud region, about 74,000. At the time we were there during the eighties, I suspect the population was lower.

Our domicile was a medium-sized house, sort of California-Balinese style, with two bedrooms and a kitchen on one the first floor, along with a dining and kitchen. We mostly ate outdoors, on a large patio. Upstairs, there was a long, covered porch looking across the valley towards the town. The kitchen had a propane stove, with a very limited electrical supply from a small generator. At night, there was an array of kerosene lamps ('lampu'), always lighted and hanging from a roof ledge, above the outdoor porch. It was all quite beautiful and functional. We were taken care of by a young Balinese family: Mahdi, Ketut and Wayan. Mahdi was the father, our driver and chief advisor; Ketut was our cook and personal advisor and Wayan was their brightly precocious son, about 6 years old.

Many things from that experience are worth discussion, but I will focus on two experiences related to death. The milieu is crucial to know.

One day Mahdi and I took a walk together to pick up some supplies in Ubud. He knew some shortcuts, and I noted we were walking through the grounds of a large, brownish building, perhaps two or three stories high, spread out over a couple of hundred feet. It looked dark and old, and the grounds we were walking through were extensive. There were lots of trees and shrubs. I asked him what kind of structure it was, and he said (to the best of my memory), 'Temple of Siwa', I was confused and asked him to clarify, and he said, 'The Lord of Death', I assumed that he was referring to Shiva, but with a different accent.[4]

I asked him whether they cremated all the dead, and he said, 'Yes, but not always right away! Lots of people don't have the money, and they wait for a rich person to have a big ceremony and they dig them up and throw them on the fire!' Since Balinese don't, to my knowledge, use an embalming process, I asked him to clarify. He said yes, I had it right. Then I sort of reactively asked him whether the bodies smelled bad after all that time, and he grinned and said, 'Yes, pretty bad!'

Mahdi may have been pulling my leg, and he did have a great sense of humour, but somehow it felt like the truth. In any case, it indicated a very different view of death than I was accustomed to in the United States. It stopped me and made me more aware of my own culturally restricted attitudes towards death. It put me more fully into a liminal space, a space of the unknowable, and tested my own defences against what seemed uncanny and enigmatic.

A more dramatic experience around death occurred ten days into our stay. Mahdi had carefully instructed us to bar the door to our bedroom, which faced onto the porch. One night, I was awakened by the sound of the door being violently shaken. I leapt up and grabbed a flashlight. The shaking stopped, and I jumped up and thought I saw, in the light of the lampu, two small figures running away. I shouted, awakening Mahdi and his family next door. He came quickly with more flashlights and listened carefully to my description. He was very concerned. I told him that, as best I could see, the intruders were small, like children. He said, 'Yes, or old people!'

I had already gleaned that old people were looked upon with some suspicion in their culture. Both men and women kept their hair dyed very black, even in very old age.

For the next few nights, Mahdi or some extended family slept on the grounds outside to guard us. They must have believed there was something amiss on a serious level. Then one day Mahdi told me that a special person was coming the next morning and that meeting with her was very important.

We were mystified but of course agreed. The next day, Mahdi gently summoned us to come with him. At the side of the house, a woman awaited us. She appeared middle-aged and emanated a sense of presence I have rarely encountered in my life. I understood that she was a sort of spiritual leader in Mahdi's home community. She brought a few simple things and asked permission to perform a small ceremony. (Chills always go down my spine when I remember this experience.) She performed a simple ritual, using air, fire, earth and water. I must have evinced a bit of reflex reaction about sipping the sacred water because Mahdi, with his usual humour, interjected, 'don't worry Doctor Hinton, it's holy water!' The woman smiled too, and shook both our hands firmly, and took her leave with our abundant thanks. My wife and I always remembered that meeting with reverence and thanks for the gift she gave us and the deep loving kindness that came from both her and Mahdi. They wanted to protect us from danger on more than one level.

Later in our stay, we learnt from Mahdi that the land where the house was built had also been a matter of contention for several decades. The family of the rich man who had died had to sell the land against his professed wishes to pay for a munificent public cremation in which all the people of the area could participate after his death. His 'evil spirit' still lurked around, and my hosts feared we could be in deadly danger from it.

These experiences of death in Bali remain clear in my mind at age 89! The effects were subtly profound, rather than dramatic. It enhanced the depth of my respect for the depth and kindness of spirit that can unexpectedly come your way in the face of possible death and evil.

**

I will now move on to discuss another experience later and closer to home. My wife, Darlene, died in 2017, after an acute deterioration from several chronic conditions. The final stage lasted about ten days, and she died a week short of our 60th wedding anniversary. She had suffered from a multiplicity of medical problems, the prognosis was hopeless and we had extensively, tearfully and painfully discussed the details of care and when she wanted to let go of life. Maintaining a mere semblance of life when there was no hope seemed degrading to her. We had once had long discussions about such a heart-rending subject with our friend, Donald Sandner, who chose not to be 'medicalised' at the end of his own life. Hospice care is excellent in Seattle, and our three sons had time to come from out of town to say their goodbyes. They were deeply present to her, as was our daughter-in-law. Our own goodbye was wrenching, and we had our final kiss in the last seconds of her life.

There were the usual rituals as we mourned together with friends and families. My old friends Tom and Jean Kirsch came for the memorial, bearing some very moving photos taken by Tom's father, James, in 1963, when we were all spending a weekend at the senior Kirsches' home in Los Angeles and Darlene was pregnant with our third son. Those pictures are haunting and still bring tears to my eyes. I am grateful to Tom for preserving them and to James, his father, for taking them.

Darlene and I had never been apart more than a day or two during almost 60 years of marriage. Of course, there were ups and downs, although rarely significant in the longer term. I would say, overall, we had a close and long marriage, and were very much in synch as parents. Our love was deep and real. After everyone had left town following the memorial, I felt like a ghost myself! I wondered how I could go on. My grief was beyond tears.

Then I had a wrenching, unforgettable dream. In the dream, Darlene and I were in Mendocino, California, a small town on the Northern California Coast that we had, in earlier years, loved for special times away. In the dream, we had just finished lunch at a small restaurant, and as we left, I paused to give some advice to a young couple who were just arriving. Darlene wandered away as we talked, and then I turned to find her. There was a small street fair outside, and I thought she might be stopping to look at some arts and crafts. Then I saw that she was walking rapidly away on the other side of the crowd. I went to catch up to her, and called out, but she didn't seem to hear me. It felt like she was in a sort of spell. She reached a set of low, adobe buildings and went into one. I neared the building she had entered, but before I could enter, I heard a loud, horrible sound like grinding, clanging mechanical gears. I awakened in shock, with the words 'The Infernal Machine!' emblazoned like a headline in my mind.

This dream filled me with horror. Was death eating up my gentle, beautiful, kind wife?! The grinding, clattering gears felt inexorable, a horrible inevitability. Not just death, but antilife in its essence! The dream vision continually assaulted me from within. I was intermittently disoriented for days, and ordinary functioning was ofttimes difficult.

However, as my mind settled down somewhat in the coming weeks, I slowly recalled that she had, in fact, 'left' me in a peaceful way that was gentle, as was her nature. After some days, I came to more fully realise that it was *my* dream, *my* experience, not hers. Her loss was a horrible event for *me*, not necessarily a mediumistic knowledge of *her* experience. This perspective felt true, and eventually calmed me somewhat, so that I could reflect more and not just react in anger and anguish at my loss. I began to accept the experience as my own.

'Infernal Machine' felt vaguely familiar to me and was immensely evocative, but I had no conscious memory of what it meant or where it came from. The voice still echoes in my mind, along with the gruesome sound of the grinding, merciless gears of inevitability. Even now, I can feel it, like a sucking quicksand that could engulf me.

However, life beckons, and the call is still strong to live my life, to be with those whom I love, my loving family and friends, and to be the best I can be in our needy, troubled world. That would, I am very sure, please Darlene.

The term 'Infernal Machine' has many connections with warfare. There was an attempt on Napoleon's life using a hidden bomb, which he later referred to as an 'infernal machine'. Hidden land mines and booby traps, which may threaten every step a soldier takes, are often referred to as 'Infernal Machines'. The hidden death that can occur anytime.

In Celan's *Death Fugue*, the very rhythm of the verse conveys the relentless clicking of the wheels of the trains heading to Auschwitz, loaded with those to be exterminated. This powerfully conveys the sense of the truth of inevitable death to come . . . the Camp as an 'Infernal Machine' of hatred and genocide.

My most significant personal association was a scene from a movie named *Mondo Cane* ('Dog's World') that I had seen in 1962, during my first year at Stanford. It was done in erratic, shocking, kaleidoscopic style – sort of a parody of a 'nice, entertaining' travelogue. It shows scenes of cultural practice from around the world in a way that created shock or surprise. One scene is a junkyard in Los Angeles, where a giant machine, clanking loudly and with indomitable intent, and loud clanging and mechanical crunches, reduces the huge pile of junked cars, one by one, into a small ball of bare metal. A cube from the crushed car metal was later sold as art in a Los Angeles gallery!

That scene had provoked many intense discussions among the residents and young faculty. We all remarked on the visceral effect of the scene. It felt as if *our* bodies were being smashed and reduced. This 'shock' movie indeed shocked us all. It has stuck with me for all these years. It powerfully captures the truth that our bodies are temporary (temporal) constructs in a very direct way. I have carried this memory for 60 years!

The ending seemed to also say that everything is ultimately for sale, after being 'processed' by the linear, mechanical world.

It often seems that the Infernal Machine is around us again, both individually and collectively, in a world that all too frequently feels mechanical and indifferent to human cares or sentiments. We see it daily in the news and on the streets: racism, drugs, brutal crimes, rampant suicide rates and wars and threats of dictators to use hydrogen bombs, the ultimate Infernal Machines, on our cities. COVID underlines the dread we already feel every day, acknowledged or not. It is urgent not to forget that our lives are now substantially being run by the new 'Infernal Machines' of high technology! 'Shock' movies can be very useful tools in waking us up to the underlying realities of our times.

My core dream/vision also raises the question of freedom versus unfreedom, at least on a personal level. The beginning scene included a young couple just setting out to explore a new place. In contrast, the uncanny, mechanical sounds came across like an inexorable force that often seems to live our lives and do its will, despite our conscious intentions. How much freedom do we ultimately have? The final monstrosity that appeared in my dream was death. My love, our love, could not defeat it. That, it seems to me, is our human fate. We do what we can.

Conclusion

Death pervades human life from the beginning. We evolve from an original, small clump of cells that must survive a life-and-death crisis in the uterus before it can become firmly implanted. The mother's immune system strongly resists the intruder. Most clumps of cells don't make it. There is a crisis of survival, which is resolved when maternal immune cells are converted to helper cells by a hormone secreted by the intruder. The majority of possible conceptions pass in the guise of a heavy menstrual period (Bassat, 2021). Uncertainty exists from the moment of conception.

The spectre of death seems to underlie our species-wide concerns about conception. Children are our most primal way of continuing into the future. As I recall, the birth rate accelerates after wars.

Death has vast psychological, cultural and historical contexts. Where is it not, whether hidden or blatant?! I could have written more about other dimensions than I have, or in more theoretical ways, but my intent was not political or sociological, but rather to reflect upon some of my experiences with death in the context of my own life. In the face of the deepest of enigmas, I wanted to speak from my core, as best I could, and especially to shun comfortable platitudes. That process has not always been easy.

I hope that the reader will find my effort of some value to others. My goal, in sympathy with the purpose of this volume, was to expand awareness of death and underline its elemental presence in every moment of life, amidst the human drama of creation and destruction. The challenge has moved me deeply, and I want to thank Luis and Murray for inviting me to contribute.

Notes

1 In more recent times, I visited the Holocaust Museum in Berlin, and part of the effect in one area was achieved by the clanging of an iron gate behind you as you entered. Then you walk on crunchy material in the semi-darkness, and that turns out to be replicas of splintered bones. Eisenman did a great job of recreating a feeling of total uncanniness. This indoor Museum affected me even more than the famous outdoor Memorial.
2 Before the lectures, there were extensive discussions with Jewish and other organisations about the ethics of using such material in teaching. They decided to use them in teaching because it could symbolically honour the death and terrible suffering involved. It might, at least, now save human lives.
3 Gregory Bateson (9 May 1904–4 July 1980) was an English anthropologist, social scientist, linguist, visual anthropologist, semiotician and cyberneticist whose work intersected that of many other fields. His writings include *Steps to an Ecology of Mind* (1972) and *Mind and Nature* (1979). In Palo Alto, California, Bateson and colleagues developed the double-bind theory of schizophrenia. (Wikipedia)
4 The Hinduism of Bali is apparently quite different from that on the Indian subcontinent, and the Balinese tend to take pride in that difference. There also seems to be a connection with Buddhism because there is a Bodhi tree in the courtyards of all their temples.

References

Bassat, S. B. (2021). "'War in a Time of Love' – Prenatal Cell Relations as a Prototype of Autistic Anxieties, Defenses, and Object relations." *Tustin Memorial Prize*. Shiri-Ben-Bassat-War-in-times-of-love-24th-FTMT-prize-winning-paper.pdf

Binswanger, L. (1958). "The Case of Ellen West." In Rollo May (Ed.), *Existence*. Basic Books, 1958.

Gunn, J. (2006, February). "Review Essay: Mourning Humanism, or, the Idiom of Haunting." *Quarterly Journal of Speech*, 92, 1, 77–102.

Heidegger, M. (1962). *Being and Time*. Harper & Row.

Hinton, L. (2015). "Temporality and the Torments of Time." *Journal of Analytical Psychology*, 60, 353–370.

Inverso, H. (2022). "Phenomenology of the Inapparent: A Methodological Approach to the New Realism." In A. Schnell et al. (Eds.), *Phenomenology and Speculative Realism*. Würzburg: Königshausen & Neumann.

Knight, C., Power C. & Watts, I. (1995). "The Human Symbolic Revolution: A Darwinian Account." *Cambridge Archaeological Journal*, 5, 1, 75–114.

Reinhardt, K. (1960). *The Existentialist Revolt: The Main Themes and Phases of Existentialism: Kierkegaard, Nietzsche, Heidegger, Jaspers, Sartre, Marcel.* Milwaukee: Bruce Publishing Company.

Chapter 2

An Interview with Ladson Hinton Conducted by Hessel Willemsen on 5th April 2021*

I: Hessel Willemsen, Interviewer
L: Ladson Hinton, Interviewee

I: Ladson, welcome to this interview for the Journal of Analytical Psychology. I think amongst your many contributions you have done a great deal for the Journal and so the Journal is interested to hear more about you and your long career in psychoanalysis and philosophy; I hope we get to talk about these today. Welcome to the interview, first of all. If you don't mind, I'm asking if we could begin, perhaps, with you talking about [the philosopher] Husserl and why, so early in your life, you think he became so important and why you spent some time studying him.

L: I ran into Husserl's work at an interesting transition period in my life, when I was preparing to go to medical school, but was ambivalent whether to stay on in philosophy and literature, my core interest for a long time. My mentor was Fritz Friedmann, who was a friend of Erich Fromm, who was very much into, we called it then, philosophical anthropology. Robert Redfield, a 'father' of philosophical anthropology, was a prime mentor for Friedmann, and their correspondence has been published. He was an inspiring teacher, but always emphasised caring as the core of one's work, and that perspective opened the way for me to continue my plan to go to medical school. At that time, I was not finished with philosophy, and had not really decided whether to become a professor of philosophy or something like that. Completing a Master's with a year of concentration on philosophy helped me in that transition. I saw that philosophy did not have to be only a matter

* Hinton, L. & Willemsen, H. (2021). An Interview with Ladson Hinton, conducted by Hessel Willemsen on 5th April 2021. *Journal of Analytical Psychology*, 66(5), 1206–1220. Reprinted by Permission of John Wiley and Sons.

DOI: 10.4324/9781003641063-3

of pundits in a university, but that everyday life was what mattered. During this, my extra year of study, Husserl was just becoming known to the English-speaking world. Phenomenology was still kind of a new enterprise in US academia, and it was a new and refreshing point of view to me. I chose Husserl's view of the transcendent for my thesis topic. I was intrigued to know what Husserl had meant by transcendent, because in the Western tradition we usually think of transcendent as akin to mysticism or something outside the realm of the ordinary human, whereas Husserl thought of it differently. He re-examined knowledge in the light of Kant, he was kind of a post-Kantian. Kant, of course said you can't know the thing in itself, the noumenon, and so Husserl focused on what you can know: phenomena. He developed a form of descriptive reflection on everyday life. This was phenomenology. At that time, only two works by Husserl had been published in English, and one writing: Cartesian Meditations, which was translated by Levinas into French. The punch-line with Husserl was that by transcendent, he didn't mean some other worldly kind of knowledge or something beyond, in a sense beyond the ordinary, but he was critiquing a pretence of knowledge in the Platonic sense of pre-existing ideas. That leaves you with existence, and then you're talking about existential phenomenology and Heidegger and so on. At that time, Heidegger hadn't been much translated into English. *Being and Time* was only translated into English in, I think, 1961. So, it was kind of a revelation because a good part of everyday thinking in the academic world and discourse was based on almost a Platonic system of 'eternal' ideas, and final principles. Phenomenology, as I experienced it in Husserl's work, was almost meditative. So, I wrote my Master's thesis on the Concept of the Transcendent and that really set me off into a whole other way of thinking. I've never recovered from that! I still follow the path of existential phenomenology, or philosophical anthropology.

I: Why Husserl, do you think? Why at that time this concept of the transcendent and what you can know? Why do you think it was important to you to study that?

L: Well, I was in kind of a mixture, undecided where to go, to go into medicine or stay in philosophy and humanities and so I was just thoroughly mixed-up and I was in a new romantic relationship, hence thinking about marriage. I met my wife in my class on existential problems in literature, where Husserl was first mentioned. A combination of a lot of things in my life at the time and being kind of dissatisfied with traditional philosophy, which seemed kind of stuffy and repetitive, as did academic psychology.

So, my decision came out of a time of intellectual and personal flux. I was in my early 20s at that time. When I first heard the name, Husserl, I remember, my mentor-to-be, Fritz Friedmann was teaching a class, Existential Problems in Literature. He was noteworthy because he was a very independent guy, a German-Jewish refugee, who later became head of American Studies at the University of Munich. He was just talking away about his thoughts on contemporary philosophies that were emerging. He wrote 'Husserl' and 'Phenomenology' on the blackboard; and he was clearly very influenced by that school of thought himself. It was intuitive, and of course influenced by my admiration for Friedmann. It wasn't really a take on a certain idea, but the way he talked about Husserl. I thought, ah, a new name and I felt his own ideas spinning around in his head for a moment, but then he went off into other things, but that name stuck with me, so I started looking at the literature and then I had to choose what to do my Master's thesis on – I wanted to read more about that world of ideas.

I: *And this also led to an interest in Heidegger, you just said.*

L: Yeah, Husserl was Heidegger's teacher. The relationship between them later on was very problematic because of Heidegger's involvement with Nazism and Husserl being Jewish.

I: *But you decided to study medicine in the end and not philosophy?*

L: Yes, I actually finished off my Master's thesis during my first summer in medical school. I studied medicine at Washington University in St. Louis. I liked the clinical part of medicine. I didn't like anatomy much, but I like it better in retrospect. It provided me with a better sense of the embodied human being in the literal sense of the word. I really liked it when I got to clinical studies in medicine. At that time, after medical school, if you wanted to become a psychiatrist, you had to become qualified in general medicine first. I went to Georgetown, then, for a year specializing in clinical studies. I could have practiced general medicine after that, but I saw that there are a handful of maladies you deal with in general medicine. If you are familiar with them, you know, things like colds, headaches, sprained ankles, so forth and so on you can practice okay. It's pretty repetitious and if you've got an interesting case, you send them to a specialist, so general medicine wasn't what I wanted to do and psychiatry was more intellectually stimulating. Actually, I discussed my future profession with my high school advisor when I was 16 years old and I told him that I had read an article by a psychiatrist on teenagers describing me perfectly with all my various teenaged preoccupations. Maybe I could be one of those? And he said, yes, I think that you're best fitted in this high school to go on to psychiatry. So, I had flirted with the idea of it very early, which was sort of different, I think. To go back to the earlier narrative: I went from Georgetown to Stanford for psychiatry, and it was a very great time in psychiatry. They were breaking away from very traditional Freudian approaches, the kind of rigidity that tended to turn Freud into a dogma. The Strachey translation of Freud was skewed toward making Freud sound more 'scientific' than I think Freud really was in the original German. Stanford was one of the main sources of explorations in family therapy and that sort of thing, and Harry Stack Sullivan was probably the main influence on the psychological approach. I worked a great deal with psychotic patients too; I worked with John Perry and I met R.D. Laing while I was there, he was a visiting professor, and Gregory Bateson was one of the founders, having invented the double-bind theory of schizophrenia, and applied it to family work.

I: And Harry Stack Sullivan influenced you too?

L: Oh, he was a big influence. One of his disciples, Don Jackson, was my first supervisor. He had trained with Harry Stack Sullivan for several years and so he was an immense influence. Don Jackson was one of these creative geniuses in a certain sense. He was very spontaneous. For instance, if a patient hallucinated that he was some religious figure, like he was Jesus, Don would get down on his knee and pray to him, asking if he could say a prayer to him. It wasn't being anti-religious, but trying to get a dialogue going, to break through the rigid bastion of hallucination, and so forth, and so I learned more about a sense of playful engagement with clinical work, as well as life. This contrasted with more traditional approaches to psychiatry and psychoanalysis. So, Don Jackson was a big influence too.

I: And this was also a time when, if I am right, you met Tom Kirsch at Stanford.

L: During my psychiatric residency, right. We were both in a group of seven people, who studied together for three years. Tom and I became close friends. He came from the background of a family very steeped in philosophy, and even though he was more extraverted, he had a deep appreciation for scholarship and intellectual curiosity. Tom died a couple of years back and I've remained good friends with his wife, Jean. Our two families lived in the same block in Palo Alto for many years. My kids were older and sometimes babysat with his.

I: A close friendship.

L: Close friendship, yeah. Over time he became much more involved in the political-organizational side of things. I was more into books, articles, lectures and stuff like that. We were to some degree an extravert and introvert pair, although there was a lot of overlap. Tom had a very scholarly side, and I was often deeply engaged in organizational things. I was a founding member of the Pacific Graduate School of Psychology, which became Palo Alto University.

I: And was it through Tom Kirsch that you then found your way into the Jungian training and Jungian world?

L: I met his father, James, who was a fascinating man. He was a tremendous scholar, and seemed to know a lot about many things, and was a very dynamic man. The family had been through the whole Jewish refugee experience. Although our pathways were different, Tom and I and remained friends through the years. He was International President for two terms, established trainings in China, and things like that. It was his calling in the world.

I: Yeah; he was really very involved in the Jungian world. So, this led you into your Jungian analytic training.

L: Yes.

I: When was that? When did you do this training?

L: I started analytic training in my last year of residency at Stanford. That was 1964–1965.

I: And you finished in the early 70s then, I think.

L: There was a lapse in my training after residency because I had to go into the Army. I'd been drafted earlier, during the Berlin Crisis, and agreed to come in later, after I finished my psychiatric training. Tom had a similar obligation, but he spent two years in the National Health Service, mostly in the Bay Area and Alaska. A lot of it was I think consulting in Alaska.

Tom and I had done independent studies at Stanford with Kurt Reinhardt, who was a well-known German philosopher and historian. He wrote a standard History of Germany – Germany: 2,000 Years – and he had taken seminars with Heidegger. He also wrote a book on existentialism – The Existential Revolt, as well as The Essential Philosophy.

Remarkably, he was the first Catholic philosopher at Stanford. It's hard to think of those times, the suspicions of Catholics being under control of the Pope, speaking for the Pope. Kurt would joke about it. For our elective in our last year of training at Stanford, Tom and I spent time with him for a morning every other week. We read Being and Time, which had just come out in English translation, and also read some Kierkegaard, I think those were the two main emphases.

These studies really reinforced my interest in existentialism and existential phenomenology. So by the time I ever encountered Jung I had already a sense of my own point of view, with existential phenomenology as the core. Archetypes always seemed a bit regressive to me, and I eventually viewed them as bastions of thought like Platonic Ideas. Despite my 'resistance' to classical Jungian theory, I never felt criticised or rejected during training and other encounters.

I: It was still a time when many of the people who taught at the Institute had themselves been in contact with Jung and/or had had some analysis or supervision with him.

L: Joe Henderson, Jo Wheelwright are good examples – the founders of the San Francisco Institute. My own first analyst was John Perry, who later got into problems with sexuality with his patients and stuff, but he was a wonderful teacher and analyst. I didn't know about all that until later. Jung was very alive and it was great openness at that time although it sometimes felt like an 'establishment'. I think the Jungians were just getting their feet wet in the States. Of course, the Freudians were much more the establishment at that time.

I: And because you did that training, did it fit with the philosophy you had studied? I was thinking about the point you made about the archetype: how did philosophy and psychoanalysis go hand-in-hand? How was that?

L: Well I think at first, it sometimes made me feel like I didn't fit in, and I went through a lot of self-doubt the first year of analytic training, like I must just not really be getting the archetype like other people seemed to do, but it just didn't ring true for me. Certainly, there are extraordinary experiences, and to a greater or lesser degree we all have those in our lives, but to call something 'archetypal' seemed to me to diminish it, like reducing it to a reflection of essences in heaven someplace, you know, pure Ideas emanating from some special circle of Illuminati somewhere far from the everyday. And so existential phenomenology spoke to me and continued to do so over the years, and I felt a little bit on the outside of the Jungian worldview, although I was always well treated and I found people quite generous and I had great clinical supervision. The clinical part of my experience was quite outstanding. The intellectual part of the training, I think, probably was not quite as good as I had had earlier on. There were notable exceptions, though. It wasn't black and white. However, my intellectual core came more from outside the Jungian world, but I tried to assimilate that with Jungian ideas as best I could.

I: But of course, there is on the one hand, the thinking about the theory, but there was also, I assume, the clinical training and seeing patients.

L: I liked the basic Jungian approach; it was very accepting of all psychic experience as having meaning. It strongly honoured subjectivity. There was a generosity of spirit, and there was a newness about things at that time, you know. It was a time when things psychoanalytic seemed new and exciting. The training was experimental – Jungians hadn't been around that long as a group. Psychoanalysis was a bit older, more intransigent. So I found the atmosphere quite congenial. For instance, the first year was preliminary at the San Francisco Institute, and after I finished my first year of training, there was a joint committee of senior analysts from Los Angeles and San Francisco, to say whether you're okay to go on for further years. I had a great conversation with the committee and everything seemed fine. We were all happy with each other and all that stuff. I thought I was calm and all was well. However, I opened a door and walked into a closet! [Laughs] And so at the conclusion of that episode, we all just laughed hilariously and so I told them, I said, well I guess I was more nervous than I had thought I was. The committee members were quite warm and lively, and we laughed and talked for a couple of minutes afterwards. That gives you an idea of the spirit of it, a really nice spirit in those early days.

I: Do you think that . . . I mean, it is a bit of a jump ahead really, but that tension between Jungian thinking and your philosophical interest that, in the end, also led to the formation of the New School for Analytical Psychology in Seattle. Did that give more of a home to your philosophical thinking?

L: Yeah, but that took many years. The New School was a later attempt to really get back to the roots of existential phenomenology, include cultural, historical, political concerns, and deeper ethical concerns. I think the final summation of my concern that way was in Jon Mills' book on Jung and Philosophy, published three or four years ago. I wrote a chapter entitled, 'Jung, time and ethics'. The main idea was that archetypes are about the eternal, while the core of human existence is temporal. We are creatures who die. Temporality is the core of our being. In many ways, Jung seemed to me to denigrate everyday human experience, to be deferential to something transcendent or eternal. The existential-phenomenological approach is that great ideas emerge out of everyday human experience, and emerge out of the sweat, passion and suffering of everyday lives. 'Archetypes' are derivative, not original.

Humans have the same bodies, the same everyday concerns, through the three-million-year history of the species as it slowly emerged. 'Archetypes', as something pre-existent, 'out there', something innate and guiding things, was never a congenial view to me. Basic ideas grew out of human experience, stemmed from human creative-imaginative thought, cultural evolution and the accumulation of cultural memories. My view is to leave the archetypes out and honour basic human experience, which of course has its somewhat consistent themes. In Jung's own seminars, his goal seemed to be always to finally 'get to the archetype', you know, as something that seemed more important to him than every-day, temporal existence. Of course, there are lots of different kinds of Jungians and they experiment with their own approaches too.

I had a dream very early in my training that I was sitting drinking beer outside a German Gasthaus with Jo Wheelwright and Jung. Jung looked very sad, and I felt his emotion and asked, 'What's the matter, Carl, you look unhappy'. And he said, 'Oh, I need somebody to translate my works into American!' And he said American, not British or English, but American. Upon awakening, I thought: the old, pragmatic American, the good side of the American spirit, you might say. The pioneer spirit, thinking things anew. There are many other, darker sides of America which have become more evident, especially in recent times! So, that was the dream. I think the dream was an expression of what I was feeling. I needed to find my own translation!

I: Yes, and the connection was still very close to Zurich. I was thinking about what you have thought and written about in your earlier paper,

'Fools, foolery and foolish' and that is also about shame. But, just thinking about that first paper, I was just wondering if you could say a bit more about it, how you arrived at that topic, which seems to be an important topic throughout your professional thinking. You focused a great deal on shame.

L: Yeah, that was a multi-determined kind of thing I think, that it's hard to pick up the exact threads, but I think growing up, I was the only male child in a fairly extended family, as well as the oldest. I had always done well in school and was athletic as well, and this led to expectations of being perfect. I ran into my first great difficulty with being perfect when I was unable to do public speaking in high school. I'd just feel paralyzed, and I couldn't proceed and, as it turned out later in analysis, it was due to shame issues. Going through the analytic process made it clear that shame was very crucial in my own development, my fear that things that were not so perfect might spill out, you know, when I was in public giving a spiel of some kind, a little talk or so forth. I substantially mastered that in medical school, in internship and clinical work, when I had to present the cases of people who had died in the hospital where I worked. The intern was stuck with presenting problematic cases before maybe 50 or 100 people who were medical school faculty and people in training. Despite my potent anxiety, I knew that I had to do it in order to get my medical licence. I just had to grit my teeth and do it, and I pretty much overcame the sense of shame, but I continued to reflect on it. I had a dread of defeat at the time. It was a core issue and I began to reflect on that, and I thought, yeah, you do have to feel shame sometimes because when you get into the unknown and you feel inadequate to the situation for inner and outer reasons, you experience shame, so that shame is, you might say always potentially there with individuation, because when you rock the boat by what you have to do or what your own emotions compel you to do, anytime you get into new territory, you feel shame and uncertainty. In a way shame saves you, it helps you to keep boundaries, you know, proper shame. It shapes who we are.

So, to continue my answer, I got into Kohut's work later on, during the 70s. In those days they had correspondence courses on professional topics, and I saw in the National Psychiatric Journal that he was giving a correspondence course that was called 'Self-Psychology' and I thought, oh, well that sounds interesting. It turned out to strongly influence my understanding of shame. I was quite influenced by Kohut, like many people were at that time. It's close to Jung in some ways. The Kohutians also talked about the self, the self as being part of everyday experience, the quality of openness that the best of Jungian stuff has. To Kohutians, shame often emerges when you get overexcited about something. There is a primary intensity related to our 'narcissistic grandiose self', overexcited in the sense of a kind of loss of an inner sense of boundaries and . . . fragmentation would be possible . . . and shame is the main resultant emotion, at least according to Kohut at that time. So, when I did my first major paper at an international meeting in the late 70s, it was at the IAAP in San Francisco, the subject was on shame and the Fool. I was also influenced by William Willeford, who was a Jungian professor of literature. He wrote a book on Shakespeare and shame, called The Fool and His Scepter. It was quite an interesting book. And then I discussed Native American concerns about shame and proper behaviour, proper in the sense of not being grandiose or destructive, but proper shame and respect for the other, for tradition and so forth. So, shame is very basic, and I believe stems from preverbal times in development. But my original preoccupation with shame was back in those teenage experiences of being unable to give talks in a group, to perform in a speech class.

I: But later, you write about shame as a teacher, really.

L: Right.

I: You see it as something that people can really use to develop reflection and so on.

L: I later gave a paper called 'Shame as a teacher' at an IAAP meeting in Zürich, in 1999 or so. There was a pre-Millennial kind of focus at the meeting, and I saw shame as about lack, as being essential in forming the capacity for a proper humility and respect for values, for the other . . . as crucial in forming a sense of boundaries. It seemed to me that this crucial dimension of life was, at that time, neglected both in psychology and culture in general, and that lack of respect for deep values was growing. Over the years, the culmination in the US has been Trump, but I think there were already signs of a looming cultural crisis at the time of the Millennium. As a consequence, I thought it was appropriate to pay more attention to the whole idea of shame and how it teaches us proper boundaries. Without proper shame and respect, real discourse is impossible. A sense of humility, a sense of our own limitations, is essential to civilised dialogue. Shame and humility are essential virtues for the continuity of what we call civilization.

I: Yes, not just focused on the individual, but also on the collective and society is what you're saying.

L: Definitely. As I recall, Aristotle wrote about shame a little bit. I think the Greek term is Aidos. The basic unit of Greek social-political life was the polis, the small governmental unit. He said the polis couldn't function in its proper way for the good of society and law and so forth and justice without proper shame, that you couldn't even begin to have a culturally significant and ethically significant discourse without there being proper shame.

I: So, would you say that currently in our day-to-day life now as we know it, society and the collective is struggling with that, that there is lack of awareness of proper shame?

L: Definitely. You could say that Donald Trump is the incarnation of the archetype of shamelessness.

I: Yes.

L: At the New School in Seattle, we have tried to retrieve awareness of the ethical purpose of shame, humility, slowing down, being able to see the viewpoints of others, as opposed to the psychopathic arrogance we see. A basic respect for others and others' ideas and so forth. We often refer to the work of Bernard Stiegler in our point of view.

I: Just thinking about some of the books you've been working on. How did temporality come alongside that concept of shame in your work?

L: Well, I think it goes partly back, of course, to my reading Heidegger's *Being and Time*. It's more theoretical, but very profound. To be in the world in time is the ethical position, whereas timelessness, as I have said, the 'timeless archetypes' seem to me almost being without shame because you're saying you have a conduit to the eternal, but the eternal is not time. Temporality is the experience of everyday time. It is part of our basic vulnerability, the fact that we know the future of us all . . . that we will die. Our basic transience, our vulnerability. There is a humility in this knowledge that is related to shame.

I: Yes.

L: The truth of human finitude, the fact that we are temporal creatures that know they will die, contrasts with Jung's emphasis on the 'Timeless'. He consistently expressed, as I have traced in his seminars, his great preference for the timeless. He was always looking for 'the archetype'. I think, as Barreto wrote about in 'Requiem for Analytical Psychology', that Jung never got past the final boundary into a certain deeper kind of exploration. His clinging to the timeless dimension kept him from launching more fully into the everyday experience of the human being, and valuing that in a primary way. We all succumb to death. That's a universal particular, so to speak. The first evidences of human culture were burial and graves.

I: Yes. I was just thinking about it and bringing shame and temporality together and there is something about it much more 'in the moment' and I was thinking about Freud's death drive and the idea of some sort of loss of hope that may be more real in the world right now. Would you see it like that?

L: The death drive, that's a complex subject.

I: It is.

L: The death drive is an illuminating topic. I like the part where Freud talks about the primeval swamp and speculates that the first creatures that emerged, the little cellular creatures or whatever they were, their main problem was to assimilate or integrate the world around them, the chemicals, the chemical soup around them and still to maintain their boundaries, or they would disappear, they wouldn't exist anymore. And then there's the other urge, that it's hard work to maintain those boundaries and the urge to kind of just say, to hell with it, it's too much work! Again, without breaking the boundaries to take in nutriment, there would be no sustained life. I look upon the 'death drive' as a kind of ambivalence about destruction and creation. Opening up is necessary to sustain life, and yet it is hard work to maintain structure and boundaries at the same time. It's a very elemental thing and I think that all the more profound schools of analytic thought or maybe all thought, and what I hope the New School people will reflect on, is creation and destruction and what were the origins of that? Part of Freud's discussion of the death drive, which took various forms later on, the parts that stuck with me were kind of the original, the emergence of organic life in some way, the whole war between structure and breaking down structure for the sake of the new to occur. It is the work involved in maintaining life, of expanding life, versus the impulse to avoid or evade the struggle.

I: That's quite important still.

L: Oh, it's very, yes, we're still struggling with that for sure. Everything seems to be breaking down so much. Shame is on the conserving side.

I: Yes.

L: It can be a terrible emotion when there's so much destruction, everything seems loaded with shame, you know, like aggression. If you don't have any aggression, you're not alive, you're buried, but too much aggression is very destructive, so of course that's where ethics comes in too. Shame, when acknowledged, pulls us toward the preservation of social structure, and a gratitude for the cultural creations of our ancestors.

I: And I suppose it is where your work on Stiegler relates to the current state of affairs in our society, his idea of symbolic misery and his work around giving technology and people a place, and the loss of individuality.

L: Stiegler is sort of a . . . he's so many-sided, he's mastered so many areas of thought, but also I deeply respect him because he was a bank robber and spent five years in a French prison, where he initially became aware, at a primal level, that he had to totally reconstitute himself or go insane. He went on a hunger strike to get his own cell so that he could focus and read all the time and he reconstructed himself. Evidently French prisons are more amenable than American prisons! He was able to get books and have his own cell. When he was released, he went directly into advanced doctoral studies. I can't remember who his advisor was . . . I think Derrida was one.

But he knew anthropology, evolutionary studies, history, philosophy. Also, I know from his translator and younger friend, Dan Ross, that they both had a very deep connection with psychoanalysis and were very interested in Laplanche, but also Winnicott and especially the whole idea in Winnicott of the cultural imagination and the transitional object, of imagination and creation as the basic human theme. That is what he called 'the use of the object', you might say, the way of creativity and imagination. Stiegler had a broadly multidisciplinary approach and was very interested in evolutionary psychology, the origins of the little human creature three million years ago and the development of tools and dimensions of memory. In particular, he talked about exteriorization of memory, which one might call culture. The capacities of the human memory are limited, as well as what we might loosely call 'instinct', or 'head memory'. Written memories, language, and archives and artifacts of every kind are what Stiegler called 'tertiary memory'. Significantly, Stiegler included digitalised, technologised memory in this concept. So I saw Stiegler combined philosophy, psychoanalysis, evolutionary psychology, history, kind of all these different disciplines and I think it makes it difficult for some people to read his work, but at the same time it seems like he put forth one of the great syntheses of our times, which hopefully will be carried further. I see there's a whole upsurge of articles inspired by his work already, just a year or so ago, since his death.

I: The relevance of his work about what is going on in the world right now, you see that as quite important, I know.

L: I do, I think it's the most successful attempt so far to create a new synthesis of the post-postmodern. He retains some of the alive qualities of postmodernism, while keeping a humility of knowing, like Derrida, that no 'truth' is final, that it is always something 'to come'. Temporality and finitude are very basic to his viewpoint. That's how I got interested in Stiegler to start with, because his primary work is called Technics and Time, technology and time. What the originary can do with a rock was not just throw it at the dinosaur that's pursuing him, but it was what he could do with that rock in various ways. Invention or imagination requires anticipating what the result might be, implying a sense of future. The disciplines of Palaeoanthropology and Palaeo Archaeology study the changes in the brain itself over the three million years, up until Palaeolithic times when the brain was kind of at its max. I think our skull, the case for our brain, might not be as large now as it was then, in the Palaeolithic times. It went down a bit in the Neolithic times, evidently because life became more difficult for human beings during the first 3,000,000 years of what we call civilization and written language. It is fascinating that the condition of Home Sapiens apparently went backwards for a time during the Neolithic period. There was significant malnutrition, and body size and skull size seemed to decrease. Only in more recent decades have those measures come back to what they were in Palaeolithic times, which is kind of an interesting social *phenomenon*, and something well worth some speculation. 'Civilization' apparently wasn't too good for the human in Neolithic times. The development of settled cities, of written language and culture seemed to have a downside. It is such problems that give perspective to Stiegler's thought. His main focus has been on Technos, technology in the broadest sense, and what effects it has had, and is having, on *Homo Sapiens* in the present.

I: Yes. He writes lots about the disconnection between people as a result of technology, the person's connection with technology, but this importance, really, of the technology we have around us leading away, perhaps, from the more human connection.

L: Yeah, the technology – Heidegger was probably more suspicious of technology than Stiegler. With Heidegger, you almost got a binary kind of thing with technology, whereas with Stiegler, he sees technology as being the essence of the human. The human with tools, time, sense of future, what we know as the human is essentially technology; if you take technology in the very broadest sense, it is technos, something that includes language, tools, all memory devices, everything we consider 'culture', but much more down-to-earth. He would see the human is really technos and that's the essential part of us. Without that, we wouldn't be what we call human, even. Stiegler often refers to technos as a pharmakon, which is something that is both poison and cure. One must always attend to the balance. Most things have that aspect.

I: No, right.

L: And so he's not seeing so many binaries involved in many people's thinking about technology, like it's this alien thing that's kind of thrust upon us, something that evokes a kind of dualism. Stiegler uses the principle of the pharmakon extensively, the basic idea is that everything is both poison and cure. Technology is both poison and cure and it's the human ethical responsibility to try to look to the curative or positive sides, the humanly enhancing side of technology, but that's the essential human, it's not that technology is this kind of alien thing from another planet or something.

I: No, no.

L: So much of talk about technology is kind of a romantic rebellion saying, oh, technology is terrible, look at all it's doing to us. Well, it's doing something to us but it's also what makes us human and you know, like right now, I use hearing aids, glasses, I take several pills. I probably wouldn't even be alive, or not nearly as functional, if it wasn't for technology. So I mean, it's writing and books and language and all those things that are dimensions of technos. I think there's a weird forgetfulness that people have about how technological we are in the broader sense, that tends to get lost in a lot of romantically-inspired discussions of loss of some perfection that we used to have. We never had perfection. Stiegler wrote a long thing against the reasoning of Rousseau, the lost 'State of Nature'. There wasn't any, as you know. Nature was always hard as hell and humans were good at making something that we call the human civilization out of that. Stiegler also lauds proper shame and humility, and gives thanks to our generations of ancestors who have created the culture that allows us to be.

I: Well, thank you.

L: Thank you. It's an honour and a pleasure to be here with you and, certainly, I personally appreciate so much the Journal of Analytical Psychology and the opportunity to be able to pass on the little dribs and drabs of things that I've thought and experienced; if it's of help to others or informative in some way, I'd be very happy.

I: Well, it's been great to have you, Ladson. Thank you very much for your time. Thank you.

END

Chapter 3

Fools, Foolishness and Feeling Foolish*

My interest in the fool originally grew out of research on humour and its relationship to the transcendent function. I sought to connect laughter and humour with an archetypal image, a primordial entity, a universally recognizable symbol. This led me to the fool, of course, in all his manifestations. And the fool, as usual gave me more than I bargained for.[1]

The fool is an intriguing being one follows through all the corners of life, a ubiquitous entity with whom we are all familiar, but who nevertheless remains elusive. We see, we "know" him everywhere, and yet to ask who the fool is, what he is, is like seeking the essence of humour and laughter. These so basic and common human experiences defy our analytical grasp, falling through our searching fingers like sand.

The image of the *Ship of Fools* (*Das Narrenschiff*) of Sebastian Brant is well portrayed in the famous painting by Bosch: it contains the idea of life itself as foolery, folie, folly. This image conveys the mystical sense that the everyday roles and structures which we take so much for granted are transient vanities, ephemeral, mere inflated illusion. From this viewpoint, one who takes himself, his role in the dance of life, with total seriousness becomes a true fool, a natural or unconscious fool, as distinguished from the artful or conscious fool. We must either dance with the fool or fall into an unconscious identification with him. When we think we have "captured" life, become like the gods, inflated and certain – we may in fact appear more like clowns, trapped in our painted masks, stumbling over the obvious. That is why we fear the artful fool so much: he reflects back to us our rigidities, the structures which block off the flow or process of life.

* Hinton, W. L. (1981). Fools, Foolishness and Feeling Foolish. *Psychological Perspectives*, 12(1), 43–51. https://doi.org/10.1080/00332928108408677, reprinted by permission of the publisher (Taylor & Francis Ltd, http://www.tandfonline.com).

DOI: 10.4324/9781003641063-4

The fool operates on the fringes, in the interstices of structure, on the edge of chaos. Indeed, he seems at times about to dissolve the whole world in chaos. The Kashore – the Hopi Indian clan of fools – keep rituals lively and effervescent; on the other hand, they have to be watched lest they dissolve the ceremony in hilarious chaos. The structured centre, often symbolised in Western consciousness by the King, like the orderly part of ritual, is the necessary counterpart and counterpoint to the fool. They require (involve/need?) one another.

In the same way that humour breaks the ice in a stiff group, the fool prevents the King from becoming trapped in senex sterility, or a ritual from becoming constrained and lifeless. The fool brings the fertility of the darkness, the fringes, the paranormal. That is why he is so frightening, so held in awe; but also why he is so beloved and so absolutely necessary.

The *hero* encounters chaos in order to conquer, to overcome, to bring a new order to the centre. He journeys to the boundaries of the known, encounters the dark unknown and seeks to bring this new meaning to the centre. The King, the old consciousness, may resist and be displaced, or may integrate the new truth as King Arthur did with his knights at the Round Table. But the hero-journey remains a drama of order, of seriousness, of ego-integration.

The fool, on the other hand, remains stubbornly unintegrated and unintegratable. On the stage, he is most often on the fringes, between actors and audience, a mediator almost like the Greek chorus. His motley costume is an apparent chaos, although most often one can observe a pattern hidden in the chaos.

Adolph F. Bandolier states that when an important council was held in the kiva, the clan chief of the Kashore, or fools, occupied a physically intermediary position between the central religious functionaries and the various delegates of the other clans, who were seated at the outer circumference of the kiva. This expresses vividly and directly the relation of the fool to the numinous centre and his role as mediator to the more mundane. He dwells in-between realities, at what has been called the *punctum indifferens*, the place which is in a sense an elusive "nothing," and yet is at the same time the wellspring, the intermediary centre where the spark of life is most truly struck.

In Ingmar Bergman's movie, *The Seventh Seal*, the heroic spiritual knight decides the whole fulfilment of his existence is to forestall Death in order that a family of fools might survive. It is as if they, in their child-like foolery, embody the moving fertile centre of life, a lifegiving spark in contrast to the sterile idealism of his crusades.

And so the fool is only marginally related to the ego, to the structured centrality of consciousness, and yet contains the very essence of life, the creative fertility of human joy and imagination. The fool, to use Victor Turner's term, seems to bring a spirit of *communitas*, of joyous wholeness, of humankind, as one rather than fragmented and in opposition. He works in the service of the Self rather than the ego per se.

It's quite interesting to note then, in empirical studies of humour in groups, that the "humorist" of a group is seen by most members as a strongly positive leader. Also, he scores higher than the group norm on an ego strength scale and has a less constricted personality. Within much of psychology, and especially among group therapists of a (the?) conventional sort, there is a tendency to label humour as regression, resistance, diversion, disruption. This is a revealing commentary on the senex position, the over-seriousness of so much of the profession, the righteous priestliness which makes psychotherapists aptly the butt of so many popular jokes.

We, of all professions, need the creative, the disorderly fertility, the lifegiving touch of the fool. We fall otherwise into a sterile structure, petty power conflicts and a sort of priestly provincialism.

The fool dances on the fringes, bells tinkling with hints of secret possibilities, motley colours clashing with our overly-ordered aesthetic sense, tickling us with his bauble which is both phallic and mocking. We fear his power like the shaman's, but we crave his inspiration, like a poet's. Yet the fool is both and neither, manifesting in his own unique way the role of mediator in the human drama.

The Tarot fool captures the essence of his being. This fool is usually pictured staring off into space, about to step over the edge of an abyss, a pole and sack over his shoulder, a dog as a companion who may be pulling down his pants to bare his buttocks.

This situation expresses the transcendent perspective of the fool. He is about to step into an abyss – an act fatal to the usual mortal. But, as we know, the fool is always miraculously saved from destruction whether he be Charlie Chaplin or Peter Sellers. An unexpected, almost miraculous factor intervenes as if by random chance. This illustrates the transcendent aspect of the fool, the unknown factor which transcends the dichotomies of consciousness and saves him – or us – when, like Parsival (?), he wholeheartedly embraces the quest of individuation. Faith, trust, purity of heart pull one through in the end – not the intellect, the comfortably collective, or even the will. When one trusts and accepts the strange pathways of individual destiny, one often feels foolish in one's own eyes and the eyes of the collective. But then one is open to the numinous, the non-ordinary – that which one can't force to happen, but just seems to run into at the most unexpected moments. The abyss, the rational pitfalls and limitations of consciousness, can be transcended if one has the fool's faith in the pregnant darkness.

The Tarot fool has a sack on his shoulder which shows him to be a wanderer and seeker (as are all wanderers). He has no stable collective home, but has his eye on the heavens, on the horizon of awareness rather than its foreground. Again, the fool seems connected with the way of individuation which must take one apart from the merely collective. Worldly ambitions, unlike wandering in search of our grail, often appear to be incompatible. Those who sit comfortably at the round table, laughing at the blundering Parsifals of life, should take pause and gaze off for a moment into the unknown, along with the Tarot fool.

The fool seems to be saying that perhaps we would all be better off to preserve what we can in our little sacks, that which is most truly ours in all its uniqueness and limitation, and cast off the complex encumbrances of power, position and persona. Jung said that simplicity is the most difficult of all things. The 19th century romantic poets liked to say, "My cup is not large but I drink from my own cup." The fool knows this secret: how to narrow life down to that little sack, to that which is most simply and truly oneself, before heading down life's path. A little humour helps so much along the way!

The Tarot fool is usually accompanied by a dog, a helpful companion. Thus, though gazing at the heavens, he remains rooted in instinct, in the earthy and earthly. [His faithful companion knows the ways of the underworld and represents the directness and fertility of the animal.] He often seems to warn the fool not to become too heavenly, too sky-borne, even ripping down his pants to get his attention, to remind him of his earthly roots. He reveals the fool's bare buttocks, his all-too-humanness.

We experience this em-bare-ass-ing aspect of the fool through the emotion of *shame*. Shame is the emotion of feeling foolish. Just as the fool is exposed, so part of his archetypal role is exposure of our own narrow-ness, pride, limitation, inferiority. He mocks our sterile rigidities, he makes fun of our pet idols, he shows us the paradoxes in our certainties. In his bare arse we see the red face of our own shame. To experience limitation is to know shame.

The fool dwells on the edge of infinite possibility, of the sacred cosmos; but this is overwhelming, bewildering chaos when seen from the perspective of the finite ego. When we experience our wretched finitude, like Adam and Eve driven from the Garden, we know humiliation and shame. We feel the ego's power and control to be that of a flea compared to a giant. Call this inferior function or what you will, the fool often makes us feel naked, vulnerable and ashamed: we *feel foolish*. Our *bare-assedness* shows. It's no mistake that fools sometimes wear asses' ears. As Kierkegaard said, the finite, as seen from the viewpoint of the infinite, appears absurd.

Shame nonetheless humbles, alchemically reduces us to that which is most essentially ourselves, leaves us with our little sack, more open to the creative fullness of the cosmos, freed from the masks which impede us. In an early version of the Tarot, the fool card was indeed labelled the alchemist. The Tarot fool thus captures much of the tortured nobility of the human situation. He gazes up at the stars but is bound to the earth: he is able to attain peaks of vision and transcendence, and yet remains naked, vulnerable, finite, all-too-limited. All these qualities seem mysteriously to require (be dependent on?) one another.

In fairy tales we see the fool expressed in the motif of the dümmling (dimwit?), the idiot youngest son of the king who has wandered with the sheep, joked with the shepherds, totally uninterested in the workings of power, of the collective kingdom, of worldly structure and ambition. We watch hopefully as the older brothers – apparently so much stronger and better-adapted – go out to discover why the golden bird is stealing the plenty of the kingdom, why things just aren't working anymore. We hope these strong-ego types will discover, conquer, maintain things as comfortable as they are – but in a better way.

As we know, they always fail. The *dümmling*, the young fool of a son of whom all respectable people have always been a little ashamed, is the reluctant last-hope candidate to save the kingdom. This shows the universal tendency to conserve an "adapted" collectivity at all costs, rather than rely on the bizarre, the unusual, the new life which at the same time always reveals our bare-assed inferiority. Fear of shame – shame, anxiety – is the great instrument of *evolutionary conservatism*, the innate resistance to change, and in which there is a purpose. But when life must move on, it is necessary to suffer shame to find the new way/the secret?.

When the *dümmling* goes (?/takes over?) out, naive and stupid in the ways of the world, yet able to connect with the new, the miraculous, in ways his more conventional brothers never could. He embarrasses us, but he is open to the weird (which in ancient times was the holy) in ways the over-adapted ego never is. Thus, he trusts the helpful fox, like the Tarot fool with his dog. He avoids the traditional diversions of fortune or lust. He steps off into the abyss, so to speak. Everyone expects him to fail, shrinking as they do from the face of shame. But the fool-dümmling is open, he contacts the forces of renewal, he transcends shame and sterility.

I wonder about the relevance of all this not only for personal development but also for the future of our own psychological collective. Will we march on with our so adapted, so successful "older brothers"? Will we strive to consolidate our public acclaim and power? Will we endlessly perfect our students so that no dangerous trace of foolishness remains? Or will we dare to trust the dümmling a bit, dare to let things be a little more shamefully disorganised? Can we worry less about the power-persona of our profession and remain open to the new, the unique, the creative, which is always on the clumsy side, somewhat strange, somewhat foolish, but full of life?

I would like to elaborate more on the idea of shame. Freud originally felt that this was a basic emotion, like love and hate, was inborn and not learned or derived from other emotions. Young children seem to experience a certain kind of shame due to their relative physical and psychological powerlessness. Shame has an intense upsurge in adolescence when increased instinctual drives combined with the cognitive complexity of the adult create a sense of inferiority. The adolescent clings regressively to group conformity in order to help maintain a feeling of control and stability. Adolescents in particular disown and despise the *dümmling*-deviant in themselves and others. Shame, the emotion of inferiority and limitation, is the predominant motif of the adolescent passage. The great fear of adolescence is appearing (as/to be) the fool.

There are many levels of shame which persist into adulthood. The most primal might be the feeling of physical inferiority, the aftermath of a creepy encounter with a shadowy figure in a dark alley; we feel again like a vulnerable, helpless child. Our cringing fear makes us feel ashamed.

Then there is the sense of fallibility before our own emotions, the times when we are helplessly tossed about by love or hate, by rage or anxiety. At the extreme is the shame of the psychotic who succumbs once again to the archetypal psyche. All these situations make us feel the victim of the dancing fool who will have his way no matter what.

Ultimately, the experience of foolishness, of shame is the experience of *ontological limitation*: our focused awareness, our ego-consciousness, our kingly demeanour, are never more than partly in control. Potential life is so much more than we can ever comprehend or be. We are in so many ways clowns strutting upon the stage of fools. To see this head-on fills one with an intense feeling of shame and limitation. It is the fool, spouting his absurd poetry, mimicking our mechanical illusions of control, speaking from the endless depths of imagination, who brings us to feel shame. The fool reminds us that we are the limited creatures we are; the fool may finally appear as death, the ultimate limitation.

All this sounds rather heavy and deflating. Of course it is true that we are all fools, full of petty strivings, ludicrously inflated, flies on the vast body of the Godhead. Yet, as we also know, foolery and humour are generally immensely invigorating, lifegiving, renewing. The fool who mocks us, frees us. A deflated ego becomes permeable, reopened to the creative depths. We can drop the inflated burden of trying to be godlike, of trying to control the whole world. As we lose the illusion of our omnipotence, we become paradoxically more open to the *presence of* what *is*. That is the joy in the dance of the fool.

To speak historically, it is true that Greek comedy, the Dionysian ritual, preceded the development of tragedy; tragedy developed out of comedy. Tragedy represents the ontological dilemma, the conflict of apparently irreconcilable planes of being. Such tragic consciousness seems very Western. The fool, comedy, humour, return us to a state of primordial whole-ness, of *communitas*, the sense of rebirth embodied in the early rituals of death and renewal. The inflated attempt to *be* the Self closes the individual or society to the renewal in the Self – a wholeness in which the ego is only a part. So only a deflated ego can really experience wholeness, the joy and relief in being *part* of a greater whole. The fool shames us and frees us from our paranoid closedness and onesidedness; he helps us transcend shame and experience wholeness.

On a more mundane level, everyone knows how relieving it is when someone makes a joke amidst an overly heavy group discussion. The fool-humorist helps the group transcend its inflated seriousness. Defensive competitiveness and suspicious self-consciousness evaporate in the face of humour. It is a fact – studied very seriously by behavioural scientists – that groups in which people know and trust one another experience much more humour than those in which they do not. Threatening, attacking comedians such as Don Rickles create less humour and spontaneity than non-threatening humorists. Thus humour, creative foolery and creative group feeling go hand in hand.

An individual or group missing the fool becomes trapped in sterility. Witness Hamlet: the fool is dead, the centre is corrupt, and Hamlet can never decide whether he is hero, mad fool or king. Thus, he succumbs to a kind of true madness. In *King Lear*, the king fails to heed his truth-speaking fool; the ego, in its closed rigidity, plummets toward destruction. Lear becomes mad, a possessed fool, wandering in the forest of chaos and inferiority. But, at the end, there is a kind of apotheosis as he recognises and spiritually transcends his worldly foolishness.

This brings to mind the dream of a middle-aged person, stripped bare by confrontation with his foolish inferiority:

> I was in a palace in which I felt alien; I was ejected naked into the streets. I had to escape and crept furtively through the streets, trying to conceal my nakedness. Then I came to an old warehouse in a dead-end alley. It seemed hopeless, with no way out. A bunch of tramps were sleeping and living there. At first, I was revolted by their strangeness and dirtiness. But they saw me, seemed to take pity on me and began to throw me clothes which I accepted. They were fool's clothes, motley and mismatched. As I accepted them, I felt an overwhelming sense of goodness and gratitude and knew the tramps and I were akin in some deep way.

Awareness of his one-sidedness, his true inferiority, had deflated him. He had to wander in humble awareness of shame and limitation. In fact, his comfortable palace of orderly existence had become more prison than home. As he acknowledged his shadowy self-indulgences and the compulsive anima moods over which he had had no control, his ego felt naked, foolish, humiliated. Only his "inferiors," the tramps, could clothe him in attitudes open to the future and renewal. His open-hearted honesty and acceptance were essential. The very deep glow of inner – and outer – community which ensued was certainly an experience of the Self. This was a true turning point in his analysis. He became much more open to the "thou," the "other," both inwardly and outwardly. There was a growing sense of renewal, and his feeling of sterile depression gradually dissipated.

At the other extreme, I have noted that people who are defensive and humorless, who fear to be the fool, rarely progress in analysis. Seriousness is, ultimately, the enemy of evolution. Typically, this is the "up-tight" person, trying to anticipate and avoid shame through clever ego-insights, "progressing" perhaps at the ego level, perhaps even memorizing and parroting

Jungian concepts, individuating-by-the-numbers. Most such individuals fail to experience true inner initiation, which always involves the pain of shame and foolishness.

One dream of such a "defensive" patient was.

I wandered through a roomful of clowns, fools. I wanted to get out as fast as possible because they seemed so strange. Finally I scambled frantically out of the door and was relieved by the light and familiar surroundings.

In another case:

I crossed a long bridge. There was a carnival on the other side. A fool or jester approached me, grinning, juggling some disparate objects. I was filled with terror, jumped in my car and drove frantically back across the bridge.

The refusal of the fool was a harbinger of difficulty for both patients. The former lived in a semi-paranoid, borderline state for a long period of time. The latter became trapped in a parade of collective "successes" which seemed sterile and unrewarding: he was chronically depressed and never seemed to reach his deeper potential.

To take off briefly on another tack, 1 would like to issue (make?) a disclaimer: the fool is *not* the trickster, in my opinion. The "tricky" aspect of the unconscious is archetypal and manifests itself in many ways when the ego is closed and defensive. The "tricky" is the demonically unpredictable: a clever but frightening animal, a shadowy pursuer, an elusive and enchanting pixie, *or* a tricky fool. That is, a fool may be tricky, like any symbolic entity. Hermes, for example, is trickster, fool, messenger, guide to the underworld, bringer of meaning; he adopts many modes, but cannot be reduced to one aspect, any more than the fool. From the standpoint of an ego committed to order, non-rational processes and creative élan appear in multiple tricky and threatening guises.

The fool and all his works are the agents of wholeness, of Self as process and evolution, of *communitas*. As Bergson said, humour frees the living from the mechanistic encrustations of the dead. Perhaps this is too extreme a statement: we do need order, modes of structure. The danger seems so often from the other direction: we tend so easily to forget that we are the shoots rather than the rhizome. There is a richness and vitality in accepting our foolishness and limitation; we restore the thread of connection with our deeper origins. There is shame in knowing we are foolish and tiny amidst the vast ocean of Being. But there is a richness and celebration in accepting limitation, sacrificing pride. Existential nakedness and shame give way *to* joy and humour when we can accept the motley of the fool.

Note

1 I would like to acknowledge my indebtedness to Bill Willeford for his very fine book on the fool, which provided me a great deal of insight and inspiration.

Chapter 4

A Return to the Animal Soul*

The future survival of humankind depends upon return to a right relation-ship to nature. The need is both inner and outer. In this endeavor, the animal soul is our most dependable guide. If we befriend the animals, they can lead us, show us what we need to know. Animals deserve our thanks, our respect, our admiration. Since we no longer hunt in lonely communion with animals, and since few of us feel called to go on formal vision quests, we have to seek ways of re-creating meaningful connection with the animal realm. Can mythology and depth psychology help us reconnect with the animal soul and reclaim a vital orientation toward life and nature?

In the *Visions Seminars*, C. G. Jung provided deeply moving and original insights about the relationship of animals and psychic evolution. Presenting a lengthy active imagination, Jung described several sequences of images that portrayed a woman's descent to pre-historical layers of the psyche. A Native American and a cortège of animals lead the way. Jung interpreted the symbolic images as manifesting a necessary regression to a deeper, pre-Christian dimen-sion of the unconscious. It is there, he said, that one rediscovers the energies of our lost pagan vitality. A major sequence of the active imagination culminates in "The Vision of the Eyes." The patient vividly described this experience[1]:

> I behold a face with the eyes closed; I besought the face, open your eyes that I may behold them. . . . Then the face becomes very dark and slowly I beheld what no man is meant to see, eyes full of beauty and woe and light, and I could bear it no longer.

* Hinton, L. & Zokowsky, P. (1993). A Return to the Animal Soul. *Psychological Perspectives*, 28(1), 47–60. https://doi.org/10.1080/00332929308404792, reprinted by permission of the publisher (Tay-lor & Francis Ltd, http://www.tandfonline.com).

DOI: 10.4324/9781003641063-5

Painting this vision, the patient fashioned the face of an animal with eyes that were indeed, "full of beauty and woe." Jung remarked[1]:

> . . . [The eyes of the animal] contain the truth of life, an equal sum of pain and pleasure, the capacity for joy and the capacity for suffering. . . . If you are within the animal, you do not feel unconscious, but it is exactly the thing that from our standpoint we call unconsciousness. . . . You see, it is possible that what we call unconsciousness . . . has a consciousness in itself . . . and so what we call the unconscious would be another form of consciousness.

Here is a very key point in understanding our awe and sense of love for the animal world: In the eyes of the animal, there is no polarity between opposites. Rather, there is a unified, whole consciousness that, without self-reflection, expresses the nature of the animal. The animal reminds us of that which we so easily forget: the immediate and simple sense of being human. The possibility of being present in the world in a whole, undivided way can be a gift of the animal. The ego, in its inflations and neurotic defensiveness, all too easily loses touch with its ground and origin. To quote Jung once more[2]:

> Many neuroses come from the fact that too good a victory has been won over the body of dark powers. . . . The old serpent has been too cruelly mauled by too spiritual a consciousness. . . . When God made animals, he equipped them with just those needs and impulses that enable them to live according to their laws. We assume that he has done the same with man. In a way the animal is more pious than man, because it fulfills the divine will more completely than man can ever dream of . . . I hazard the conjecture . . . that the [deepest] layers of our psyche still have animal characters. Hence it is highly probable that animals have similar or even the same archetypes.

Is this the mystery we see in animals – the archetypes, or ancient patterns of natural being, manifesting through the animals like Platonic ideas, eternally repeating themselves through time? Do the animals comfort us because they are born already knowing and being what they wholly are? Do the animals remind us of an innate "knowing" we have forgotten – an intrinsic sense of the patterns for being human that we have lost due to technology and the extreme pressures of collective live?

In 1904, Chief Letokots-Lesa of the Pawnee tribe spoke of the time of creations[3]:

> In the beginning of things, wisdom and knowledge were with the animals; for Tirawa, the One Above, did not speak directly to man. He sent certain animals to tell men that he showed himself through the beasts, and that from them, and from the stars and sun and moon, man should learn. Tirawa spoke to man through his works.

In the mythos of the great hunting cultures, God (or Tirawa) manifests directly in animal forms. Such a view of life dominated Paleolithic Europe, Siberia, and eventually North America; this was the landscape at the "Great Hunt"[3]:

> This landscape was typically a spreading plain, clearly bounded by a circular horizon, with the great blue dome of an exalting heaven above, where hawks and eagles hovered and the blazing sun passes daily; becoming dark by night, star-filled, and with the moon there, waxing and waning. The essential food supply was from the multitudinous grazing herds, brought in by the males of the tribe following dangerous physical encounters. And the ceremonial life was addressed largely to the ends of a covenant with the animals, of reconciliation, veneration, and assurance that in return for the beasts' unremitting offering of themselves as willing victims, their life-blood should be given back in a sacred way to the earth, the mother of all, for rebirth.

In the shamanic cultures of the Paleolithic Great Hunt, communion with the divine occurred mainly through animals. The phenomena of the world were imbued with Being. The cultures of the jungle in the equatorial belt of the world lived in a contrasting universe. In its endless inevitability, the vegetative cycle of nature vividly dominated their awareness. The leafy canopies above, decaying vegetation below, and the swarming struggle for life in-between, presented a world of inexorable bloody death and rebirth. There was little seasonal change, little variation of terrain, as opposed to the dramatic seasons and geography of the Paleolithic Great Hunt[3].

This "jungle" view of life, which sees the world as an endless repetition from which one must seek liberation, has dominated our traditional religions. In this view, the phenomena of the world are the source of sin and temptation, and life is lived in bondage to the endless wheel of change. The only hope is detachment or the "Via Negativa" – a dying to the world. In

Christianity, this view has often approached a near-hatred of life – life seen as *Original Sin* rather than *Original Blessing*.

The shamanic vision-quest world of the hunting peoples has heavily influenced depth psychology. The dream, the symbol, the personal and collective myths – all are rooted in, and give direct access to, the divine. The world, emotions, and symbols are welcome manifestations of Being, not merely illusions to be resisted. The inner voice is a guide rather than a tempted.

A world view dominated by the observation of the order of the heavens later supplanted both mythologies. Through the nascent science of astronomy, the five visible planets with their lord, the moon, became the focus of mythic concern. The world was now perceived as mathematically ordered, and that which could be recorded in writing and mathematics was seen as most real and true. This was a radical shift from the idea of a divine energy observable and immanent in nature, brought to us in the endless forms of animal messengers. It became man's task to decipher, and to put himself in harmony with, a power that was transcendent and celestial rather than immediately tangible in human beings, plants, and animals. We are living amidst the results of this paradigmatic shift: the alienated condition of the modern person, estranged from Being in a cold, uncaring universe.

Mythologically speaking, return to the animal soul would involve a return to a more primordial ground of existence. From such a perspective, one experiences the divine as directly accessible. By returning to the mystery of the animal, the "eyes of the animal" in the words of Jung, we can begin to see through the veil of our rationality. We come closer to our natural origins. Through the animal, we can regain connection with the intersecting web of life as it manifests in all beings.

Animal Messengers in Our Dreams

Animals often manifest themselves to the modern Western person during the analytic process. They come most frequently in dreams. By comparison to earlier times, our contemporary connection may seem impoverished. However, considering the sterility of our technological culture, the persistence and vivid proliferation of animal life in the modern psyche stands out all the more remarkably.

One example is a dream reported by an unmarried, 33-year-old man:

First, there is a herd of cows. I am milking one, or trying to. The whole herd starts mooing or barking. I'm frightened! Next, I'm backing my car out of a parking place. I hear a very loud yelp – I think it's a cow. I jump out of my car, thinking something terrible has happened. But the car is only on the cow's hoof and it seems okay. I pull back into the space.

This was the dream of a highly intellectual person, who had major problems relating to women. He tended to become infatuated with very attractive but unstable females who led him "around in circles." He was troubled by moodiness, with a kind of testiness and hypersensitivity that sometimes caused problems with colleagues. He often felt alienated and gravitated toward a self-imposed isolation. In discussing his early life, he described his mother as a "witchy" woman who abused him physically and emotionally.

Together, we pondered this dramatic and mysterious encounter with the cows. The eyes of the cow are deep, soft, and mystical – they seem bottomless. The cow generally appears to be passive, although a cow or cows may become aggressive when provoked. Mostly, the cow ruminates, chewing quietly, turning the grass of earth into milk. Its tongue is gentle, soft, warm, enfolding.

In Hindu belief, bull and cow often represent the active and passive generative forces of the universe. Gandhi once said about the cow[4]:

"Cow protection" to me is one of the most wonderful phenomena in all human evolution; for it takes the human being beyond his species . . . man through the cow is enjoined to realise his identity with all that lives.

Another beautiful description of the cow's meaning is provided by Helen Luke[4]:

The cow is the passive feminine heart of unremitting attention without which there can be no transformation by fire . . . all of us have somewhere buried the capacity for image-making, and the little spark can be nursed into a blaze only if we will care for our cow. She must be milked without fail, morning and evening, or she will sicken and die. We must draw the milk and drink it.

Cow-consciousness, then, was the order of the day for this man. Through analysis, he was getting deeply involved in the unconscious. His efforts at milking evoked a response that frightened him. Pervasive fear and anxiety, due mainly to the early experiences with his mother, had continually interrupted his efforts to forge ahead in life. The future direction clearly entailed more patient, receptive caring for the soul – respect for the cow nature.

In the second part of the dream, he would like to back out: The analytic process has stirred up the unconscious and the ego-consciousness wants to regain a sense of control. However, cow-consciousness has developed sufficiently to voice a strong protest. He heeds the warning. The patient is beginning to discover the re-wounding that results from disowning inner and outer possibilities. The inner witch-mother, with her frightening affects, had constantly blocked his development. The cow strongly calls attention to other, more nurturing, possibilities. His nature is an innately vital one, and the cow offers the prospect of fuller creative expression of that life energy. Everything is now possible – if he stays parked long enough!

Another animal dream from a professional woman in her forties:

An older woman, a psychologist whom I admire, comes to my house to observe me with a client, who is a depressed, withdrawn woman. Someone tells a dream and my mentor watches. Then I'm in the kitchen with her husband. He's telling me about the bad termites in their house. I say I have them too, but they're subterranean and not in the basic structure, so they're not a serious problem.

I had worked with this person for about two years. She suffered from chronic depression and low self-esteem. Fulfilling the scapegoat role in a large family, she had difficulty believing any good would come her way. By contrast, her relationship with the mentor in the dream had been an exceptionally good one. On the other hand, she had a pattern of overidealizing people and then being disappointed.

The termites are the most enigmatic part of the dream and greatly puzzled the patient. She thought they seemed dangerous and alarming.

Termites are the little things we can't get rid of, no matter how hard we try. Everyone is bugged by such things. They are tiny, almost invisible, working deep below the surface, eating away at structure. They are highly organised and live for the whole, to feed the collective. They are industrious and rather linear. The queen is proliferative, endlessly laying eggs. In mythology, ants are an attribute of the Earth Mother, Demeter. Ants helped Psyche, the evolving feminine soul, in a difficult part of her task.

In this dream, the admired woman – the older, wiser spirit – is coming home. She is becoming a part of the inner life of the patient. No longer is she merely projected into the world. However, there is also a danger of falling into depression, of identifying with the withdrawn woman, when the knowing eye of the idealised mentor takes over the house of the psyche. Then someone tells a dream – another dimension enters the picture. The mentor's husband appears. One would expect that he would know about the non-ideal side of his wife. They are in the kitchen, the place of alchemical transformation. The husband confides that *they* indeed have termites, of a sort even worse than hers.

This shows a healthy process of balancing and compensation. *Everyone* has termites! All of us are prone to the petty annoyances of life. All of us need to become small in order to appreciate the detailed immediacy of things. We can't be soaring eagles all the time! In these bugs one senses the inexorable vitality of life, the determination to be, no matter what neat structure is undermined, no matter how banal the task at hand. These termites live in the earth, which is *humus. Humility, humor*, and ultimately *humanness* come from this earthy connection.[5] If we are in touch with our ant- or termite-consciousness, it is hard to become inflated. When we see the bugs of others, it's much harder to overidealise them. It brings them down to human proportions, and thereby frees us.[6]

A 44-year-old woman dreamed:

I am presented with a certificate. It seems mass-produced, not valuable. I don't want it, but I have to accept it. Then as I accept it, it becomes black silk. It's a death certificate! It shimmers! I use it like e bullfighter's cloak, and I am enticing bulls with it, moving gracefully out of the way, like a dance.

At the beginning of analysis, this woman was leading a deeply unsettled life. Divorced after many years of marriage, she continued to experience a disturbing degree of ambivalence in intimate relationships. She would become close, and then experience deep dread of becoming engulfed. When her life became too difficult, she often returned home for an extended visit with her aging parents (she was the youngest and only daughter in a large family). She regained a sense of groundedness during these visits . . . something that came both from the containment of family and the nourishment of native soil.

At the beginning of this dream, she did not want to accept the certificate – it seemed "too ordinary." This reflected an underlying grandiosity in her character: She subtlety disdained "submitting" to analysis and to working out life and relationships in an earthy, everyday way. A part of her felt she should be "above" all that. Her family prided itself on aesthetic and social superiority. They clearly conveyed this attitude to their only daughter, who was in many ways the "princess." However, her sense of entitlement had not led to a fulfilling life, but to intense fear of failure, because nothing was ever good enough. She suffered from painful feelings of inferiority and at times felt like an "impostor," as if no accomplishment was "real." A tyrannical inner judge, severe and perfectionistic, evaluated every experience. This judge was also projected into relationships, including the analyst-patient relationship.

In her dream, she *must* accept the "mass-produced" certificate. This sense of the necessity of submission often comes from the Self. She must submit to analysis, to suffering through emotions and relationships, in order to experience the vitality of being fully alive in the world. When She does so, there is a remarkable transformation. What seemed like a death certificate becomes a black, shimmering cape. In the ordinary, which she had treated as death-like, she found the extraordinary. Then the fascinating dance with the bulls ensues. She wields a dark, silken power over the bulls, which seems erotically connected and almost Dionysian. It was this last scene, with its surprising transformation, which stood out the most for her. Bulls have been revered since Paleolithic times. They are wild, red-eyed, snorting, strong, fertile, quick to take offense, territorial. They are often associated with the sun and its fertility (as in Egyptian and later in Mithraic rites); their horns are connected with the moon, and their bellow with the movements of the earth and earthquakes. The ancient Cretans performed a ritual dance with the bull, in which the dancers' greatest achievement was a somersault over the horns of the animal. In this way, right relationship could be established with the core of the bulls' strength and fertility. Rather than fleeing from or feeling engulved by this elemental life force, the patient was gaining a sense of controlled relatedness. She connected with the raw vitality of her inner depths – something so powerful it could overthrow the tyranny of the inner judge, who would sacrifice life on the altar of perfection. The vitality of the bull-energy was fully active, not killed or repressed. It was indubitably *real*! The black silk cape represented an ancient knowledge that was now hers. She had gained an instinctive relationship to the energies from the Self, brought to her by the bulls. It required a delicate balance between connection and distance. One should not forget that submission to the scorned and "ordinary" certificate is the means of access to this archaic wisdom. It represented the routine and "ordinary" ritual of analysis, as well as the necessity for enduring "ordinary" life,

A 38-year-old woman dreamed:

> *I walk into a large arena-like area. It is full of caged animals. There is a wild energy present, like e circus. The cages are in ornate geometrical patterns. There are bands of guards, with bows and arrows. The groups seem to argue. A huge elephant with sad eyes stares at me. I want to leap on its back and ride out, breaking down all the cages to free the sad animals. The unfriendly guards sense my intention and point their bows at me. They look angry. I am afraid and hesitate to act.*

This extremely bright, single, university science professor was the oldest of four children. She had been the responsible caretaker in her family. Her mother was alcoholic, and she strongly identified with her father, a successful scientist. Her youngest sibling's suicide precipitated her entrance into analysis. She felt somehow to blame. Although her intellectual achievements were impressive, she did not find meaning in her scientific career. She attracted many men, but the relationships did not evolve into long-term commitments.

In the dream, she enters into a circus-like world, a sort of Dionysian panorama of life. However, there are geometrically shaped cages. It is a world of the extraordinary, what with all the people, animals, and wild energies. It contrasts strongly with her ordinary world where she tries hard to be the good daughter: predictable, dependable, and rational. There is argument going on, meaning that parts of her psyche are becoming dynamically interrelated rather than carefully compartmentalised. Her fear of the hostile guards – representing the old ruling principle of her psyche and her lifelong character structure – inhibits her desire to lead the animals out into the world.

Elephants are huge, ponderous, majestic animals. They are slow, weighty, and deliberate. Their adult life begins late and they live long. They mate in secret and adultery is rare. Wise and intelligent, they have a kind of patience and long memory that projects an aura of timelessness. In myth, they are often noted for their invincibility in overcoming impediments. In the Hindu pantheon, an elephant carries the world. The elephant Ganesha, the "Lord of Obstacles," breaks a path for his devotees. Elephants are the bringers and bearers of weight.

Elephants have a thick-skinned resistance to the slings and arrows of the world. They are slow to anger, to gestate, and to die. They are vegetarians and love the green world. They are the most magnificent land animals, often alone in their wise and dignified way. As we all too sadly know, poachers now kill them ruthlessly for their ivory tusks, threatening to make them an endangered species.[7]

Such a weighty animal seemed auspicious for this attractive but frail-looking woman, who felt so insubstantial in both the inner and outer worlds. In the non-rational world of the unconscious, she finds a wild circus of energies as well as the wisdom, solidity, and commitment of the magical pachyderm. This is the strength she needs to overcome inner and outer obstacles, and to bear the emotional repercussions she will experience if she dares to break new pathways. She will need the strength of the elephant to take the potential life found in the circus into the everyday world. She will also need that strength to withstand her critical and angry inner authorities, which would always maintain the status quo.

Birthmark of the Animal Soul

In 1843, Nathaniel Hawthorne wrote a visionary short story entitled, "The Birthmark." This story contains extraordinary insights into the plight of the contemporary world. It begins with the marriage of Aylmer, a natural scientist of world renown, to a beauty named Georgiana. They are quite happy until he notices that his wife has one flaw: On her left cheek she bears a crimson birthmark resembling a tiny animal paw. He becomes quietly obsessed with Georgiana's mark of imperfection, "the indelible mark of the human." The birthmark is the visible sign of the animal soul: "The crimson hand expressed the indelible grip in which mortality clutches the highest and purest of earthly mold, degrading them into kindred with the lowest, and even with the very brutes, like whom their visible frames return to dust." It is the mark of imperfection, including the ultimate imperfection of death.

When she discovers the source of Aylmer's discontent, Georgiana becomes equally obsessed with her "imperfection." Aylmer has a terrible dream, in which her husband and his servant Aminadab (*bad anima* spelled backwards!) attempt an operation to remove Georgiana's birthmark. They cut deeper and deeper, until it becomes apparent that the roots of the birthmark go clear to her heart. The dream ends as Aylmer resolves to cut or wrench away the grip of the animal paw upon his beloved wife.

Georgiana finds out about the dream and begs him to remove the hated birthmark, whatever the risk to herself. He declares confidence in his science and ability and goes to work with Aminadab in his laboratory, The story notes that, earlier in his career, Aylmer had failed in experiments to fathom or create life because of "the truth . . . that our great creative Mother, while she amuses us with apparently working in the broadest sunshine, is yet severely careful to keep her own secrets and, in spite of her pretended openness, shows us nothing but results. She permits us to mar, but seldom to mend."

The mystery of birth, of new nation, belongs to the realm of the dark Mother, and masculine logos can approach, but never decipher, that enigma. Even Aminadab expresses doubt about the enterprise. However, the possessed Aylmer and Georgiana move their quarters into the lab, so as to continue the research uninterrupted.

As the experiments progress, the couple become more and more intoxicated with the enterprise. There are many failures. At last, Aylmer concocts a potion that makes spots disappear from the leaves of a plant. Georgiana herself insists on partaking of the experimental elixir. She quaffs it down and falls into a deep sleep. The mark grows more and more faint; but, as the last sign of the animal paw fades from her cheek, she dies!

This prophetic story presages the growth of faith in rationality, with its deadly one-sidedness. Blind faith in reason is faith in the "perfectibility" of life. However, in the world of nature, blemishes form a part of the wholeness of things. To take away the "flaw" may well destroy the complex totality. In medieval times, they referred to the *felix culpa* – the fortunate flaw – in individual character. What to the rational mind seems a flaw is often a profoundly mysterious key to the secret of individual life. We live in a culture addicted to perfection of mind and body, which yet suffers from aimless violence, discontent, and illness. Reason and logic cannot grasp the mystery of the uniqueness of life, of creation and individuality. Shades of light and dark, of rough and smooth, of strangeness and familiarity, are deeply intertwined in the human character. To arbitrarily eliminate one dimension of personality is to destroy the whole. When we pathologise human foibles in our relentless way, trying to subdue and "purify" life, we kill the soul.

Hawthorne's story describes the plight of the modern psyche. In America, we struggle with a Puritanism that begets witch-hunts and scapegoating. This stems from fear of the enigmatic mystery that life is. We want to eliminate the "evil," the troubling "flaw," and we end by destroying life. Society abounds in Torquemadas. The worst things are always done "in a good cause." Social and moral perfectionism becomes hatred of life itself, very different from a true morality that respects and revered the individual. Perfectionism's real temple is the temple of death, and at root, it is the stillness of the necropolis that it craves. Creative life is constant change movement, messiness. When we cease to embrace life as it is, in its turbulent essence, we indeed become worshippers of death. We become secret servants of the Lord of Death and enemies of the animal soul.

Our cultural obsession with perfectionism touches everyone. We feel entitled to life without flaw or dysfunction, but the world is a messy whirl of constant change. With our Puritan tradition, we tend to blame our problems, our malaise, on someone or something that can be "corrected" or eliminated. We try to starve the animal soul, perfect it, do away with its messiness, outlaw it. We attempt to drug it out of existence, legally or illegally. It rebels in eruptions of personal and social violence. Puritanism foments the dark pathology it most fears.

We all bear the print of the animal, and in that we can find salvation. Zest for life comes from living in accordance with the animal soul, from listening to its messengers. To survive and thrive, we must honor its voice wherever we find it. Dreams and solitude, walks in mountains and forest, the company of animals, all may help attune us. However, it is not an esoteric pursuit. We must never forget that the animal soul requires *fully living* all the dimensions of our humanness. "*Amor fati*," love your fate, Jung liked to say. We must *live* our nature to "know" nature. If we passionately and *consciously* embrace the raw reality of life in all of its messiness, the animal soul will in turn reward us. We will experience renewed meaning, energy, and purpose. We will feel deeply in accordance with nature. That is the animal's gift.

This does not involve a sentimental romanticizing of nature, Nature is everywhere. We *are* nature. Much of the simplistic adulation of nature we see is, at root, the child's regressive longing for the eternally good mother. It is poetic and understandable, but is another way of disowning the messy business that life is. Such "love" of nature becomes another subtle form of the hatred of life. It is often a shadow-Puritanism, which disdains life as it *is*, with all of its animal smells and creative ferment.

If we acknowledge and embrace this animal zest within us, if we can stay attuned to its voice, the energy of life will flow. The only antidote to nihilistic perfectionism, to cynical skepticism, is an honoring of (to paraphrase Santayana) that dark inner glow of animal faith in life that transcends all reason and is the ground of all creation.

Notes

1 Jung, C. G. (1976). *The Visions Seminars*. Zurich: Spring Publications.
2 Adler, G. (Ed.). (1975). *The Selected Letters of C. G. Jung, 1909–1961*. Princeton: Princeton University Press.
3 Campbell, J. (1983). *The Way of the Animal Powers*. San Francisco: Harper and Row.
4 Luke, H. (1970). The Cow. In: *Man, Myth and Magic*, Vol. 4. New York: Cavendish Corporation.
5 Luke, H. (1986). *Woman, Earth and Spirit*. New York: Crossroads Press.
6 Hillman, J. (1988). Going Bugs. *Spring*, 48, 40–72.
7 Hillman, J. (1990). The Elephant in the Garden of Eden. *Spring*, 50, 93–115.

Chapter 5

The Hunt for the Wild Unicorn

Containment, Sacrifice and Evolution*

Introduction

In 1966, my wife and I visited the Cluny Museum in Paris at the sugges-
tion of a German graduate student – whom I have thanked many times
over in my mind! The Lady and the Unicorn tapestries at the museum had
a powerful impact on us.

Later, I became acquainted with the tapestries at the Cloisters in New
York – the Hunting Series. These reinforced my fascination with the enigma
of the Unicorn. Over time, I became more entranced by the Hunting Series
because it is more vital and emotional, whereas the Cluny series is a more
abstract reflection on the senses.

The mystery of the magical beast that never was captured my imagination. Later, I connected this mystery with the animal paintings of the Palaeolithic caves and the animal rituals of the Native Americans, along with
the animal as key to dreams and fairy tales (Hinton, 1991, 1993). As the
earliest human beings contemplated their place in the universe and tried to
comprehend their own presence in the world, they consistently focused on
the Magical Animal.

This dimension of the life of the psyche has not changed with the decline
of hunting cultures, for we continue to see an endless proliferation of animals in our own dreams and those of our analysands.

The tale of the Wild Unicorn expresses the strangeness of the Unknown
when it impacts our familiar world, continuing the long fascination of the
human race with the mystery of the Magical Animal. What is the meaning of
this strange, powerful animal that emerges out of the Unknown? How can we
contain it so that it feeds our souls with its aliveness and does not destroy us?

* Paper first presented at the National Conference of Jungian Analysts. Santa Monica, California, in
2001.

DOI: 10.4324/9781003641063-6

There is a strong connection between this mystery and our analytic work. The Age of Reason and the increasing pressures of collective life and technology have led to an alienation that Jungian and other analytic approaches have sought to heal. We, and most of our patients, suffer at times from feelings of psychic deadness. We are often Hamlets who do not know what to do or how to be.[1] In contrast, animals know how to be what they are. The Unicorn tapestries derive from a time – perhaps the last time in the Western world – when the gods and goddesses were felt to be alive, and everyday existence was imbued with meaning. With a potent emotional immediacy and aliveness, the Unicorn embodies a primal vitality stemming from the Unknown. It expresses something we have lost and need to recover to heal others and ourselves.

The vicissitudes of the Hunt for the Wild Unicorn illustrate, in their way, elements basic to the analytic process – most especially containment, sacrifice and evolution. By participating in the drama of the Unicorn, the Hunt and capture, we enter into the ancient human mystery of the Magical Animal that appears out of the Unknown.[2]

I will speak here of 'the Unknown', meaning something like the Kantian 'thing-in-itself' that can never be known. Paradoxically, it is also the ground of our aliveness. This concept is related to the Jungian Self (big S) or Uroboros, to what Bion called 'O', and what Grotstein has named 'the Ineffable Subject'. Dwelling with the Unknown produces or provokes surging movements of affective life, thereby keeping experience free and open. This is a 'cleansing' effect that rescues us from a deadly literalness and enhances the capacity to use symbolic thought (Eigen, 1996, p. 45ff). Keats used the expression 'Negative Capability', by which he meant, 'when a man is capable of being in uncertainties, mysteries, [and] doubts, without an irritable reaching after fact and reason' (Symington & Symington, 1997, p. 169). Freed of the strictures of the literal, truth and insight may be unveiled, and inner space can expand.

Encountering the Unknown also provokes a constantly moving stream of emotions that often makes us overfull. This inner flow is always evolving from containment to containment and, in the best case, towards differentiated inner and outer life. The philosopher and psychoanalyst Jonathan Lear describes the psyche as functioning with an inherent tendency towards disruption (Lear, 2000, p. 106ff). There is an 'over-fullness' in the system that it cannot contain. As a result, life is lived under conditions of tension, and, to quote Lear,

. . . Because we are always and everywhere living under pressure, we must live with the possibility of breakthrough in any psychological structure we have thus far achieved. . . . There is always and everywhere the possibility of being overwhelmed.[3]

On the one hand, our ongoing encounters with the Unknown may unveil small epiphanies, such as the Unicorn tapestries, or may emerge in ordinary experiences, such as a meal, a meeting with a friend or an analytic session. On the other hand, we flee from the terror of being overwhelmed, often becoming reactively stuck in concreteness, rigidity and sometimes deadness. The overload of emotions may be 'too much', causing dissociation and fragmentation of the self (little s).

Encountering the Unknown deeply affects consciousness, and yet the Unknown remains wholly Other. The need to contain and transform our surplus of emotion is part of the necessity of the human condition. To evade the anxiety of the Not-Knowing, we employ an endless bag of defensive postures such as paranoia, schizoid detachment and manic denial. From infancy onward, we struggle to maintain emotional regulation, striving to contain and transform our overfullness into something that is humanly connected and creative.[4]

However, even though we may be dominated and, at times, overwhelmed by our overfullness, still we also *seek*; we Hunt new experiences at the expense of containment. Pribram has written of the brain as a stimulus-seeking organ. Jung's description of individuation is certainly not a path of contentment and avoidance of stress! We have a hunger for aliveness, Truth and meaning that overrides our dread of the Unknown. The presence of the Unknown foments a disruptive overfullness and at the same time creates openness and opportunity.[5]

Seen in this context, the tale of the Wild Unicorn can be seen as a complex parable of our overfullness: a story of the Unknown impacting on the Known. As a Hunt, it is a quest for something enigmatic and unpredictable. There is both fascination and danger in this enterprise. We seek contact with the Unknown because it brings aliveness and meaning. We dread it because the experiences it provokes may overwhelm us.

After the events of September 11th, comparisons of our own time with the time of the Tapestries have come to my mind. The overfullness of much of the world psyche has come to our doorstep in terrifying fashion. We are so overwhelmed that it has been very difficult to even begin to get a handle on events so huge.

One thing that has been recurring to me is a contrast between *Moby Dick* and the Unicorn Tapestries. The 19th century was the height of the Age of Reason, and one could see Moby Dick as its shadow. To the possessed Ahab, the great whale, symbolising the enigma of life and the Unknown, has become the enemy. The wounds inflicted by the whale feel deeply *personal* to him – narcissistic injuries. In his wounded, monomaniacal fury, he wants to destroy it. The enigma of life has become a *personal* enemy rather than a part of the mysterious round of life and meaning. It must be eradicated. Such a dark, magnetic vision of destruction lurks in the contemporary psyche, a reaction to the confusing diversity of a globalising world.

From within this perspective the world must be made pure. That is the core of the genocidal and terrorist mentality. A Marxist paradise, the Third Reich, an Arcadian Cambodia or the purity of Heaven after a martyr's death are similar visions of taintlessness. The adherents of these views identify with the pure and split off and project the impure. The idea is to eliminate the impure. Life being at root impure, the end result is the overt or covert nihilism that manifested in the genocide and terrorism of our times.

I invite you to contrast this modern attitude towards the white whale with the cultural attitude towards the Unicorn around 1500. As you will see, there is violence and destruction in the Unicorn Hunt, but it is contained. The Unknown is a moving thread in the midst of life. Being and becoming are, at root, one. By contrast, in these modern and postmodern times, we have lost our containers, lost the possibility of enlivening ritual contact with the Unknown. Instead it feels out of control, a haunting demon.

Analysis is one small container for ritual contact with the Unknown, but we lack meaningful containment on the community level. We can only live with what we have and hope that new structures of meaning come into being over time. If we consciously bear our almost unbearable tensions, a new vision may emerge, like an unexpected dream. Otherwise, globalisation and the modern Western state remain the white whales, assaulted by endless Ahabs filled with narcissistic rage. Seen psychologically, much of the world is in a massive crisis of overfullness. The contemporary question is whether the mind/brain/soul/psyche can evolve to creatively encompass it. In the meantime, we can only sadly envy the rich symbolic containers of other times in history, such as the era of the Unicorn Tapestries.

The Unicorn was a creature of dread and Mystery. Only a virgin could finally entrap and contain it. Its pursuit and capture illustrate multiple dimensions of containment and breaking of containment. It is like the analytic process, during which the potent new life that we encounter forces us to break free of the concrete and expand our world.

Five hundred years old, the Unicorn tapestries were woven in Belgium and were created for a wedding. The identity of the couple is not known, although their initials are visible in most of the scenes. The Late Middle Ages was a time of cultural transition when Christianity was losing its authority and pagan ideas forcefully reasserted themselves. Alchemical ideas also emerged during this time.[6] Gods and goddesses were portrayed in everyday clothes, and there was an air of excited and almost dreamlike extravagance in the significant human activities.

To quote Huizinga (1996, p. 1):

When the world was half a thousand years younger all events had much sharper outlines than now. The distance between sadness and joy, between good and bad fortune, seemed to be much greater than for us; every experience had that degree of directness and absoluteness that joy and sadness still have in the mind of a child.

The Unicorn tapestries were created in a feverish atmosphere when the old order was breaking down and the new was not yet. Typical of the strange extravagance of the times, the cost of such tapestries was great.

Later, the tapestries barely survived the French Revolution, having been taken and used for decades by peasants to cover haystacks and such things before they were recovered by the Rochefoucauld family.

John D. Rockefeller, Jr. obtained the tapestries in 1923. This event twice appeared as front-page, headline news in the *New York Times*! They quickly became one of his most beloved possessions, and he built a special room for them that became his most cherished place of retreat. In 1937, he donated the tapestries to the Medieval collection of the Metropolitan Museum that was being established at the Cloisters, a beautiful amalgamation of French convent buildings in a forested setting overlooking the Hudson River.

The Unicorn myth originated in China or India, emerging in the Western world around 300 BC. In Chinese legends, a Unicorn announced the birth and death of Confucius.[7] In India, it sometimes assumed the form of a pursuing destiny. In our own times the Unicorn is often depicted in a sentimental, Walt Disney kind of way. However, to the medieval mind, as in the Asian context, it was a daemonic creature with uncanny powers. And it had a raucous bray!

Typical of late Medieval times, the Unicorn tapestries utilise multiple mythologies. Christian and pagan endlessly intermingle. Every flower and every animal had a symbolic meaning. These were employed in rich narratives that could easily be read by ordinary people. I will only touch upon a few of these meanings.

Created in an age when the Unknown world was closer to the everyday, the rich emotional symbols and contexts of the tapestries give them a power and beauty unique in their directness.

The drama of the Unicorn Hunt illustrates the many ways we contain, sacrifice and evolve during encounters with the emotional life provoked by the Unknown. This speaks to the core of the analytic task. The drama of the Unicorn Hunt evokes clinically relevant questions such as: What are the varieties and levels of containment that we see? Which lead towards evolution of consciousness, and which tend to abort the enterprise?

To reflect on such questions together, I will show you slides of the seven tapestries in sequence, commenting briefly on the central symbols of the evolutionary process that is depicted. I will weave in commentary connecting these depictions with relevant dimensions of the analytic experience. There is a great deal of material, but I hope that the beauty of the tapestries themselves will provide a fine container for any overfullness!

The Start of the Hunt

I think of this scene as Breaking out of Containment. A period of stasis is about to change. This fits with the season of *early Spring*. The animated conversation of the three nobles in dapper dress contrasts with the darkness of the background forest. A *cherry tree* stands in the middle of the scene, ripe with fruit. This signals the possibility that something new may emerge.[8]

The forest itself is outside cultivated areas, outside the usual boundaries of the self, and dimensions of the Unknown dwell there. This is where the analytic process often begins.

The *Divine Comedy* commences with the words (Luke, 2000, p. 4):

Nel mezzo del cammin di nostra vita
mi retrovai per una selva oscura
che la diritta via era smaritta.

Or, in English:

Midway through this way of life we're bound upon,
I woke to find myself in a dark wood,
Where the right road was wholly lost and gone.

The dark wood is the threshold of the journey. For the individual, a joyless mood may dominate the soul, with no way out visible. Perhaps a tormenting sense of psychic deadness pervades the psyche. Waiting for a better season seems to be the only choice. Here, the cherry tree suggests new possibilities, and the scout signals that he sees something worthy of note.

The smallest new openings may signal the presence of the Unknown. These are exciting occasions because of their potential. Such nuclei of meaning can eventually gather more bits of significance around them, eventually unveiling some new aspect of Truth and Being. Spots of aliveness bring hope and excitement, but also dread. That is because to explore them requires a journey into the dark wood of emotions and psychic presences conjured by the Unknown.

The scout calls out the new possibility. The handlers prepare the hounds, and the Hunt is about to begin!

In Medieval times, there was a belief that Christ remained in the Underworld throughout Winter and arose in the Spring. This was intermingled with the myth of the Oak King of Spring, who superseded the Holly King of Winter. From both viewpoints, the 'Silent Power of the Possible' is more manifest in early Spring.[9] Christ is in the Underworld, the world of the Unknown, and when He re-emerges in the Spring like the Oak King, He can re-vivify the world.

Eros' pursuit of the Lover was also a prevalent motif in the late Middle Ages. The well-dressed Hunters probably represent Eros, or Love, and the quarry is the Unicorn: the Lover they seek. One is drawn into the Unknown by desire for Love and connection.

The hounds were known by names such as Beauty, Kindness, Intelligence, Courage, Largesse, Gentleness and Sincerity (Freeman, 1983). Sometimes they were connected with the Archangel Gabriel. They represented the virtues of differentiated feeling that serve relationship and consciousness. Shame is a crucial element in shaping the emotional self, and most of these virtues are shame-based (Hinton, 1998). Such probity is essential in containing the raw emotions provoked by contact with the Unknown. Without a steady sense of integrity, catastrophe is all too possible.

There are times during analysis when interpretations seem endlessly fruitless, and both parties may wonder about the point of it all. Then an awkwardness of mind, a strange bit of emotional turbulence, appears, and finally something that stands out in a new way (Rhode, 1998). It may be something quite disturbing, like seeing some new aspect of the shadow. From that point, the process may take on a renewed sense of life and possibility.

It is difficult to know why such openings surface at one time rather than another. Until they do, we can only proceed with faith and bear the tension of Not Knowing. This requires the quiet, persistent Eros of the Hunter. It is often tempting to stir things up artificially or to take the 'unproductive' darkness as a sign of failure. But one must keep the hounds leashed until the quarry is sighted, else the analytic enterprise founders.

The Unicorn Dips Its Horn in the Fountain to Rid It of Poison

I call this one The Time of Choice. The Hunt has not fully begun. This is the darkness of *Winter*, the night of the world. The legend was that the serpents of evil intruded to poison the wellsprings of life for the other animals. The Unicorn bends its horn into the water to rid it of those poisons. There was a generalised belief in the Middle Ages that the Unicorn had this power, and drinking vessels made from 'Unicorn Horns' – in actuality, usually horns of the narwhal – were prized for their protection from poisoning.

Psychologically, the Unicorn's action can be seen as a decision to emerge from defensive postures and take responsibility for the toxic poisons of one's own psyche. In this tapestry, we see a *choice* that can be a powerful, moral moment in life as in the analytic process.

The Unicorn is contrasted to the *Fountain*, which is actually the *Fountain of Narcissus* (Williamson, 1986, p. 102). Two pheasants sit on the edge of the fountain. One gazes at its own image. In Medieval times, it was believed that placing a mirror in a cage could trap the pheasant. The story was that when it saw itself in the mirror, it thought it was a rival, struck at the mirror and was thus caught! It succumbed through its jealousy and envy (Freeman, 1983, p. 82).

This is an apt depiction of defensive, narcissistic containment. The possibility of real relationship or change – any contact with the Unknown – is seen as a threat. Life is sought on the cheap – stolen, manipulated, seduced. Symbolic thought, when it exists, is misused in a concrete way, rather than used to expand mental life. Stagnation results, for there is no living connection with the stream of renewing emotion. In this state of avoidance, the terror of the Unknown grows. Evasive behaviours and addictions multiply, substituting false hungers for the deeper but terrifying hunger for Truth and Being. Jealousy, envy and paranoia increasingly predominate.

Many analyses seem to get stuck in this deadening container. The 'analytic couple' often falls into a comfortable sharing of the same perceptual and conceptual universe.[10] It is a mutual defence against the Unknown with its strangeness, suffering and terror. Lear calls this the attitude of 'already knowing', which kills the possibility of reflection or imagination (Lear, 1998, p. 43ff).[11] It results in a subtle stasis at best and severe pathologies at worst. The analyst bears more responsibility than the analysand does for these situations, since he or she espouses the vocation of awareness.

The potential, symbolised by the stone pomegranate at the top of the fountain, is never actualised unless one submits to the stream of life, with its passion and suffering. The Water of Life is flowing from the Unknown into the Known, but what we do with this mystery is a matter of choice and attitude.

Some authorities equate the 12 men here with the Disciples of Christ (Williamson, 1986, p. 118). There is a sense of awe and respect at the scene. The animals present are mostly connected with the fight against serpents and evil. The panther in the foreground is interesting in that, in medieval legend, it represented the scent of the divine. The sweetness of the panther's breath was equated with resurrection and immortality.

In Egyptian religion, the scent of the body of the Pharaoh was likewise connected with his eternal nature. This seems to equate with a deep intuitive awareness of the Unknown in its paradoxical fruitfulness. We smell it, we know it, but it may not be apparent to everyday, pragmatic thinking. This is also a function of the helpful hounds of the psyche, who scent the invisible in a way that is not accessible to the ego.

In analysis, as in life, there are times of choice. We may follow the scent of the Unknown or we may not. For the most part, these are not conscious, cognitive choices but are made with one's very being. Probably the process of choice begins very early in life. As analysts, we can only help bring the individual to the place of choosing, for we cannot actually choose suffering for another.

Narcissus holds desperately to his image in the Fountain, sensing that everything changes when the Unknown encounters the Known. Teiresias had warned Narcissus that he would remain eternally youthful only if he did not know himself. Therefore, he holds tight to the present.

Often the choice is not overtly dramatic and frequently seems acausal. The analysand may come in and announce a new awareness or behaviour. Symington describes a case when a severe alcoholic, sitting on a bench outside a hospital ward from which he had been banished, suddenly decided to quit drinking (Symington, 1996, pp. 90–91). The decision simply surfaced in him. Symington speculates that, if a helpful therapist had come up at the moment of decision with a fine set of insights, it would have aborted the enterprise. The lineaments of truth would have disappeared back into the depths, perhaps never to return.

In this tapestry, we see the Unicorn's moment of choice as it braves the dangerous waters. In our personal lives or in the analytic process, there may be an inner choice we face, like owning some destructive presence in the subjective world. At other times, it may have more to do with Truth in relationship. Whatever the case, the choice is crucial and highly moral.

Like the Hunters in the tapestry, the analyst must stand by at this time of choice and allow each individual to confront the mystery of the future.

The Unicorn Crossing the Stream

Now there is commitment. The preliminaries are over. It is time for the full engagement of the Unknown with the Known and all the fateful processes of containment and sacrifice that entails. I call this tapestry Danger and Possibility.

The predominant, leafy *Oak tree* in the foreground shows that the season is *May*, the time of the Oak King. A *hawthorn* silhouettes the body of the Unicorn as it crosses the stream.

This was a crucial time for farming people. If there was an early drought or late frost, they could starve the following Winter. As a consequence, there were important Maytime rituals to protect the still-vulnerable crops.

Here, the Unicorn is fully immersed in the Water of Life, the Stream of Life. One could see this as an act of acceptance of the Unknown future – an act of faith. The descent into the water by the god, whether in antiquity or in the Christian baptism, was an auspicious event that brought good things to the community (Williamson, 1986, p. 124).

May Day was celebrated especially by the gathering of hawthorn, a tree connected with the goddess Maia, who had both benevolent and malevolent connections that are appropriate for a precarious seasonal change. Sharing of food expressed great joy in the abundant aspect of Nature, and a sense of Unus Mundus – the wholeness of the human community. These occasions included fertility rituals, symbolised by the Maypole, that sometimes scandalised the conservatives of the time (Williamson, 1986, p. 128). In the tapestry, we see the Oak tree in the foreground, emphasising the Maypole connection.

This scene can be seen as depicting the crossing from one state to another. Crossings create a liminal space where we meet the Unknown. There is a small bridge on the lower right, emphasising this symbolism. The Iris next to the bridge represents the rainbow, which connects worlds. The crossing and the bridge underline a process linking the Unknown – the Unicorn – with the everyday world. The hunting party and their dogs seem to be carefully containing it, herding it onward in its crossing. It cannot be killed by ordinary means but can be contained and directed.

This is a picture of full engagement, fraught with feelings of both fertility and danger. It is like a time in analysis when stasis has been fully broken, and there is excitement and possibility, but no clear-cut sense of direction. There is a danger of acting out and dissipation of the energy of evolution. The analysand may be a bit manic, and both analyst and analysand are tempted to be overly optimistic about the course of things. The excitement of the crossing is a time of ambivalence. There is danger that the entire enterprise could go awry if the sense of manic excitement is not adequately contained. Astute herding is crucial, although heavy-handed interpretations may abort the process.

The Unicorn Defends Itself

An *orange tree* centres this tapestry, along with the battling Unicorn. To the Medieval mind, the orange was connected with the sun and with fruitfulness. It is the time of the *Summer Solstice*. The *Holly Tree* now predominates over the Oak, signifying a new phase of the cycle. This scene is full of action. The Unicorn has no ears in this or the following tapestry. The time for fine words, for reason and debate, has ended. Therefore, I entitle this Total Commitment and Terror. The Unknown has begun to impact the Known, and vice versa. There is a sense of inevitability, mutual wounding and sacrifice.

The figure blowing his horn at the lower left is believed to be the Archangel Gabriel. On his scabbard is the inscription, *Ave Regina C[oelorum]*, which translates as 'Hail Queen of Heaven' (Williamson, 1986, p. 158). It was a common belief in medieval times that Christ was reluctant to undergo incarnation and His inevitable Passion. Gabriel represents God's will, and he often had his own hounds. The Divine Hunter was often seen to be a messenger of God. An old German folk song describes how the 'hunter who hunts the beautiful unicorn' came 'from the throne on high' (Freeman, 1983, p. 23). This brings a profound dimension to the scene of Total Commitment. When the Will of God comes to bear, there is no further choice. We must fully commit to the encounter with the Unknown in its terrifying depths. This is the voice of Anangke, or Necessity.

Such times occur in analysis, manifested by a sense of inevitability regarding some especially difficult task. Often it is summarised in a dream, where there is something to be done or something to be faced that seems almost impossible to bear. Sometimes the task is an external one, such as a call to vocation or a demand for a new level of Truth in relationship. These are often special times in analysis: nodal points that are never forgotten.

To speak more of the tapestry: at the upper left, there is a felled beech tree and a young man with an axe. The young man seems to be giving an unhappy-looking older man some instructions. The beech was symbolically equated with the oak. The theme of death, of sacrifice, is clear. The time of the old Oak King is waning. The Oak King has conducted the course of the drama to this point, but his capacity to contain is now exhausted. The drama must move forward to another level of containment, symbolised by the younger man, the Unknown future. This is potentially fruitful, as exemplified by the orange tree – but fruitfulness is yet to come.[12]

Both analyst and analysand may sense that the time has come for a painful but deeply necessary sacrifice. Old defensive containers, often at the narcissistic core, are about to be given up. This new level of commitment to the process risks exposure to a terrifying, out-of-control, over-fullness. A profound vulnerability, fuelling ambivalence and volatility in the analytic relationship, is frequently present. Fluctuations between dependent longings and angry accusations are common. The analyst feels the intensity of the blame and the discomfort and perhaps some guilt at the pain created by the analytic process itself. The analysand desperately wants containment of the flood of emotions and may inject these into the analyst – to his or her distress.

This is exemplified by the wounding of a hound by the Unicorn. The blood of the dog flows on to a clump of blue violets – a flower that had close associations with the goddess of love, Aphrodite (Williamson, 1986, p. 147). Love always has an aspect of wounding, and this certainly includes the analytic relationship. As mentioned earlier, the dogs represent shame-based virtues. When such developed patterns of the self encounter the primal intensity of the Unknown, there is wounding. This is a sacrifice in the service of containment and transformation.

When defensive and destructive presences pierce us, we can respond with the endless rage of a Captain Ahab, or we can accept the voice of Necessity. Mutual wounding is often part of the process. Projective identification is its usual guise. One must struggle to remain aware that these are wounds in service of the Magical Hunt and are intrinsic parts of psychological evolution.

The Unicorn Is Tamed by the Lady

This tapestry continues the theme of wounding. I call it Love and Betrayal. The time is *Early Fall*. Here, the Unicorn is lured into the container of human relationship by Love.

The Unicorn is for the first time overtly in an enclosure: the *hortus conclusus*, or enclosed garden. In the centre is an *apple tree* with abundant fruit (in the original weaving, the apples were interwoven with silver-gilt thread, which has now tarnished; this would have created a shimmering effect).

The enchanted animal is apparently staring into the face of a Lady, whose arm and hand are all that remain (note the fabric for reference to a later scene). However, the surviving fragments are extensive enough to convey profound layers of meaning. The Unicorn's eyes seem almost demonically possessed, and it still has no ears. It is so entranced that it does not appear to feel the wounds being inflicted by the hounds.

There is a maiden visible who has a sly and deceptive expression. She seems to be betraying the Unicorn by signalling to a Hunter, who blows a horn outside the enclosure.

A Holly tree stands inside the enclosure as well, and just outside is an Oak. Roses cover the fence.

The enclosure is an old emblem for Mary's virginity. It was a predominant belief that only a virgin could capture a Unicorn. Hildegard von Bingen suggested that several maidens were better than one to effect a capture! (Freeman, 1983, p. 23). Some depictions of these dramas were overtly erotic. And if the maiden was found not to be virginal, she often suffered a bloody death.

This is a profound drama of attraction, innocence and betrayal.

In my opinion, the emphasis on virginity is related to the basic stance that the analyst must try to maintain – an openness that is, in Bion's terms, without memory or desire (Symington & Symington, 1997, p. 166ff). Jung frequently said to put away all books and theories when entering the consulting room. An overemphasis on the past as the 'cause' of the present, or on future goals, including teleology, may impede the analytic task. In this view, the crucial element is genuine openness to the Unknown. If there is an excess of reductionism or too much attachment to concrete goals, the process is aborted. That is the Unicorn destroys the maiden because she is not virginal. Psychologically speaking, that means the horizon of the Unknown has been lost because of the failure of the analytic container. Evolution cannot ensue, and there will have to be a return to the beginning.

The state of calm relaxation or reverie is highlighted in much of the analytic literature (Hinshelwood, 1991, p. 420; Ogden, 1997, p. 107ff; Symington & Symington, 1997, pp. 168–169). An analyst's capacity for reverie is crucial for the evolution of the emotional core of the analysand. This can provide a transforming island of calm spaciousness.[13] It is what the infant requires from its mother in order to transform its terrifying overfullness into tolerable bits of emotion and symbol.[14]

It is important to note that the Unicorn is powerfully attracted to the Lady. Seemingly, this animal stemming from the Unknown *desires* and *seeks* evolution into a more coherent, humanised form.

This picture is complicated by the treacherous betrayal that we see. This is the other side of the picture. The innocent, guileless Unicorn is delivered to the Hunters by a maiden who is apparently an alter ego of the embracing Lady.

This hints of a universal drama that we all experience. In discussing the myth of Isis and Osiris, Neumann spoke of the ambivalence of the Mother who both nurtures and betrays (Neumann, 1970, p. 79). Those who bring us into the world cannot protect us from the pain and suffering of life, and it stifles us if they try too much. The analytic process – and therefore the analyst – cause pain by uncovering the past and bringing Truth closer (Grotstein, 2000, p. 236). Guilt over the necessity of causing pain seems intrinsic to life and evolution. The betraying maiden is as crucial to evolution as the accepting one. There must be a sacrifice of the containing oneness, or evolution would cease. We would return to the narcissistic well of self-absorption. The containing reverie of the mother/analyst would become a trap and a sort of chronic psychological death. We would return to an envelope of self-absorption like the well of Narcissus.

When the analyst is too 'kind' and avoids becoming the betrayer, the analysis can end in a chronic stagnation, or worse. In order to evolve, we must first use and then, in our imaginations, destroy that upon which we were originally dependent for protection (Grotstein, 2000, p. 241). That is to become free beings, we must break out of the fantasy of dependency and develop a sense of personal courage and destiny.

Some form of betrayal is essential in development, whether it comes from within or without. Otherwise, we end up in an attitude of paranoid defensiveness against the terror and sacrifice that the process of evolution entails. Such fear often creates a hypersensitive 'envelope' of narcissistic containment that is like a subtle tomb of deadness.

The Unicorn Is Killed and Brought to the Castle

Here we see the violence of a Medieval Hunt. I call this The Somber Transformation. The emotional pathos of the scene is especially moving and, to our modern eyes, may seem brutal. The subdued Unicorn is in its death throes. Most of the observers have a very serious demeanour, as they witness and accept this tragic side of life.

This is very different from the air of celebration that accompanied an ordinary hunt.

A well-dressed lord and lady are there, ready to receive the body. In this scene, *Oak trees* predominate in all directions, both near and far. The death scene and the noble entourage are separated by a watercourse that is, due to fading, only barely visible. At the lower left, a hazel tree conceals a squirrel.

Both an Oak and a Holly tree silhouette the dying Unicorn. In fact, the only Holly is behind the animal, signifying another shift in the sequence of seasons. The iconography seems to signify the *mid-Winter Solstice*. The eternally green Holly tree is the repository of fertility when the earth is encompassed in winter. The death of the Unicorn – at one and the same time being the Oak King who will be reborn – was often connected with Crucifixion and the wintry time of Christ in the underworld (Williamson, 1986, p. 175ff). The Oak signified the potential new life, the reborn sun and the Resurrection. The Unknown fluctuates in its manifestations and may become invisible to consciousness at times but is always potentially there.

The Unicorn is brought to the Lord and Lady. Since the overriding dedication of the tapestries is to marriage, one could see this as a final evolution of the energy from the Unknown into human relationship. The material of the Lady's dress seems to identify her as the same Lady that tamed the Unicorn and brought about its capture.

A Hunter catches the blood of the dying Unicorn in his horn, like a chalice. This is another Christ metaphor and underlines the importance of the death of the animal for the entire community. Psychologically speaking, this container signifies that the transformation of these toxic effects stemming from the Unknown is complete. The Unicorn's sacrificial death makes participation in a transformative Communion possible. The emotional overfullness fomented by the Wild Unicorn can now foster the renewed abundance of everyday life.

A squirrel on the lower left runs up and down the embryonic World Tree, showing there is now a living connection between worlds. The wreath of Oak around the Unicorn's neck shows an underlying identity with the Green Man and fertility. Swans in the distant pond epitomise commitment in relationship.

Marriage, communion, the swans, the World Tree and the Green Man underline the themes of commitment and fertility evolving from the Unicorn's sacrifice. These are the boons that may come when the Known accepts the suffering and turbulent emotions provoked by the Unknown. Broadly speaking, this is the cycle of death and rebirth that must be maintained to ensure the fertility of the land and its people. Certainly, this seems true of the individual as well. The alternative is the Waste Land.

A sacrificial death has occurred. We mourn the loss of our original vision of beauty and perfection – the Unicorn in its untamed magnificence. This mourning releases us, opening us to a more vigorous embracing of the everyday. Loss is thus a paradoxical gain, since it transforms our relationship to self and world and can eventually foster an enduring bridge to the transcendent dimension.

Parenthetically, it should be noted that the couple in the castle tower seems to be in a sort of jail. Perhaps this is the harbinger of a new cycle, when the container again becomes a prison that must give way!

The Unicorn in Captivity

This to me is a misnomer, since the situation of the Unicorn seems entirely voluntary. I wonder whether this title reflects our modern, individualistic view of 'total freedom'. We think so much of freedom from rather than freedom to. I think of Jung's statement that freedom consists of doing gladly that which one must do!

It is a *perpetual Springtime*. The Unicorn drips not with blood but with the juice of the ripe *pomegranates* from the tree above.[15] The Unicorn's decorative collar and chain, resembling those of the loyal hounds, are no impediment for such an all-powerful beast. It must have assumed them voluntarily. It could also leap the small fence in one bound. This enclosure is a place of equipoise between the wildness of the Unicorn and its perfect containment. I call this the Position of Faith.

The botanical images are connected with copulation and fertility. The *hortus conclusus* is here a heavenly enclosure, a fecund paradise where male and female unite. Evil may not enter, and many of the plants have the property of repelling and destroying serpents (Williamson, 1986, p. 199ff).

To quote Williamson,

[This scene is] the apotheosis of the Hunt, in which the resurrected Unicorn symbolises the rebirth of Christian and pre-Christian vegetation gods. This tapestry is an epigram or coda to the yearly cycle, mirroring the death and ultimate resurrection of the fecund seasons, and the sexual powers of plants and animals – a reflection of heavenly perfection, where there is perpetual springtime, abundance, and an absence of malign forces.

Clinically, this would seem to coincide with the transcendent position. To quote Grotstein,

Transcendent means having the ability to transcend our defensiveness, our pettiness, our guilt, our shame, our narcissism, our need for certainty, our strictures in order to become 'one with O,' which I interpret as becoming one with our *aliveness*, or with our very *being-ness*.

(Grotstein, 2000, p. 300)

This is the position of faith vis-à-vis the Unknown.

Called by many names, this is the foundation of our other endeavours, enabling us to go on in the midst of pain and terror, loss and sacrifice. We are granted small glimpses of the Unknown in all its promise and fecundity. This gives us faith. Without such moments of vision, life would not be worth living, and the analytic enterprise would not be possible.

The ultimate container may perhaps be this potent vision itself, this on-going glow of animal life at the core of our being. It is both Unknown Presence and container. This Unknown Presence makes possible the small and great epiphanies of life and underlies faith, the ultimate container. Such faith, won through sacrifice and suffering, fosters a continuing connection to emotional aliveness – the truest 'joie de vivre'.

Conclusion

The story of the Unicorn stems from the intense imagination of a culture on the brink of the Unknown future – what was to become, ironically, 'The Age of Reason'.[16] The Catholic Church was losing its hold, the fascination with old 'pagan' symbols surged to the fore and yet Christian symbolism was still quite alive. The time was intense and overfull.

As a consequence, the need for containment was pronounced. The Unicorn tapestries depict a noble attempt at containment, sacrifice and transformation. What useful perspectives have we gained from this astounding work of art, and how do they relate to the analytic process?

The steady patience of the hunters stands out prominently. Jung was fond of saying that the main ingredient of change was 'patientum': the capacity not to act precipitously but to let things emerge from the Unknown.[17] At the same time, the hunters were experts at their art and the habits of the game they pursued. They have faith in the enterprise, and they are totally committed. Patience, knowledge of the lore of the Hunt, faith and commitment stand out as crucial traits of the Hunter – and not bad ones for an analyst!

The hounds, the basic virtues, are of crucial importance. Integrity of presence is deeper than cognition. The civilised and civilising affects of the core emotional self must be congruent with the task at hand. Without an embodied psycho-affective presence, there will be no deep analytic work and no fruitful evolution. The hounds work by scenting the Unknown in ways the ego cannot. Only such evolved affects can contain the turbulence of the human psyche in its encounters with the Unknown.[18]

The willingness to be wounded, like the hound gored by the Unicorn, is part of the enterprise. The process must touch analyst as well as analysand. The relationship itself becomes overfull. Out of this a third thing may be created, something more than the mere addition of two separate psyches (Ogden, 1994, p. 61ff). This is also a container that endures.

Nature is a profound container implicit in the tapestries, and the circularity of the seasons underlies the entire drama.[19] The various plants and animals are there to amplify and supplement the narrative meanings. One envies the wonderful familiarity that people of the Late Medieval times had with nature. Everything was alive and could be read like a book.

There is a social container. The tapestries were made for a marriage, and there are people and castles all around. An order and stability in the social realm contain and enable the task. Indeed, the death of the Unicorn seems to mainly serve the social group centred on the castle and its lord and lady. The aura of Marriage and relationship pervades the enterprise.[20] The final death scene seems to involve the whole community as well as the noble couple. There are hints as well that another cycle of change will ensue and that this container will eventually be superseded by another encounter with the Unknown.

The Virgin and her entrapment of the Unicorn is a fulcrum of the series. Due to our inherent 'over-fullness', we long from birth for such transforming reverie to contain us. The attuned maternal container takes in our painful surfeit of emotion. These raw elements must be returned in a transformed state as tolerable affects and the basic elements of thoughts and symbols. The affective core of self is also shaped and patterned. This is an essential part of the analytic task.

This profound reverie culminates in the Unicorn's betrayal and death. There is guilt in this, and yet it is only through such a sacrifice that the emotions from the Unknown can enter into everyday life. For evolution to occur, maternal reverie must finally become an inner container or organ of perception – what Jung called the anima. At some point, the outer container must be sacrificed. Grief and mourning are appropriate parts of that experience because there is a true loss of a kind of beauty and innocence. In this process, psychic structures become internalised, and inner space evolves. Useful symbolic thought can take place. The ultimate, internal container that can result is such a self with true dimensionality (Horne, 2000).

The Unicorn in the enclosure summarises fulfilled containment and is the ground of faith. It is that which is and always was, that for which we yearn, that which makes the whole undertaking worth the cost in pain and suffering. Submission to the turbulent stream of life is the prime attitude of transformation. This experience of the Unknown is mainly emotional and embodied. *Amor Fati*, as Jung was fond of saying: embrace your fate!

There remains the containing and entrancing figure of the Unicorn itself, the animal that never was and yet endlessly fascinates. In analysis and in life, we know it intuitively, feel it emotionally, but cannot possess it. It is a manifestation of the Unknown that, at special moments, graces us with its presence. And yet those moments make the endless effort of our Hunt worthwhile.

Acknowledgments

I would like to thank Darlene Hinton and Michael Horne for their help in editing and in clarifying the ideas in this chapter.

Notes

1 It is interesting to see that the recent interpretations of Shakespeare interpret him as a transitional author between the Medieval and modern, rather than as a Renaissance figure per se. In fact, the Renaissance is being re-thought as a late manifestation of the Medieval, rather than merely the beginning of the modern era. Thus, Hamlet's tragedy is that of a man caught between eras – postmodern in a sense!
2 In the story of Acteon and the Hounds, the identification with the Magical Animal is complete. That is Acteon becomes one with the Hunted. This could be seen as a sort of apotheosis of the mystery of the Hunt.
3 To look at this in a more cognitive way, one could say that our worldview is constantly being tested and is chronically limited in its ability to contain our fullness. While this situation can be terrifying, the Unknown frees the individual from a concrete way of thinking and being and keeps the worldview open and creative.
4 The words of Li Tai Po express these ideas more poetically: 'No one can embrace . . . The Moon on the Yellow River'.
5 Interestingly, there is one ideogram in Chinese that represents both danger and opportunity (Knight, 2001).

6   Alchemy has an air of abstraction and detachment that connects it to the modern scientific tradition. In contrast, the Unicorn tapestries fully display the emotional reality of the process of spiritual and psychological evolution.

7   Jung wrote on the Unicorn in *Psychology and Alchemy* (Jung, 1968). He was mainly interested in the alchemical allusions of the Unicorn. He considered the Unicorn as a manifestation of the Spirit Mercurius, and saw the pairings (in other depictions than the Hunting Series) of Lion and Unicorn and Lady and Unicorn as illustrations of the dual nature of Mercurius. In my opinion, this does not take into account the unique dimensions of the Hunting Series as an evolving sequence. In addition, unlike Mercurius, the Unicorn in this series does not change into other forms or manifest overt duality. It may be that Jung was not familiar with the entire Hunting Series, since he refers only to the well-known tapestry of the Unicorn in Captivity. Be that as it may, those who find the alchemical model to their liking can find much in the Unicorn lore to feed their interests.

8   The cherry is the earliest tree to bloom and was lauded for its 'courage' in both Eastern and Western lore. For this reason, it is a frequent subject in Korean, Chinese and Japanese painting.

9   This is a term from Martin Heidegger.

10   Theodore Dorpat has discussed this phenomenon extensively in his book, *Gaslighting, The Double Whammy, Interrogation, and Other Methods of Covert Control in Psychotherapy and Analysis*.

11   Lear also analyses the Oedipus myth in this light. Oedipus is the man who 'already knows', who will not stop to reflect. His impatience and impulsiveness are at the root of his tragic character. The modern person is viewed as similar to Oedipus in his/her impatience and lack of reflectivity. Oedipus is, in this sense, quite contemporary.

12   The heron on the lower right is both an icon of silence and a symbol of the end of a preliminary cycle. The Unknown is close. The heron is connected with Hermes and Thoth, conductors of souls to the other world after death. This underlines the theme of the death of the Oak King and is a foretelling of the coming passion of the Christ/Unicorn.

13   In the last half of the first year of life, shame normally begins to shape and refine these containing patterns. As development progresses, these become our basic values, the faithful hounds within us (Schore, 1994, pp. 32–33 and pp. 461–462).

14   The infant's embryonic self encounters the Unknown, resulting in a terrifying overfullness. To survive and evolve, the infant needs to insert this incoherent, intolerable set of emotions into the mother's mind. The mother's mind must be in a state of calm receptiveness to take in these emotions and give them meaning. Such attuned reverie can transform the overfullness into contents that can be tolerated and eventually used as elemental thoughts and symbols. The analytic attitude at its best is a cultivated, virginal receptivity, a reverie without attachment to past history or future goals.

15 Jung refers to this tapestry as 'Mandala of the Unicorn and the tree of life', in his discussion of how the Unicorn includes both masculine and feminine components: both horn and cup (Jung, 1968).
16 This is like a Kuhnian paradigm shift. See his *Culture of Scientific Revolutions.*
17 This is Kairos, the right time or the Moment of Opportunity (Knight, 2001).
18 Antonio Damasio, a philosophical neuroscientist, has written of the layers of the emotional self in very experiential and yet empirically grounded terms. In my opinion, we chronically undervalue the complexity of the layers of the 'affective self' (my term) and the crucial importance of affects and feelings in consciousness itself (Damasio, 1999).
19 An entire additional study could be made of the importance of circularity in this drama, such as the role of the goddess of the changing year, Nemesis and the Triple Goddess figure. This is evident in the Lady, and the three women in the sixth tapestry. Among other things, they symbolise Birth, Love and Death (Williamson, 1986, pp. 170–171, 174–175, 188).
20 The concrete ritual of marriage and preparations for marriage are a vast theme that would require an entire work of its own. The pursuit of the Lover, the submission and the hymeneal blood are but a few of the important motifs here. Among other related works, see *Le Roman de la Rose.*

References

Damasio, A. (1999). *The Feeling of What Happens*. New York: Harcourt Brace.
Eigen, M. (1996). *Psychic Deadness*. NJ: Aronson.
Freeman, M. (1983). *The Unicorn Tapestries*. New York: Dutton.
Grotstein, J. (2000). *Who Is the Dreamer Who Dreams the Dream?* NJ: Analytic Press.
Hinshelwood, R. (1991). *A Dictionary of Kleinian Thought*. NJ: Aronson.
Hinton, L. (1991). "The Goose Girl: Puella and Transformation." In *Psyche's Stories*. Vol. 1. Wilmette: Chiron.
Hinton, L. (1993). "A Return to the Animal Soul." *Psychological Perspectives*, 28.
Hinton, L. (1998). "Shame as a Teacher: 'Lowly Wisdom' at the Millennium." In *Florence 98*. Switzerland: Daimon.
Horne, M. (2000). *Dimensionality and Experience: Finding Self in the Interstices in Space*. Paper Presented at the Northwest Alliance for Psychoanalytic Study Forum 2000, Seattle.
Huizinga, J. (1996). *The Autumn of the Middle Ages*. Trans. R. J. Payton & U. Mammitzsch. Chicago: University of Chicago.
Jung, C. G. (1968). *Psychology and Alchemie*, CW 12. pp. 435–471. NJ: Princeton University Press.
Knight, M. (2001). Personal Communications.
Lear, J. (1998). *Open Minded*. Cambridge: Harvard University.

Lear, J. (2000). *Happiness, Death and the Remainder of Life*. Cambridge: Harvard University.

Luke, H. (2000). *Dark Wood to White Rose*. New York: Parabola.

Neumann, E. (1970). *The Great Mother*. NJ: Princeton University.

Ogden, T. (1994). *Subjects of Analysis*. NJ: Aronson.

Ogden, T. (1997). *Reverie and Interpretation*. NJ: Aronson.

Rhode, E. (1998). *On Hallucination, Intuition, and the Becoming of "O"*. New York: ESF Publishers.

Schore, A. (1994). *Affect Regulation and the Origin of the Self*. NJ: Erlbaum.

Symington, N. (1996). *Narcissism: A New Theory*. London: Karnac.

Symington, J. & Symington, N. (1997). *The Clinical Thinking of Wilfred Bion*. New York: Routledge.

Williamson, J. (1986). *The Oak King, the Holly King, and the Unicorn*. New York: Harper & Row.

Chapter 6

Black Holes, Uncanny Spaces and Radical Shifts in Awareness*

The Genealogy of the Term 'Black Hole'

The term 'Black Hole' has become a familiar part of our everyday 'languaging' of things. It apparently originated in the semi-fictional tale of the 'Black Hole of Calcutta'. In 1756, 150 or so Europeans and others supposedly suffocated when the Nawab of Bengal held them captive in a small room with little ventilation. The expression took root in the collective imagination, evoking a terrifying image of claustrophobia and death.

However, the details of the tale were dubious, and it seems to have been largely an English fantasy. Meetings between cultures often provoke jarring gaps in discourse, along with a sense of the uncanny. A classic example is the terrifying cave in Forster's (1924) *Passage to India*. The 'black hole' signifier seems to have had its modern origins in the shadows of Western civilization, signifying the 'unknown other' that allures, and yet threatens when one approaches the limits of the culturally familiar (Said, 1978).

In modern astrophysics the Black Hole refers to the phenomenon in which infinite gravitational forces have compressed the mass of a collapsing star into an infinite density. The potent centre of the Black Hole is called a singularity. Black Holes are only known by their indirect effects on normal stars. In 'Black Holes' the laws of physics break down and there is no escape. They seem to stifle new star formation. One could say theoretically that, within this singularity, an entity becomes so densely particular that the usual laws no longer apply. According to the Big Bang model, a singularity is also the point from which the original expansion of the universe began. This phenomenon has provided a rich metaphor for certain troubling psychic states.

* Hinton L. (2007). Black Holes, Uncanny Spaces and Radical Shifts in Awareness. *The Journal of Analytical Psychology*, 52(4), 433–447. https://doi.org/10.1111/j.1468-5922.2007.00675.x. Reprinted by Permission of John Wiley and Sons.

DOI: 10.4324/9781003641063-7

The 'Black Hole' as an Enigmatic Signifier

In contemporary philosophical as well as analytic discourses the 'black hole' is used as a signifier for an indescribable 'nothing' that, paradoxically, is both the origin of the subject and the immaterial font of creativity and freedom (Daly & Žižek, 2004). Its 'negativity' creates a space for renewed consciousness and imagination. 'Black hole' conjures other emotionally potent signifiers such as abyss, vortex, void, lack and emptiness. It is a sign that emerges when we are 'stopped short' by a failure to 'language' experience in our usual language. Appearing in gaps and lacunae in discourse, it may evoke the new events of possible, but as yet unrealised, meaning that we call 'imagination' and 'consciousness' (Castoriadis, 1998, p. 3; Chandler, 2003, pp. 74–77; Davis, 1989, pp. 8–33). In a similar way, Stanton Marlan (2005, p. 190) describes the Black Sun and the other 'black spots' in alchemy as connected to a 'continuous deconstructive activity . . . necessary for psychological change'.[1]

In psychoanalytic discourse, 'black hole' imagery has been depicted as pointing towards possibilities for becoming that are not yet represented (Stern, 1997), or due to a deficiency of internal self-object relations (Tustin, 1990; Green, 2001; Hopper, 1991; Kinston & Cohen, 1986), or ultimately due to the unrepresentable (Barnard, 2002, pp. 160–181; Dyess & Dean, 2000; Nobus, 1999, p. 171).

The 'deficiency' model has many permutations. One of the more common describes 'holes' in the psyche that are due to 'primal repression' resulting from early trauma. This is different from the 'secondary' repression that occurs after psychic structure has developed, leading to the impression of elements as yet unformulated, but relatively accessible. In contrast, 'Primal repression . . . is the site of catastrophic, unthinkable, past-but-ever-present trauma and associated confusion and terror, hopelessness and loss of self-preservative function; while it can serve as the "frail bud of psychic structure" . . . from which growth occurs' (Kinston & Cohen, 1986, p. 340). All these dimensions often manifest themselves during full analyses (Kinston & Cohen, 1986, p. 337).

The evocations of the 'black hole' tend to have a spatial significance, but there is no final, essential 'something' that they signify. In their various ways, they refer to gaps in experience that cannot be conceived, a lack of 'somethingness' (Hauke, 2000, pp. 191–222). Therefore they often convey a negation of familiar discourses, accompanied by intense affects and disturbing currents of the uncanny. The sense of terror, loss and grief may open a space for the creation of new signifying elements and an enriched presence in the world (Colman, 2006, p. 21; Kristeva, 1980, pp. 16–17).

Traumatic and premature exposure to the experience of such 'black holes' may cause chronic and severe psychological conditions. One must be aware of the dangers involved in such clinical phenomena. On the other hand, therapies that are mainly ego- and symptom-focused are in danger of cutting off the flow of life. Experiences at the edges of the 'known' seem to be at the basis of consciousness and creativity, and intensive suppression or denial of the 'black hole' experience in order to treat symptoms may result in 'throwing out the baby with the bath water', and result in a way of life that is sterile and contrived.

The 'Black Hole' and Embeddedness

Our embeddedness in the sensuous surround of our culture – things such as languages, spaces, social customs, rhythms, rituals, tastes, smells, taboos, economic life, and technologies – comprises an extremely complex, ongoing signifying structure and process that is largely outside of consciousness. It creates us; it is us, so to speak (Muller, 1996, pp. 1–60; Hurley & Chater, 2005). These signifiers vary greatly from time to time and place to place (Howes, 2005). We take them for granted, like the air we breathe. Jung once said:

> The spirit of an age gains . . . uncanny power. It is . . . a phenomenon of the greatest importance . . . a prejudice so deeply rooted that until we give it proper consideration we cannot even approach the problem of the psyche . . . It is an ethnopsychological problem, and as such cannot be treated in terms of individual consciousness.
>
> (Jung, 1931, paras. 653–657)

The experience of the 'black hole' disrupts this sense of complacent embeddedness. It 'foments' an opening that can make the emergence of the human subject possible, along with increased dimensions of freedom and creativity. Neumann mentioned the invariable connection between negation and consciousness (1954, p. 121).

The 'black hole' is a floating signifier that can be traced through history and culture, varying greatly in the ways it has been 'languaged' (Levy,

2006). It involves a cluster of experiences involving acute anxiety and terror that has had many names (Hauke, 2000, pp. 211–214; Kjellberg & Ivanhoe, 1996, pp. xiii–xx). The impact may be dramatic. A sense of reaching some absolute limit, chaos, or a terrifying abyss may evoke rapidly shifting experiences of place and space. Terror and anxiety may be intense along with a powerful sense of the uncanny.

These radical changes may create an opening for the appearance of novel elements of meaning 'at the edge of the abyss'. Emerging from this penumbra, things may stand forth more fully in their rich particularity. Encountering the 'black hole' in its various significations can be at the core of shifts in awareness, the creation of new signifying elements, of new images and metaphors, of radical changes of perspective on individual and culture (Castoriadis, 1998). Eric Rhode has colourfully described this process as 'Hallucination, Intuition, and the Becoming of O' (Rhode, 1998).

A Clinical Case History

Some years ago an analysand presented several emotion-laden dreams and images that encompassed the black hole, uncanny spaces, and transformation. Because of this person I added the 'black hole' to my psychological vocabulary, and I deeply thank him for that.

Todd was in his middle thirties when he entered analysis due to depression and anxiety. He had recently separated from his wife of several years. From his description, she was a very unstable, probably borderline person. He had previously been in intensive analytical therapy for 3–4 years and described it as 'a waste of time'.

Todd described his family home as 'the mausoleum'.[2] His mother worked fulltime and was rather cold and unavailable. His father, a butcher, was a severe alcoholic who was often emotionally violent. A rigid veneer of conservative Roman Catholic moralism concealed the psychological realities.

From the beginning he was very anxious and critical of me. As a result, I often found it difficult to be with him. It was as if he 'had no space' for my words or my presence, and that I was 'squeezed out'. He was 'encapsulated' in his defensive terror (Hopper 1991). I was the 'alien other' as well as the secret hope that he dared not consciously entertain.

In our interaction, I referred to this underlying thread of hope in various ways. For instance, I might make some comment about 'the mausoleum' and the connection with his mood of anxiety and despair, and he would say, 'That's no help at all . . . you've told me that stuff before and I feel just the same. I might as well ditch this analysis'.

My responses were generally simple, empathic and observational, such as, 'I know that you are in a lot of pain and feel discouraged, but I also sense a bit of optimism beneath your protests'.

Or, 'You haven't had much reason to trust others in your life, and you need to try me out and see whether I'm trustworthy, and whether I can be of any help'.

After a year or more of constant testing he confided in me in a new way. Gazing intently at me in an almost desperate manner, he burst out with a new revelation. He said he had long been tormented by a 'black hole' 'deep inside' him, and was terrified as to whether this meant that he was psychotic like his wife. There was a slightly 'mad', desperate look in his eyes as he spoke. I sensed a shift that was quite moving at the time, a thread of trust that I had not felt before.

This troubling experience continued as time went on, and I suggested that we sit together with 'It' – the black hole – during some of our sessions. He agreed, and this led to some very intense meetings. Looking shaky and almost desperate, he sometimes angrily blamed me for his pain. At other times he seemed comforted by my presence. Describing the black hole as something inchoate, devouring and horrifying, Todd often felt that he had no ground under his feet, nothing to hold on to, and was falling into an abyss.

Todd would often say, accusingly, 'This crazy stuff is just making me worse! Why in hell should we just sit with it?!'

My responses were along the lines of, 'The black hole is just what's there. It appeared on its own. If we evade it, it will just come back to haunt you. I don't know why it's there or what it is, but I will be with you as we try to understand it'.

Usually such remarks were reassuring to him.

Then he began to have panic reactions during the night. Hardly able to bear the depth of his terror, he thought of suicide as an escape. He called me several times late at night but calmed down pretty quickly when we talked. It was clear that the analytic relationship had become a place of safety and containment. I believe that my implicit and explicit faith in the meaningful-ness of his uncanny experience, and my ability to maintain a state of reverie and containment in the face of it, were the most important factors in the evolution of the analysis.

Through endless trials and driven by curiosity about objects around them, children expand their sense of space (Horne, 2003). This was what Todd was beginning to do in the analytic process. His growing acceptance of my presence as a helpful 'object' made expansion of space and place a possibility. Now we were both there with 'It'. He was no longer stuck with the 'Thing', all alone.

James Grotstein quoted Tustin to the effect that the 'black hole' is

a universal . . . image in the internal world and seems to represent where the mother used to be, but ripped herself away prematurely, leaving a 'gaping hole'.

(Grotstein, 1990a, p. 42)

Such separation is not only a 'loss of the object' – the point emphasised in much of the literature – but the experience of being left alone with 'It': the Black Hole. It is the gap between the 'Fort' and the 'Da' (Freud, 1961, pp. 7–8).[3]

This psychological image seems to reflect an ontological – or pre-onto-logical – condition that is fundamental to human experience, not merely an aspect of psychotic or borderline conditions (Barnard, 2002). If endured over time and contained in the analysis, the traumatic impact of such 'black holes' can provoke a basic rearrangement of our personal narratives. This enduring gives us an expanded base, though still 'on the edge of the abyss', that can allow such changes to occur. A light grasp on the part of the analyst – a kind of non-directive openness, a hovering attention, and a state of reverie – is a necessary condition for the emergence of novel signifying elements.

Jung generally emphasised the transcendent function as the process of enduring 'the opposites', thesis and antithesis, with the eventual appear-ance of a 'third', new meaning that is a superior 'mediatory product' (Jung, 1971, paras. 826–828). In his alchemical writings he often seemed to por-tray the continual process of change as transcendence (Jung, 1970, para. 257). However, he also reiterated his earlier definition of the transcendent function, and referred to the transcendent function as a 'psychic process of assimilation and integration' (Jung, 1970, para. 261). In the 1958 revision of 'The transcendent function' Jung described the 'third thing' as 'a quality of conjoined opposites' (Jung, 1931, para. 189). Assimilation, 'conjoining' and integration imply a larger 'totality' or image of 'wholeness', in which the particulars, or 'the opposites', are subsumed.

What I am describing as the 'black hole' and 'transformation' is a more enigmatic, often disturbing, and sometimes terrifying experience that does not have to do with thesis, antithesis and synthesis. Rather, gaps in discourse provoke a troubling, deeply challenging sense of 'absent' meaning or 'lost' meaning. In this process of negation, any resultant 'transformation' has to do with 'opening more space' for the particulars of the personal world. The particulars are not subsumed to a 'superior image of wholeness' that is created. Rather, in this expanded space, they can emerge more fully as what they are 'in the flesh', in their singularity. This expanded spaciousness allows disparate elements of cultural and personal experience to coexist and flourish, along with novel signifying elements (Rhode, 1998, pp. 12–13, 52–64, 209–210).

Such an emergent process is not a synthesis. It is endlessly dialogical: the ongoing 'heteroglossia' of life (Bakhtin 1981, pp. 271–275). Giegerich has described a 'dissolving' through the process of negation into a more spacious ground or clearing, an expanded interiority in which the particulars of existence may emerge more fully in the form of what they always, already were (2005, pp. 5–8).[4] Negation – so to speak – removes the cobwebs of unconsciousness so that a new level of reflection and symbolization becomes possible. We can then experience more dimensions of what is (2005, pp. 20–22). This is an ongoing process, not a telos that is ever finally achieved.

A few months after Todd first confided in me about the black hole, he had his initial big dream. Up until this point, his dreams had been sketchy and fragmented. This dream, told to me in an intense emotional burst, was as follows:

I'm in Hong Kong, then on a trip to Red China. It's a backpacking trip to see the sarcophagus. I'm with some guys. We have to sneak across the border. There are some warning shots and we have to scamper up the hill. Then we cross the desert to an underground passage. We come to a crowded room where the sarcophagus is supposed to be. I see some porcelain and granite bulls with red horns! The bulls pull all my attention rather than the sarcophagus.

I want to take a picture . . . A guy is in there with two bare-breasted women and he tells me to stop looking, that he's going to kick the shit out of me. I knock him against the wall and break a chair over his head.

We head for the border. There is a gorge with only a plank across it. A rock falls from above toward me. [My buddy] Mike stops it somehow. I feel the presence of my father and am terrified. As I start to walk the plank, a helicopter lands. I know it's my father because I see his feet. The plank is slanted and I start to slip. Mike helps me. I say I'll just fall into the gorge and swim, but I really think I'll die and that's okay. Then we go across and reach the border. Mike says you have to run 30 yards or more after you cross . . . you can't just skip across. I see buses crossing the border freely. Guards begin shooting at us. I keep running and running and they keep shooting and shooting. I crawl gasping up an incline, pulling on a railing. We're suddenly at 40,000 feet! I can look out and see clouds. Mike says to come on. I'm not sure what to do.

He finished telling me this dream with an air of relieved exhaustion as if he had delivered a baby. He expressed amazement that such a creative achievement came from 'inside' him.

In the dream the multiple movements in space are striking. First he takes a stand on the earth to make a crossing beyond the known world, at an interface of cultures. To do that you have to sneak, you have to find a new way. The old, conventional approaches won't work anymore. Then he's under the ground where he finds the dramatic porcelain bulls, which he chooses over the deadness of the sarcophagus. These animals have an earthy vitality and penetrating red horns, but a cold and brittle porcelain skin. He gazes at the bare-breasted women, perhaps sensing nourishing possibility rather than lack.[5] However, there is a problem when he tries to take photos, to make permanent images. It is always a struggle to take such experiences back to the everyday world.

He has left the boundaries of the known, and this had a disorienting effect. As he returns to home base, the experience of space becomes more uncanny and terrifying. He has to cross an abyss. Perhaps this is the unsignifiable that always lurks in the background of experience. He has left the pseudo-safety of the 'dead mother' and this opens up the terror of the 'black hole'.

He can barely glimpse his father. However, this glimpse of him and Todd's capacity to dream it and verbalise it were the beginning of representation of the life energy of the father/bull. The terror involved had to be faced for him to open new spaces, to create room to be. Surrendering to the experience, he confronts his fear and is willing to die. Such a level of surrender seems to be crucial for transformation to occur. Only with the containing support of the transference was such a shift possible.

The spatial shifts emerged like a giant whipsaw. After being down below he must cross a gap, an open space. This constellates a panicky reaction and his sense of place and space shifts violently. He is suddenly high above. It is as if the 'sheltering sky' has itself become a version of the 'black hole'. Mike, the steadfast transferential analytic companion, continues to help.[6] Dimensions of space have radically shifted, through his owning of his life energy that has emerged via his capacity to endure the black hole.

I was as surprised as Todd at the emergence of this dream. It seemed to embody a leap in his capacity for reflection and symbolization. The content was intense and full of conflict, but his affect was one of satisfaction and almost peace.

The dream came up intermittently in subsequent sessions. He continued to be somewhat in awe that such a dream could 'come out of me'. This was a shift in the whole sense of himself as a subject with a 'rich, creative interior'. I supported this more positive sense of self with comments such as 'It's really hard to bring this life back to the everyday world, like in the dream. It may look like it's easy for others, but I don't think there's ever an easy way. It's our job to see that you don't lose connection with the life you found there inside yourself'.

We also explored the specific symbols. I noted that it was the bulls that attracted his attention, not the sarcophagus. They were encased, but seemed full of potential life. The need to fight for his experiences, and to endure the terror of his father, were other foci of attention.

Often, he would merely smile and nod at what I said, then go on with his own associations. We had developed a wordless trust that often seemed sufficient.

His dreaming self was able to articulate the violent shift into a more spacious world with more room for life. Significantly, the 'black hole' did not reappear in pure form during the remainder of the analysis, and his terror and panic subsided. A richer set of possibilities continued to emerge, furnishing a broader base for life. Over the next few months there was a series of dreams with facets that connected with the big dream. He had remarried and his new wife was pregnant. Another dramatic dream expressed this change (dream slightly edited for the sake of brevity):

My wife and I are in downtown Seattle. A friendly dentist is working on my teeth. We leave, and decide to drive our new van around the city.

We want to walk around; it would be good for her, since she's pregnant. A guy takes us on this walking tour. We get to a huge plaza, like in Rome. He says this is a Spanish-Mexican area of town. People are running toward us. It's a mass of humanity. A guy has a pack of Pall Mall (cigarettes), and points to a mall pictured on the package, like that's where we'll be safe.

I get separated from my wife. I realise people are running from the bulls. It's Pamplona! Something has me from behind. I call to my wife but she can't do anything. The bull has me but it turns into a person with a cat's head. It is a tall, sinewy man, very muscular, who is strong and controlling. I want to get free but he says, 'No, you can't!' He takes me to a stage where there are three cauldrons filled with warm, dark fluid. I think he is going to cook me! He has me get into each cauldron so as to put my body scent into each one. There are also herbs and spices that I add.

The reliable dentist works on his teeth, like the focused, hard work of analysis.[7] Then there is a tour of a mall – the agora – led by a guide. In his company, Todd confronts his psychological agoraphobia, his personal constriction, and his fear of space. The dizzying abysses of space that were evident in the earlier dream were now something to be navigated and explored with transferential help.[8]

In the dream, the bulls surge through the streets. They are alive, not fixed in cold porcelain capsules, but also not out of control. The spaces of the city streets contain their powerful movement, and the enigmatic cat-man conducts a ritual. There are vessels in which Todd's scent will intermingle with the warm waters, in contrast to his past encasement in a cold, rigid shell. He must also include spices! In this dream there is a mood of deep interiorization that is quiet, disciplined, and serious.

Smells permeate boundaries and are part of our most embodied presence. They are often related to shame.[9] We frequently judge odours to be signs of danger or pollution and try to conceal the smells that seem to signify abjected parts of self-experience (Kristeva, 1982). The socially excluded or disempowered are often said to smell bad. We spend huge amounts of money on perfumes and deodorants. Smells remind us of our body with its vulnerability and death. Hard shells are a sometimes-desperate means of clinging to an illusion of permanence, sameness, and purity that never stinks! To allow these all-too-human taints into the core of awareness represents a basic shift that dramatically contrasts with Todd's initial encapsulation.

He seems to be more grounded, 'in place' in a way that does not require a rigid shell. His raw body smells and the new spices intermingle in their rich particularity. He is more present 'in the flesh', immersed in the smelly richness of life. His space is more fluid and in circulation. The hierarchical encapsulations have radically given way to a flowing, contained sense of openness and possibility.

Some Developmental and Philosophical Perspectives

The 'black hole' first appeared in contemporary analytic discourse when Frances Tustin used the term. Interestingly, she did this before the astro-physical entity had been described (Grotstein, 1990b, pp. 39–40). During treatment of autistic children she noted a frequent terror of falling into something they referred to as a 'black hole' that was accompanied by a sense of living as a shell-like 'nothing'. Due to their underlying terror, these children 'nullified' anything that seemed 'other' because it could loosen their fragile grip on reality and condemn them to 'falling forever' into an inchoate nothingness. They seemed to feel they had nowhere to go, no safe space for symbolization (Tustin, 1990).

Adults create complex, ongoing narratives of words, body language, emotions, images, rituals, and meaningful objects to articulate their worlds. However, these eventually fail to contain affect-laden eruptions (Chandler, 2003, p. 2). The experience of the 'black hole' looms when we reach this limitation. Hegel called this point the 'anstoss', referring to an enigmatic 'something' that 'stops us', that defies signification (Zizek, 1999, p. 34). We are just there with 'It'. Our psychic space begins to 'turn topsy-turvy', and feels uncanny. This has been described as 'annihilation anxiety' that stems from the threat of madness or psychic death (Gediman, 1995, p. 4).

The 'black hole' feels as if it is *too much*, an overwhelming opening in experience that exceeds one's capacity to signify (Merleau-Ponty, 1964, p. 21). Awareness of all that we are *not* disrupts the stability of our personal world. This overwhelming 'presence' is the 'other' for which we lack signi-fiers. It is, perhaps, the ultimately unsignifiable, the unknowable (Nobus, 1999, p. 171).

If this experience can be contained and 'suffered through', being 'on the edge of the abyss' may bring forth new signs and symbols. A broadened, more expressive narrative may emerge from the upsurge of primal sensory elements that the 'black hole' can engender. This manifests within a sort of penumbra, a cloud, a 'beam of darkness' (Bion's term) – not 'out in the light' (Rhode, 1998, p. 24). The understanding that this experience generates can be so distinctive that the individual's presence in the world radically shifts.

To feel solidly *in place* in the world involves creating a base in image and language. The process of making meaning through signification, and the creation of narratives, is simultaneously an expansion of spatial experience. The richness of our significations, our ongoing stories, gives 'breadth' and 'depth' to our worlds. This is personal and experiential, not space considered as an objectively-given, measurable substance 'out there'.

The 'Black Hole' and Contemporary Art

Anselm Kiefer's work situates the 'black hole' in contemporary cultural history. Something resembling an alchemical Nigredo – perhaps yet another signifier for the 'black hole' – lies at the core of much of his work (López-Pedraza, 1996). 'To the Supreme Being' depicts a mass of blackness at the far end of a huge hall reminiscent of Nazi-inspired architecture (Arasse, 2001, pp. 66–95). In the place where one would expect to find an altar there are three black panels (Taylor, 1992, pp. 301–307). Ironically, the perspectival lines in the painting evoke Leonardo's 'Last Supper' (Steinberg, 2001).

In Kiefer's painting, there is no transcendent Last Supper, but only darkness and an overwhelming sense of lack. 'This desertion does not leave in its wake mere absence, nor does it promise the arrival of presence' (Taylor, 1992, p. 303). There is 'no Christ and his disciples, no food, and no windows opening onto nature. Only the room itself, where nothing is happening, opens out before us, and we cannot even tell what function the space has been designed to hold . . .' (Gilmour, 1990, p. 20). It vividly depicts the uncanniness of the black hole, the sense of void that has so strongly emerged in contemporary culture. The perspectival lines draw us into a vision of blackness that pervades the horizon of the painting, and by implication the tragic events of modern history. This is the contemporary bleakness that we confront in our patients and in ourselves.

Although he never shrinks from blackness, Kiefer (2002) has attempted many new syntheses, most often utilizing sources outside the modern tradition.

Swathes of 'starlight' appear in some of his later paintings. However, he is constantly wary of any final answers, and has stated that the hallmark of his art is *ambivalence*. For instance, one of his recent paintings depicts the 'Seven Heavenly Palaces', which seems to be a vision of the Divine deriving from the Cabbala. In the following painting he depicts similar 'heavenly dwellings', but now surrounded with menacing fox traps! Such startling paradoxes starkly and somewhat humorously illustrate his determination not to be trapped in reified forms, or in an overly romanticised view of the universe.

Conclusion

It is an endless challenge to be present as persons, without seductive adornments, at a specific time and place in history. Whatever its chains of signification over the centuries, the 'black hole' seems prominent in our own times. Black holes, voids, vortices, and gaps pervade contemporary Western culture. These entities are consistently there in our patients' everyday experiences, not merely in extreme or 'borderline' conditions. If not articulated in culturally creative forms, this reality may well find expression in violent and unforeseeable ways, individually and culturally.

The 'black hole' or 'void', the no-thing, can open the space for the emergence of new elements. This experience may precipitate trauma and disruption, but also a 'rearrangement' or 'transformation' of subjectivity as well as cultural creation (Castoriadis, 1998). If imaginatively articulated – as we saw with Todd and in a glimpse of the art of Anselm Kiefer – a life with increased dimensionality and consciousness may become possible.

From time to time we always reach the limit of what we can signify, and must face the 'gaps and abysses' of life once again. Bearing of 'not-knowing' lies at the heart of analytic work at its best, and is a precondition for the emergence of new personal and cultural forms. This paradoxical 'negative' reality is the basis of the human subject, with its humble portions of dignity and freedom.

Acknowledgments

My thanks to my son Devon Hinton and to my friend and colleague Michael Horne for their important contributions to this writing.

Notes

1 Marlan appropriately cautions against seeing the alchemical blackness as merely a 'stage' in a 'process of transformation'. When viewed within a system such as alchemy, there is always the danger that the particular experience is subsumed to some 'larger whole'. Although transformations may occur at the edges of experience, stuckness, chronic paranoia, destruction and death are also real possibilities. There is always real risk.

2 The motif of the 'mausoleum' certainly reminds one of the 'dead mother'. At the beginning of the analysis, some basic representations of selfs and other had been achieved, but Todd's life energy remained neither dead nor alive (Green, 2001). To give it up is to risk losing all familiar orientation to life, however unsatisfactory such a suspension between 'safe' deadness and terrifying aliveness may have been. New life requires transit of the terror of the 'abyss of unknowing', the 'black hole'. As will be seen, the reservoir of potential life is connected with the father who is despised and very dangerous in the Oedipal sense. Only if the terror is faced and the 'black hole' traversed is there any hope of symbolizing something like the bull-like energy of this father.

3 Fort/da means gone/here. In analytic thought this refers to Freud's observations of his grandson when his mother had left the room. The child played with a cotton reel whose back and forth movements he could control. As he exerted this control, he said 'fort' when the object was at a distance, and 'da' when he reeled it in. This originally stimulated Freud to consider aspects of representation and sublimation. The point here, emphasised by many Lacanians, is the gap that exists, a sort of 'black hole' during the movement between the 'fort' and the 'da' (Golan 39, pp. 154, 202, 225).

4 This brings to mind the old Zen aphorism, 'Before the ass is gone, the horse has already arrived'. Paradoxically, the ass is already the horse, and vice versa (Safran, 2006). We do not wait for a resolution of the 'ass complex' or a synthesis of ass and horse, but they are already there in their particular ways of being.

5 The bare-breasted women may indicate the beginning of the transformation of the 'dead mother' and his willingness to fight for more life. He has seen the still-encapsulated aliveness of the bulls, and seems to have 'chosen' them over the deadness of the mausoleum sarcophagus.

6 'Mike' could be seen as an emerging capacity for 'object usage' in the transference. I had been fairly active and available in our interactions. This seems to be an important factor in the analysis of such patients (Green, 2001, pp. 183 & 193; Winnicott, 1969).

7 Modifications of teeth are common parts of initiatory rituals, and often have that meaning in dreams.

8 Agoraphobic panic emerged in the late nineteenth century as a primal distur-
   bance of spatiality (Hinton in press). Todd's malady could be seen as part of a
   more general malady of our times.
9 Varieties of shame are often indicators of the level of development of consciousness (Hinton, 1998; Mogenson, 2000).

References

Arasse, D. (2001). *Anselm Kiefer*. New York: Harry N. Abrams.

Bakhtin, M. M. (1981). *The Dialogic Imagination*. Austin: University of Texas
  Press.

Barnard, S. (2002). "Diachrony, Tuché, and the Ethical Subject in Levinas and Lacan." In E. Gantt & R. N. Williams (Eds.), *Psychology for the Other*. Pittsburg:
  Duquesne University Press.

Castoriadis, C. (1998). *The Imaginary Institution of Society*. Cambridge: MIT Press.

Chandler, D. (2003). *Semiotics: The Basics*. New York: Routledge.

Colman, W. (2006). "Imagination and the imaginary." *Journal of Analytical Psychology*, 51, 1, 21–42.

Daly, G. & Zizek, S. (2004). *Conversations with Zizek*. Cambridge: Polity Press.

Davis, W. A. (1989). *Inwardness and Existence: Subjectivity in/and Hegel, Heidegger, Marx, and Freud*. Madison: University of Wisconsin Press.

Dyess, C. & Dean, T. (2000). "Gender: The Impossibility of Meaning." *Psychoanalytic Dialogues*, 10, 50, 735–756.

Forster, E. M. (1924). *A Passage to India*. London: Edward Arnold.

Freud, S. (1961). *Beyond the Pleasure Principle*. Trans. J. Strachey. New York:
  Norton Publications.

Gediman, H. K. (1995). *Fantasies of Love and Death in Life and Art*. New York:
  New York University Press.

Giegerich, W. (2005). "'Conflict Resolution', 'Opposites/Creative Union', Versus
  Dialectics and the Climb up the Slippery Mountain'." In G. Mogenson (Ed.),
  Dialectics and Analytical Psychology. New Orleans: Spring Publications.

Gilmour, J. C. (1990). *Fire on the Earth: Anselm Kiefer and the Postmodern World*.
  Philadelphia: Temple University Press.

Green, A. (2001). "The Dead Mother." In *Life Narcissism, Death Narcissism*. London: Free Association Books.

Grotstein, J. S. (1990a). "The Black Hole as the Basic Psychotic Experience: Some
  Newer Psychoanalytic and Neuroscience Perspectives on Psychosis." *Journal of
  the American Academy of Psychoanalysis*, 18, 1, 29–46.

Grotstein, J. S. (1990b). "Nothingness, Meaninglessness, Chaos, and the Black
  Hole II." *Contemporary Psychoanalysis*, 26, 3, 377–407.

Hauke, C. (2000). *Jung and the Postmodern*. London: Routledge.

Hinton, L. (1998). "Shame as a Teacher: 'Lowly Wisdom' at the Millennium." In M. Mattoon (Ed.), *Proceedings of the 14th International Congress for Analytical Psychology*. Einsiedeln: Daimon Verlag.

Hinton, L. (in press). "A Short History of 20th Century Theories of Panic in the United States: From Irritable Weakness to DSM-IV to the Cognitive Model of Panic." In D. Hinton & B. Goode (Eds.), *Culture and Panic Disorder*. New Brunswick: Rutgers University Press.

Hopper, E. (1991). "Encapsulation as a Defence against the Fear of Annihilation." *International Journal of Psycho-Analysis*, 72, 4, 607–624.

Horne, M. (2003). "Opening Space in Space: Insights from Infant Observation." In M. Mattoon (Ed.), *Proceedings of the 15th International Congress for Analytical Psychology*. Einsiedeln: Daimon Verlag.

Howes, D. (2005). *The Empire of the Senses*. Oxford: Berg Publishers.

Hurley, S. & Chater, N. (2005). *Perspectives on Imitation*. Vol. 2: *Imitation, Human Development, and Culture*. Cambridge: The MIT Press.

Jung, C. G. (1931). The structure and dynamics of the psyche (R. F. C. Hull, Trans.; H. Read, M. Fordham, & G. Adler, Eds.). In *The collected works of C. G. Jung* (Vol. 8). Princeton University Press.

Jung, C. G. (1970). Mysterium coniunctionis (R. F. C. Hull, Trans.; H. Read, M. Fordham, & G. Adler, Eds.). In *The collected works of C. G. Jung* (Vol. 14). Princeton University Press.

Jung, C. G. (1971). Psychological types (R. F. C. Hull, Trans.; H. Read, M. Fordham, & G. Adler, Eds.). In *The collected works of C. G. Jung* (Vol. 6). Princeton University Press.

Kiefer, A. (2002). *Merkaba*. New York: Gagosian Gallery.

Kinston, W. & Cohen, J. (1986). "Primal Repression: Clinical and Theoretical Aspects." *International Journal of Psycho-Analysis*, 67, 3, 337–354.

Kjellberg, P. & Ivanhoe, P. J. (1996). *Essays on Skepticism, Relativism, and Ethics in the Zhuangzi*. Albany: SUNY Press.

Kristeva, J. (1980). *Desire in Language*. New York: Columbia University Press.

Kristeva, J. (1982). *Powers of Horror: An Essay on Abjection*. New York: Columbia University Press.

Levy, M. (2006). *Void in Art*. Putney, VT: Bramble Books.

López-Pedraza, R. (1996). *Anselm Kiefer: "After the Catastrophe"*. London: Thames & Hudson.

Marlan, S. (2005). *The Black Sun: The Alchemy and Art of Darkness*. College Station: Texas A & M University Press.

Merleau-Ponty. M. (1964). *Signs*. Chicago: Northwestern University Press.

Merleau-Ponty. M. (1986). *The Visible and the Invisible*. Chicago: Northwestern University Press.

Mogenson, G. (2000). "Slinking towards Bethlehem: A Prospective View of Shame." *Spring*, 67, 19–37.

Muller, J. P. (1996). *Beyond the Psychoanalytic Dyad*. New York: Routledge.

Neumann, E. (1954). *The Origins and History of Consciousness*. Princeton: Princeton University Press.

Nobus, D. (1999). *Key Concepts of Lacanian Psychoanalysis*. New York: Other Press.

Rhode, E. (1998). *On Hallucination, Intuition and the Becoming of "O"*. New York: ESF Publishers.

Safran, J. D. (2006). "Before the Ass Has Gone, the Horse Has Already Arrived." *Contemporary Psychoanalysis*, 42, 2, 225–232.

Said, E. W. (1978). *Orientalism*. New York: Pantheon Publications.

Steinberg, L. (2001). *Leonardo's Incessant Last Supper*. New York: Zone Books.

Stern, D. B. (1997). *Unformulated Experience: From Dissociation to Imagination in Psychoanalysis*. Hillsdale, NJ: The Analytic Press.

Taylor, M. C. (1992). *Disfiguring: Art, Architecture, Religion*. Chicago: University of Chicago.

Tustin, F. (1990). *The Protective Shell in Children and Adults*. London: Karnac Books.

Winnicott, D. W. (1969). "The Use of an Object and Relating through Identifications." In *Playing and Reality*. London: Tavistock Publications.

Zizek, S. (1999). *The Ticklish Subject*. New York: Verso Press.

Chapter 7

The Enigmatic Signifier and the Decentred Subject[*]

General Introduction

The view that everything should or can be understood or spoken into exist-ence (Frosh, 2006, p. 372), and that psychological life could be seen as a teleological or evolutionary process, guided by a strong ego, dominated the early decades of analytic thought and practice. The hope of this modernist viewpoint was illustrated by Freud's dictum (1933, p. 112; Frosh, 2006, p. 364):

> to strengthen the ego, to make it more independent of the superego, to widen its field of perception and enlarge its organization, so that it can appropriate fresh portions of the id. *Where id was, there ego shall be: it is a work of culture, much like the draining of the Zuider Zee.*
>
> (Italics mine)

The human challenge was to tame the wildness of nature and put it to use. Everything could be known, classified, and utilised. This was the 'Enlight-ened' Western ethos (Frie & Orange, 2009, pp. 3–6; Elliot, 2001, pp. 10–11; Harvey, 1990).

World wars, genocides, ecological threats, terrorism, and economic up-heaval have put these ambitious and optimistic beliefs in doubt. Such spec-tacles of useless suffering disrupt our illusions of meaning and coherence, and to subsume it under the rubrics of a 'higher purpose' or 'telos' seems, at the least, callous (Bauman, 1989; Edgar, 2007; Levinas, 2000, pp. 91–103).

This background has impacted analytic thought and practice. We now know that the communications of both analyst and patient are not 'pure',

[*] Hinton L. (2009). The Enigmatic Signifier and the Decentred Subject. *The Journal of Analytical Psychology*, 54(5), 637–657. https://doi.org/10.1111/ j.1468-5922.2009.01811.x. Reprinted by Per-mission of John Wiley and Sons.

DOI: 10.4324/9781003641063-8

but are invariably influenced by unconscious elements (Ferro, 2006, 2009). A postmodern ethos has emerged focusing upon an 'otherness' that cannot be finally understood or spoken (Levinas, 2000). The 'subject' develops out of the ambiguous interface between enigma and our always-incomplete attempts at discursive understanding.

Within analytical psychology, this changed milieu has provoked rethinking of archetypal theory and the question as to whether the self is 'found' or 'made' (Zinkin, 1991/2008). The classical view of a Self or centre that guides development, and of archetypes as a priori structuring forms, has come into doubt. As a result, with varying degrees of success, there has been a multiplicity of efforts to reconsider Jung's ideas in the light of developmental theories, cognitive science, dynamic systems theory, neuroscience, and postmodern perspectives (Hauke, 2000; Kugler, 2005; Colman, 2008; Hogenson, 2009; Knox, 2004, 2009). Giegerich has created a substantial and original work that is heavily influenced by Hegelian concepts (2004, 2007). Whatever its merits, this work has also not been accepted by all (Hillman, 1994; Drob, 2005).

In psychoanalytic theory, recastings of subjectivity have shifted away from Freud's 'Oedipal' structures and inborn 'drives', toward more ambiguous perspectives often termed 'pre-Oedipal' or 'pre-object relations', and from a Lacanian-inspired theory of the linguistifacation of the subject to a post-Lacanian theory of pre-verbal, imaginary significations (Anzieu, 1989; Kristeva, 1989; Castoriadis, 1997; Elliot & Spezzano, 2000; Fairfield et al., 2002; Zizek & Daly, 2004). However, as in analytical psychology, none of these speculations has been universally embraced. As Elliot (2005, pp. 25–26) describes the contemporary situation: 'these far-reaching investigations have raised afresh the question of human creation, the question of representation and fantasy, and the question of the imaginary constitution of the socio-symbolic world'.

One generally accepted premise that has emerged is that an isolated mind in which development occurs, or in which the self or subject is constructed out of pre-existing contents, is no longer tenable. The developing individual is immersed in an ocean of signification from the beginning, and subjectivity develops from that enigmatic matrix. And yet, the value of reflection and articulating experience – the process of the development of the human subject – remains central to the analytic ethos (Astrachan, 2005). We are left with some challenging dilemmas. Jean Laplanche has fully engaged this formidable gap in psychoanalytic theorizing, and created a profound and thought-provoking metapsychology.

Laplanche and Metapsychology

Laplanche: Introduction

Laplanche navigates these circumstances by carefully tracing the lineaments of the enigmatic core of psychological life, emphasizing the role of
the other in the development of subjectivity. The study of his ideas regarding the enigma of the other, as seen in the transference and in the discourse
of analysis, provides a unique perspective that is invaluable in clinical work.
One feels the excitement of an original, learned mind on a quest – whose
perspective enlarges and enlivens one's own.

Now in his eighties, Laplanche studied under Merleau-Ponty, starting his
career as a phenomenological philosopher. He then became a psychiatrist
and psychoanalyst. Originally associated with Lacan, he later developed his
own version of analytic theory and practice. In his university-based psychoanalytic school in Paris, the Association Psychanalytique de France or APF,
work with analysts of any school was encouraged. At the time, this openness was unique in analytic institutes. While remaining part of the International Psychoanalytic Association he also made major changes, such as not
adopting the training analyst hierarchy, in the organization of his institute
(Laplanche, 1991; Kritzman, 2006, pp. 99–100).

His theories integrate psychoanalytic tradition with important trends in
contemporary thought. While acknowledging the basic need to put experiences into words, he points out that our attempts are always incomplete
because our efforts are limited by an enigmatic element stemming from an
original helplessness and dependence upon an adult other – an other whose
messages are partially enigmatic to both the child and the adult 'sender'.

He refers to his view of the decentred self as a 'Copernican Revolution'.
According to Laplanche, we are born into a 'Copernican' world in which
our 'centre' originally develops only in relation to an 'other', like the earth
circling the sun. Later we become 'Ptolemaic', as the ego spins narcissistic
illusions of 'centrality', 'wholeness' and self-sufficiency, defending against
the 'signifying stress' of the other's messages (Santner, 2006, p. 33). The
sun once again orbits the earth! That, according to Laplanche, is the view
of ego psychology. Finally, through analysis or life experience we may return to the Copernican perspective, realizing that indeed we are decentred
subjects, dependent on the enigmatic otherness of unconscious and 'world'
in the Heideggerian sense (Laplanche, 1999, pp. 52–84).

Primal repression is, for Laplanche, the very condition for the establishment of subjectivity. Freud first developed this idea in his early writings (1900, p. 603): '. . . in consequence of the belated appearance of the secondary processes, *the core of our being, consisting of unconscious wishful impulses, remains inaccessible to the understanding and inhibition of the unconscious'*. These memories and impulses are like fixations, estranged from later conscious recall and direction. However, they are 'forgotten' only in a literal sense; actually *they exert a powerful influence on all later mental events through their wishful force* (Freud, 1915, pp. 141–158; Frank & Muslin, 1967, pp. 59–61). Freud later replaced his idea of primal repression with a biologically-based 'id': an upwelling of *innate* drive forces that must be subdued and directed by a 'secondary' repression. This later form of repression, epitomised by the breakup occasioned by the Oedipal complex, subsequently became the main basis for Freud's elaboration of psychic structure (Elliot, 2005, p. 27; Laplanche, 1999, pp. 18 & 86). For Laplanche, in contrast, an unconscious 'otherness in me' due to primal repression is responsible for a *gap* between self and other. 'I' am 'other' to 'myself'. Subjectivity develops in the face of the otherness that one always already is (Elliot, 2005, p. 27).[1]

Laplanche is consistently critical of Freud's increasingly biological orientation, as well as his tendency to reduce the present to the past. He views Klein as even more biased toward innateness, noting in her theories a kind of biological idealism (1999, p. 125). This leaves out the crucial importance of the other – particularly the parental other – as a source of messages. As a result the other becomes, 'only . . . an abstract protagonist of a scene or a support for projections . . .' (1999, p. 159). In Laplanche's estimation, Klein never asks the crucial question, 'what does the *breast* want?' (1999, p. 126).

Laplanche adopts the term 'enigmatic signifier' from Lacan, but redefines it to mean the gestures, actions or words of the other – the enigmatic messages of the other – in the situation of what he calls 'primal seduction' (1999, p. 12, n. 13). He was strongly influenced by Lacan, but disagrees with his view of the child as a 'symptom of the parents' (1999, p. 160, n. 15). In his opinion, that disregards the creative activity of the nascent subject, 'the break, the profound reshaping, which occurs . . . and which may be likened to a metabolism that breaks down food into its constituent parts and reassembles them into a completely different entity' (1999, p. 160).

The presence of an enigmatic, destabilizing nucleus of experience pro-vokes the development of an ego that seeks to 'bind' the over-stimulating inputs. These enigmatic elements have an ongoing, destabilizing effect on personal and cultural structures, and at the extreme may feel like 'black holes' (Hinton, 2007). The unsayability of those things that are the gaps in our 'reality' may evoke a sense of loss and melancholy. However, they are also the basis of our freedom to re-translate or re-imagine them (Butler, 2003, 2005; Frosh, 2006; Kristeva, 1989; Zizek & Daky, 2004, p. 78). These imaginative 're-translations' of the enigma create 'new situations' in a way that seems akin to what Jung called the *transcendent function* (Jung, 1960, para. 167; Martin-Vallas, 2005, pp. 289–290; Miller, 2004, pp. 21–22).

Following Freud, Laplanche often employs a German word for the 'other,' *das Andere*, emphasizing the neutral article, the '*thing*-ness' that is inserted into the background of our experience (Laplanche, 1999, p. 17).[2] It is always already there in its otherness, 'something that eludes phenomenal manifesta-tion', and yet it is the opaque core around which our descriptions circulate (Critchley & Schürmann, 2008, p. 135 ff.). Our ego, our thought and charac-ter, all emerge around it. The ego is born to 'manage' it (Caruth, 2001, pp. 27–38). And yet we can never grasp it. It plagues us like an ongoing riddle, or as Lacan says, it is like finding a 'hieroglyph in the desert' (Lacan, 1977, p. 194). Our subjectivity and what we call 'the unconscious' is indeed formed out of relation to this inevitable 'otherness' (Laplanche, 1999, pp. 84–116).[3]

These elements that are the results of primal repression lose their capac-ity to signify any particular object or event, but retain an elemental aura of intentionality . . . they retain the capacity of '*signifying to*'. This often con-jures a strange and uncanny feeling. From infancy we are confronted with the enigmatic question of what the other wants from us. To quote Lacan quoting Cazotte, the primal question is: *Che Vuoi? (What do you want?)* (Laplanche, 1999, p. 147; Pluth, 2007, pp. 69–72).

To quote Laplanche's mentor, Lacan (1981):

all the child's 'why's' reveal not so much an avidity for the reason of things, [but] a testing of the adult, a 'Why are you telling me this?' ever-resuscitated from its base, which is the enigma of the adult's desire.

Lacan suggests the metaphors of the hieroglyph in the desert, or of cu-neiform characters carved on a tablet of stone. In such cases the signifier may lose what it signifies, without thereby losing its power to signify to

(Laplanche, 1989, pp. 44–45; Santner, 2006, p. 34). For Laplanche, such enigmatic experiences lie at the core of the subject.

Primal Seduction, Primal Repression and the Enigmatic Signifier

The vast discrepancy between the complex dimensions of adult communications and the unformed psyche of the child is at the core of 'primal seduction'. Laplanche describes the interaction with the nursing mother as an example of what he terms 'primal seduction'. He points out that the breast is an erotic organ, and the mother's experiences and fantasies are far beyond the comprehension of the infant (Laplanche, 1997). The mother often seductively speaks to her baby, perhaps caressing its naked body while meeting its needs (Rotmann, 2002). Such interactions are largely unconscious. Empirical studies confirm that infantile sexuality is paradoxically the most unmirrored activity between infants and mothers (Stein, 2007, p. 191; Fonagy, 2008). Laplanche uses the term 'seduction' to include not only erotic fantasies, but also the broader meanings signified by the German noun Reiz, which conveys a sense of provocation, charm, allure and stimulation (Laplanche, 1999, p. 227). Laplanche emphasises that such mother-child interactions are the usual state of things, not aberrations, not psychopathology.

We usually think of repression as what Freud called 'secondary repression'. This describes the activity of the psyche in putting aside experiences that might create anxiety. However, this secondary repression presupposes psychic structures that can judge and discriminate, that can evaluate experiences at some level and take protective actions. In Laplanche's view, primal repression is much more significant in the development of the subject (Laplanche, 1999, pp. 18 & 85–86; Kinston & Cohen, 1986).

Experiencing such enigmas may create dread and anxiety, and the danger of psychic collapse (Stack, 2005). The loss of a sense of intactness often results in deep grief and melancholy (Kristeva, 1989). On the other hand if one can weather such gaps, transformation and renewal may emerge, with a renewed spaciousness and sense of play. We endlessly navigate and retranslate these enigmas throughout our lives, in our relationships, careers, and creative endeavors. In a related spirit Jung defined a living symbol as one that retains a disruptive element, an unknownness; otherwise, it is a dead symbol or sign (Jung, 1971, para. 817).

The Analytic Process

Laplanche has well-developed ideas about the analytic process (Laplanche, 1999, pp. 214–233). He sees the 'offer' of analysis as resembling the original 'seduction' of childhood, implying a sort of 'promise' to resolve the enigma. The analyst therefore tends to be seen as 'the one supposed to know'. In order for the process to evolve it is crucial for the analyst to remain in touch with his/her own enigmatic core. By refusing to 'know' – or, more accurately, being aware that he/she does not know – the analyst provides a 'hollow' in which the process can evolve.

In this basic 'hollow' two, usually intertwined, types of transference come to rest. One is the reproduction of forms of behavior, relationships and childhood images. This is the *transfert en plein*, the 'filled in' transference. The other dimension of transference concerns elements in the relationship that have an enigmatic character. This latter is the *transfert en creux*, the 'hollowed out' transference. In practice these are usually mixed. The enigma is the means that enables 'analysis' to take place – the 'lysis' part of analysis.[4] The impact of the enigma may create a kind of opening, a gap, a crack, a cleavage plane in the ordinary 'filled in' process of things. If not for the enigma, there would be no analytic work and no dismantling of old patterns (Laplanche, 1989, p. 160; 1999, pp. 228–229).

Analysis may foster a kind of *opening up* that can be maintained and transferred to divergent fields of otherness and inspiration. This is very different from sublimation (Kumar, 2009, pp. 486–487; Laplanche, 1997, p. 663, 2002, p. 42). Laplanche calls this the 'transference of the transference', or 'the transference to the enigma as such'. By this he implies 'not some loss of being, but the possibility of being surprised, seized, traversed by the endless questioning of whoever comes to encounter us' (Laplanche, 2002, p. 50).

Laplanche talks about 'translation' rather than interpretation. In his view interpretation implies knowledge of some factual situation. Much interpretation has the purpose of giving us a [falsely] comfortable sense of 'recognition': rediscovery of what we already know (Stack, 2005, p. 69). We can retranslate the enigmatic core of what we are, but we never achieve the final, structural understanding that 'interpretation' implies. 'Translation means that there is no factual situation . . . if something can be translated it's already a message . . . you can only translate what has already been put in communication, or made as communication. That's why I speak of translation rather than interpretation' (Caruth, 2001, p. 14).

He sees transference as a general phenomenon, not limited to analysis. The analytic method – the *lysis* aspect of analysis within the safety of the analytic situation – provides a unique and valuable human experience, but this experience is not generically unique to analysis. Intermittently, 'windows in time' present themselves for translation out of the situation of analysis and into cultural forms.[5] Laplanche warns that the analyst's narcissism can block new translations by automatically interpreting such movements as resistance (Laplanche, 1999, pp. 230–233).

For Laplanche, analysis ends not so much as a 'termination', but as a recognition of the deepened capacity for re-translation or 'transferring' life into different sites, different relationships. The end of analysis also involves a mourning that is not just about the loss of the object, but includes an awareness that all discourses remain unfinished. It belongs to the analysand to transfer this dimension to another place (Laplanche, 2002, p. 50).[6]

Like the basic enigma, transference is never in essence 'resolved'. He says that theoretically, seen from this perspective, 'analysis is also interminable' (Laplanche, 1989, p. 164; Rotmann, 2002, p. 269).[7] In a more poetic moment, Laplanche compares the analytic process to the task of Ulysses' wife Penelope in her daily unweaving in order that a new weaving may take place tomorrow – so that a new pattern in the fabric of life may appear (Laplanche, 1999, pp. 250–254).[8] In a similar sense analysis tends to dissolve old structures, in the hope that new patterns may be created that enable a fuller life.

Case History

The following case narrative illustrates elements of Laplanche's metapsychology such as primal seduction, thing-like enigmatic signifiers, and enigmatic sexuality as they developed in the transference and through the 'lysis' of analysis and life events. I thank my patient for allowing us to use his story to help us understand some important psychological processes.

Initial Situation

Ralph was in his mid-fifties when I first saw him. In appearance, he was a carefully controlled, stocky man, well dressed in a casual fashion, with a slightly intellectual air. He had already interviewed two other analysts before we met, but found them both 'too cold and formal'. In contrast, he found me both 'warm and lively' and 'knowledgeable'. He had no previous experience of analytic therapy.

Initially, he was somehow both reticent and confident in his manner. After a brief time, he suddenly broke into anguished sobs. Between flurries of deep emotion he began to tell me about his situation.

His wife of thirty years had died a year and a half before. They had had a 'companionable marriage', had raised three children, but he said that there had been minimal spontaneity or passion. However they had been profoundly connected in many ways, and he had deeply mourned her loss. He had been a successful biotechnologist, and had retired after selling his company a few years before. Since that time he had travelled a great deal, mostly alone and usually focused on philanthropic projects.

A few weeks before I saw him, he had suddenly become involved in a passionate love affair with a woman near his own age. It had been the most intense, abandoned sexual experience of his life.[9] He insisted that they be together almost constantly because he couldn't bear any separation. 'All I think about is her!' he said. After a time she had apparently found the situation frightening and declared a moratorium, refusing to see him. He felt shattered and bereft, and was sleepless and extremely anxious, constantly beseeching her for some form of contact. Both she and his friends told him that he must seek therapy.

His first dream, reported at our second meeting:

> I am in an oppressive, miserable prisoner-of-war camp or maybe a concentration camp, with some family and others. There has been a terrible event, and we are full of sorrow. Then someone or something enables us to tunnel out, to get out to a freer space.

He spoke tearfully of his grief, both for his wife and for the loss of his lover and the 'new life' he had experienced. Now these seemed like two catastrophes that had left him feeling sad and alone, and hopeless. He said that a sense of loss and desolation had haunted him his whole life. The surprisingly hopeful event in the dream indicated a positive transference, a shred of hope.

Despite his somewhat distant and reticent manner, I felt a sense of rapport. I said little, but was supportive in my demeanour. He seemed grateful to be able to have the safety and containment of the analytic frame, and continued to easily break down in tears, especially when he fell into a state of near-desperation from his longing to see his woman friend and his fear that he had lost her forever. My schedule was very crowded at that time, but I managed to fit him in three times a week. I regretted that we couldn't meet even more often because of the powerful emotional eruptions that periodically wracked him.

Gaps

Early on during the first couple of years of analysis, an important theme appeared. One day he came into the room and sat down, staring at me very intently and silently. I felt a wave of powerful emotions, a kind of primordial awfulness impossible to capture in words. His face was contorted in indecipherable waves of expression, but he said nothing. Moved, puzzled, a bit frightened, I wondered what this inchoate mélange of emotions might be. Was it loss, longing, despair, deep anxiety, grief, and anger all bundled together? As came out in time, bits of all these emotions were indeed there, but I later discovered that there was something more. Now I think of this as the presence of the enigmatic signifier, the 'thing' – *das Andere*. I was stunned, deeply moved, and somewhat bewildered. The sense of the uncanny was powerful, and evoked my own enigma in the form of a slight sense of panic, and a kind of psychic dizziness. I struggled to stay in touch with unknowing and not reactively close off the emotions.

After a tense couple of minutes – that felt much longer in subjective time – he gathered himself and began to speak about the vicissitudes of his thoughts and emotions regarding his lady friend. Still in a bit of shock from the intensity and 'otherness' of the emotions, I interrupted and remarked upon the abrupt turn back to the everyday. He said that he couldn't stand to be in that place, and he really couldn't say what 'it' was. We sat silently with that fact for a few minutes and then he continued on, remaining closer to the everyday. I had a sense that if I had pressed him there would have been a strong reactive, defensive closure, probably intellectual. I knew that this material was very deep, perhaps dangerous, and that it was crucial to patiently track and articulate its uncanny reality.

This became a theme that appeared intermittently during the first two years of analytic work. Perhaps once a week we would sit in extended silences of several minutes. Over time when I inquired about what he was experiencing, and increasingly at his own initiative, he began to tell me the bits and pieces of what was going on.

The most common topic was his very 'cold' mother. Dead many years, she had been a very attractive woman who always seemed emotionally removed. She was a CPA who practised part-time during most of her life. Never, in his memory, was she physically affectionate with him, although she took good instrumental care of him and his sister who was four years younger. He was told that he was breast-fed for only a brief period of time. There were, around his childhood home, photographs of her as a young, happy-looking, very pretty girl and young woman. 'That was the mother I never knew, the one I always wanted to know. It was really weird – a total mystery – that the woman in the photos could be the same person I knew as my mother'. Sometimes he caught glimpses of that 'other' mother when he saw her at a party with professional friends of his father, but that was very rare.

His father was a gruff and rather distant scientist who provided little emotional support, and indeed often felt 'dangerous' as a result of mood swings and bursts of angry criticism. He tried to get Ralph to play sports, but Ralph was awkward and self-conscious and usually ended up with a sense of injury. He grew to fear sports and groups of rowdy children, and was generally terrified of personal interactions at school or at home. His outstanding intellect brought some sense of self-esteem in the form of good grades and awards, and with much effort he was able to form some relationships. He said that he would 'latch onto' a girl as a friend and do anything she wanted in order to maintain the connection. This pattern had persisted throughout his life, including his long marriage.

He slowly became able to articulate small, spontaneous bits of his experience of the gaps. Then one day some words suddenly tumbled forth from the core of his being. Staring at me angrily and accusingly, he burst out in a voice that trembled with emotion, 'I just couldn't figure out what you *wanted*!' The deep pain was caused by my unknown-ness, my enigmatic presence. I was indeed the other, the enigmatic *other* whom he could never seem to satisfy.

All his life Ralph had, often desperately, created different translations, different responses, firstly and most importantly to his mother and later to other women, hoping to find something that would be the key. After he was able to articulate some of this to me – and to himself – the gaps continued but were somewhat less fraught with emotion. He felt safer in the container. From this point his presence seemed steadier than before.

It reflected, I think, a growing sense of reliable space for his subjectivity. I was 'other', but unlike his parents he could trust me to manage my own enigma. I demanded little from him, which left him free to play with his own translations.

Gradually, the sense of infatuation and loss abated, his anxiety decreased, and he began to enter more fully into his daily life.

Laughter Intrudes

After about three years of fairly insightful, productive work we had lapsed into a sort of habit of discussing his past relationships. In contrast with the early dramatic process our work had become somewhat routine, a little deadened. In retrospect, I wonder whether I had been relieved that we had successfully navigated a very difficult period, and was reticent to rock the boat.

One day he came into the room and lapsed into a pained silence that felt very different than the silence of the 'gaps'. Then he suddenly gave me a piercing, angry look and burst out, 'What in the hell are we doing here?!' With little hesitation the words sprang from my lips, 'Fuck if I know!' I was totally startled by my own words, as was he. It was very tense for a moment, and time seemed strangely suspended. After this pause in some atemporal-seeming space, he flushed and I flushed, and we broke down in mutual peals of deep belly laughter.

Laughter, according to Bergson, 'removes the mechanical from the living' (Bergson, 2005). In a similar vein, Bakhtin said that laughter 'de-grades', in the sense of dissolving 'monogogic' structure and freeing the dialogical process (Bakhtin, 1984, p. 21). Laughter shows that the 'serious' structures of things have no inevitability, no necessity (Critchley, 2002). To speak in Laplanchean terms, we could say that laughter performs a kind of 'unbinding' function, as well as a deflation of the fantasy/longing that the analyst be *'the subject supposed to know'* – *'le sujet suppose savoir'* (Laplanche, 1999, p. 49; italics in original).

The unbinding of structure on these levels, the transferential shift and the related shift in subjective processes, both reflected and enabled a creative contact with the core human enigma, the enigmatic signifier in its creative aspects. Over-generalizing a bit, one could say that the experiences of the 'gaps' involved the terrifying aspect of the enigma. After repeatedly nego-tiating the passage through the gaps, a dimension of openness to the other appeared. This is what we shared. Our enigmas touched, opening a space for renewed life in our relationship, and a new spaciousness in his being as a subject. It seemed to involve a shift or partial re-creation of his subjectivity that one could call 'the transcendent function' (Hinton, 1978).

Having weathered the earlier, tormenting transitions he had developed trust that neither he nor I would be destroyed by his disruptive anger. The result was a timeless moment between us and a capacity to experience his core enigma as creative rather than merely as a terrifying and destructive gap. It seemed to make possible a mutual experience of the enigma, and an example of what Laplanche called the 'hollowed out' transference – the 'transfert en creux' (Laplanche, 1999, pp. 50 & 111, 214n; Rotmann, 2002, p. 274).[10]

This was an important turning point as there was much more flow in our relationship that in part resulted in a quiet humour. There was a subtle increase in his capacity for reflection. We never really 'analysed' the laughter and the accompanying emotions, but referred to it from time to time, usually in moments of intimacy, with a few words such as 'that wild laugh we had together'. The experience did not fall into a distant, unconscious place but continued as a living process both between us and, as became increasing clear, in his interactions with others.

A Major Dream

Following the above changes, things began to move along. He met a new woman and the relationship worked out well. It came across as dynamic and multi-dimensional, with an intensely sexual component. About six months after the 'laughter' incident he had the following series of dreams:

It is a surreal landscape, like a jungly area in Central America where I've done volunteer work.[11] A young woman is walking along a trail on the side of a hill ahead of me, but suddenly disappears off to the side, like into a cave or something. I plunge ahead, wanting to find her or help her. There is a wall of dry board at the entrance to the cave . . . I break through it, looking for the woman. (Note: I immediately felt a different energy in the room; he had seldom been so directly aggressive in fact or in dreams.) There are claw marks on the wall and I know that there is an invisible monster there in the cave. I felt absolutely terrified!

At this point Ralph looked very apprehensive and somewhat anxiously went into some associations: the young woman reminded him of the photos that he had seen of his mother as a beautiful, happy young woman. 'That's the mother I never knew', he said.

Slowly and seriously he went over his lifelong feelings of loneliness and abandonment, and his ongoing terrors as a child – feelings that we had re-visited many times. He had never been able to say what terrified him. It seemed uncanny and unknowable. The mere thought of it had made him feel paralysed and unable to think.

He continued:

> Then I see some balls, and I think that I can distract the monster. I don't see it but I know it's there. It seems like I can do it: distract it.
>
> Then it seems like the monster is different, like it has become playful. The whole mood becomes different.

He said excitedly that it was the first time he had ever been able to hold his own and act in the face of such feelings of terror whether in dreams or in everyday life, that he felt like he'd spent his whole life in activities and relationships to try and make things safe. The anxiety and terror had always been like an invisible presence that – whatever his successes – kept him on edge, vigilant, unable to play. Underneath, he had always felt lacking, like 'half a man'.

Due to his rich associations I said very little except for non-verbal acknowledgements. The associations were very much in tune with the earlier analytic process. These dreams seemed to summarise much of what had transpired during the course of analysis. He left the session smiling, seemingly enlivened, feeling very good about what had transpired. I shared in the good feeling and wondered whether, too, I was the enigmatic monster of the gaps with whom he could now play.

Speculations

The analytic process had been precipitated by an intense and highly sexualised relationship, and then he had been 'abandoned', left alone in a 'gap' with an unbearable excess of emotion.[12] This desperate state of crisis, a threat to his very survival, forced Ralph to undertake a process that led to the awareness of his enigmatic core. The pursuit of the young woman in the dream, like all his lifelong pursuits, stemmed from a longing to find the – impossible – key to the enigmatic longings of his unhappy, somewhat schizoid, mother. He had come into being as a subject in his attempts to respond to her messages, to know what she 'wanted'. This stimulated his subjective development, but the concretization of his fantasies, in particular relationships, had left him endlessly vulnerable to loss and the fear of falling into the 'gap'. The result was an avoidant, deadened life.

Monsters tend to appear when unnameable emotions and experiences surface (Astrachan, 2005; Connolly, 2003; Kearney, 2003). The analysis had begun from such a situation. We had faced this elemental state repeatedly, until he was finally able to laugh and play with me. A new and more meaningful re-translation of his subjectivity seemed accomplished. The enigma was now a source of not only 'deconstructive' terror but also playful creativity.

His intellectual prowess had given him some sense of control and efficacy, and through strong ego development he had been able to bind his terror, to bridge the gaps, alleviate the depression, and lead a life as a creative scientist and businessman, husband and father. In late midlife, with the aid of analysis, he had re-translated the enigmatic core of his subjectivity into an ongoing possibility of creative play, of fantasy and imagination – the essence of the transcendent function (Jung, 1971, pp. 106–107; Miller, 2004, pp. 46–47).

Heretofore in his life he had withdrawn at perceived slights or rejections. Any new interpersonal context had been fraught with hesitation and anxiety. Now this had shifted. He was still prone to similar emotions, but he was much more aware that these stemmed from him and not the other. As he said, 'I knew that I projected all over the place before, but now I *really* know it and it doesn't control me'.

Another aspect of this was the expansion of the ability to imagine the reality of others, including their unknowability, their own enigma. Such awareness 'deconstructs' the tendency to want to make the other a colony that fills one's lack. In this vein, Ralph described much more capacity for intimacy, and said that he was generally happier than ever before.

Last Part of Analysis

The remaining eighteen months of analysis had a different tone. Our relationship was more spontaneous and sometimes playful, and he continued to use the time productively. Ralph discussed his relationship with his new woman friend a great deal. The fluctuating issues with her were often at the foreground. He no longer became mired in long periods of defensive withdrawal from her. He felt it was the best relationship he had ever had.

A simple dream summarised his new situation:

Fish are jack-knifing in paroxysms in a pool – they think that they will die without a mate. Then a cell phone rings, and they get a message of some kind and swim peacefully.

(His association was that was how he felt as he began to get caught up in the old mood, of being abandoned to terror and nothingness if there was a gap in relationship.)

This illustrates Ralph's emerging reflective capacity in the face of 'gaps'. He could now recognise and re-translate what had been almost unbearable, inchoate emotion.

We mutually agreed that things were going well, and we set a date for ending. He brought me an interesting little object from his travels as a parting gift, and we both shed a tear at the last session.

Conclusions/Reflections

Laplanche rarely provides us with clinical material in his own writings because of his views regarding the intrinsically defensive nature of most clinical narratives. 'Histories' lend themselves to the fantasy that the present is 'caused' by the past (Laplanche, 1999, p. 141). We must be careful, he says, because 'there can be *no linear causality* between the parental unconscious and discourse on the one hand and what the child does about these on the other' (Laplanche, 1999, p. 160).

However, the richness of his metapsychology does whet one's appetite for more examples that demonstrate that 'his structures have legs' (Copjec, 2006). For instance, Charlie Chaplin's movie *City Lights* provides a scenario humorously illustrating Laplanche's concept of the enigmatic signifier. In the film, Charlie accidentally swallows a whistle, and it haunts him. He wants to fit into the 'sophisticated' life of the city, but the whistle sounds off erratically from his belly, disrupting his best efforts to be 'normal'. Such 'messages' are eternally disruptive, and yet they rescue us from becoming collective zombies, automated cultural products that are not capable of an ethical stance (Hinton, 1978). This scene illustrates how we cannot get rid of the 'thing' that is, in part, us.

Some take Laplanche's emphasis on 'primal seduction' to indicate a pathologizing of mothers and infants (Solomon, 2002, pp. 282–283). He endlessly emphasises, however, that this 'seduction' is the normal course of events and not pathological. He sometimes uses the German term *Reiz* instead of 'seduction', and this has a broader set of meanings such as allure, provocation, charm, stimulation, or sex appeal (Laplanche, 1999, p. 227). However, it might be helpful if he were to discuss the growing capacities of the infant/child and how it can, increasingly, contribute to the dyadic interaction.

To think more broadly, a seductive 'excess' may be the basis, the 'driver', of personal, cultural and spiritual development (Stein, 2008; Kumar, 2009). Indeed, creative endeavours of all kinds tend to be filled with sexual imagery, and often entail a quest for the lost object (Kristeva, 1989). One could regard the excess of enigmatic stimuli – excessive in terms of what the ego can as-similate – as an upsurge of desire that creates turbulence, but can create new openings in relationships and world. In Jonathan Lear's terms (1998), we are born 'overfull', and what we do with this overfulness expresses the heart of who we become. The enigmatic messages that we meet in everyday life end-lessly evoke our responses. To quote Laplanche (1999, p. 224): 'the cultural [itself] is an address to another who is out of reach, to others "scattered in the future" as the poet says', and he asks, 'why does the Dichter Dicht – why does the poet poetise – except in response to an enigmatic other?'

One could, if so inclined, readily make connections with more philo-sophically speculative theories (Kumar, 2009). The thought of Levinas is an outstanding example, especially when he refers to the enigmatic quality of subjectivity as deriving from a 'trace of the infinite' that cannot be reduced to personal – or even ontological – terms.

The concrete sense of seduction and enigma in its many dimensions makes Laplanche's work distinctive. His work expands awareness of the enigmatic core of subjectivity . . . a core that is also, paradoxically, the source of our dignity and freedom.

Acknowledgments

My thanks to Michael Horne for his faithful editing and his unfailing dia-logical presence.

Notes

1 It is interesting to note the resemblance of Sartre's observation about shame: 'J'ai honte de moi devant autrui' (Sartre, 1943, p. 337). Or, 'I am ashamed of myself before the Other' (Sartre, 1956, p. 289). It would be an interesting exercise to tie together shame experience and the enigmatic signifier. Shame indeed became very important in Lacan's later thought (Copjec, 2006).

2 The masculine form, *der Andere*, would be used to refer to another person. These two forms actually illustrate two moments in the act of 'primal repression'. First, the message of the other person of inscription and implantation, followed by primal repression of the untranslatable elements of the 'message'. This untranslatable 'remainder' becomes das Andere, a thing-like 'enigmatic signifier'.

3 [Laplanche describes] this 'otherness' [using] a neologism in French – not just *etrangete*, strangeness, foreignness, alienness, but *etrangerete*, stranger-ness, foreign-ness . . . 'alien-ness' (Laplanche, 1999, p. 47).

4 Laplanche repeatedly makes a point about the analytic process as Lösung, or 'dissolution' (1999, pp. 252–253). It is the enigmatic signifier that makes 'unbinding' possible. The defensive ego tries to bind things into a whole. The enigma rescues the psyche from determinism through the 'lysis' of – often imprisoning – patterns (1999, pp. 45, 49, & 252–253).

5 Laplanche uses the metaphor of a rocket launch and the 'windows in time' during which it would be possible to send a rocket to Saturn (1989, p. 164).

6 He describes this as another potential form of inspiration, which sounds similar to the views of Julia Kristeva on the relationship between melancholy and creativity (Kristeva, 1989).

7 In this light, it would be interesting to revisit the disagreement between Tresan (2007) and Connolly (2007) regarding the meaning of time and length of analysis.

8 There is a certain similarity to Jung's depiction of the 'analytic' and the 'synthetic' aspects of the analytic process (Jung, 1966, pp. 80–90).

9 Helen Gediman has provided a related, fascinating study of the 'annihilation anxiety' associated with sexuality. Fantasies of death and longings for rebirth or immortality are often intimately connected (Gediman, 1995).

10 Levinas describes a moment of 'otherness', a 'subjection' to otherness, which goes 'all the way to the laughter that refuses language' [jusqu'au rire qui refuse le langage]. That is, laughter can be a moment beyond words, an experience of the unsayable (Levinas, 1998, p. 8; Wall, 1999, p. 36). Wit or humour at their best touch on such dimensions, but are more clearly related to the realities of human culture and psychology. The deepest laughter just 'takes us over', takes us to a different space. It is sudden and unexpected, even a little 'mad'.

11 For Ralph, these 'exotic' places had been full of 'enigmatic signifiers', as they have been for Westerners for many centuries (Lyotard, 1979).

12 Ruth Stein has written a fascinating and wide-ranging discussion of the meaning of sexuality and excess. She sees such experiences of excess as frequently

being manifestation of the 'human longings to grasp the elusive, ineffable quality of the sexual other', to bridge the gap between self and other (2008).

References

Anzieu, D. (1989). *The Skin Ego*. New Haven: Yale University Press.

Astrachan, G. (2005). "Naming the Unnameable." *Quadrant*, 35, 1 & 2.

Bakhtin, M. M. (1984). *Rabelais and His World*. Bloomington: University of Indiana Press.

Bauman, Z. (1989). *Modernity and the Holocaust*. Ithica, NY: Cornell University Press.

Bergson, H. (2005). *Laughter: An Essay on the Comic*. Mineola, NY: Dover Publications.

Butler, J. (2003). "Violence, Mourning, Politics." *Studies in Gender and Sexuality*, 4, 1, 9–37.

Butler, J. (2005). *Giving an Account of Oneself*. New York: Fordham University Press.

Caruth, C. (2001). "An Interview with Jean Laplanche." http://www.iath.virginia.edu/pmc/text-only/issue.101/11.2caruth.txt.

Castoriadis, C. (1997). *World in Fragments*. Stanford: Stanford University Press.

Colman, W. (2008). "On Being, Knowing and Having a Self." *Journal of Analytical Psychology*, 53, 3, 351–367.

Connolly, A. (2003). "Psychoanalytic Theory in Times of Terror." *Journal of Analytical Psychology*, 48, 4, 407–431.

Connolly, A. (2007). "Frozen Time and Endless Analysis: A Response to David Tresan's 'Thinking Individuation Forward'." *Journal of Analytical Psychology*, 52, 1, 41–45.

Copjec, J. (2006). "May '68, the Emotional Month." In S. Zizek (Ed.), *Lacan: The Silent Partners* (pp. 90–115). New York: Verso.

Critchley, S. (2002). *On Humour*. New York: Routledge.

Critchley, S. & Schürmann, R. (2008). *On Heidegger's Being and Time*. New York: Routledge.

Drob, S. L. (2005). "Giegerich and the Traditions: Notes on Reason, Mythology, Psychology and Religion." *Journal of Jungian Theory and Practice*, 7, 2, 61–73.

Edgar, A. (2007). "The art of Useless Suffering." *Medicine, Health Care and Philosophy*, 10, 395–405.

Elliot, A. (2001). *Concepts of the Self*. Cambridge: Polity Press.

Elliot, A. (2005). "The Constitution of the Subject." *European Journal of Social Theory*, 8, 1, 25–42.

Elliot, A. & Spezzano, C. (Eds.) (2000). *Psychoanalysis at Its Limits: Navigating the Postmodern Turn*. New York: Free Association Books.

Fairfield, S., Layton, L. & Stack, C. (2002). *Bringing the Plague: Toward a Postmodern Psychoanalysis*. New York: Other Press.

Ferro, A. (2006). "Clinical Implications of Bion's Thought." *International Journal of Psychoanalysis*, 87, 989–1003.

Ferro, A. (2009). "Transformations in Dreaming and Characters in the Psychoanalytic Field." *International Journal of Psychoanalysis*, 90, 209–230.

Fonagy, P. (2008). "A Genuinely Developmental Theory of Sexual Enjoyment and Its Implications for Psychoanalytic Technique." *Journal of the American Psychoanalytic Association*, 56, 1, 11–35.

Frank, A. & Muslin, H. (1967). "The Development of Freud's Concept of Primal Repression." *Psychoanalytic Study of the Child*, 22, 55–76.

Freud, S. (1900/1958). *The Interpretation of Dreams. S.E. 5*. London: Hogarth.

Freud, S. (1915). *Repression. S.E. 14*. London: Hogarth.

Freud, S. (1933). *New Introductory Lectures on Psycho-Analysis. S.E., 22: 1–182*. London: Hogarth.

Frie, R. & Orange, D. (Eds.) (2009). *Beyond Postmodernism: New Dimensions in Theory and Practice*. New York: Routledge.

Frosh, S. (2006). "Melancholy without the Other." *Studies in Gender and Sexuality*, 7, 4, 363–378.

Gediman, H. G. (1995). *Fantasies of Love and Death in Life and Art*. New York: New York University Press.

Giegerich, W. (2004). "The End of Meaning and the Birth of Man." *Journal of Jungian Theory and Practice*, 6, 1, 1–66.

Giegerich, W. (2007). *The Soul's Logical Life: Towards a Rigorous Notion of Psychology*. Bern: Peter Lang.

Harvey, D. (1990). *The Condition of Postmodernity*. Malden, MA: Blackwell Publishers.

Hauke, C. (2000). *Jung and the Postmodern: The Interpretation of Realities*. New York: Routledge.

Hillman, J. (1994). "Once More into the Fray: A Response to Wolfgang Giegerich's 'Killings'." *Spring*, 56, 1–18.

Hinton, L. (1978). *Humor and the Transcendent Function*. Presented at the National Meeting of Jungian Analysts, Asilomar, CA. Unpublished Manuscript.

Hinton, L. (2007). "Black Holes, Uncanny Spaces and Radical Shifts in Awareness." *Journal of Analytical Psychology*, 52, 433–447.

Hogenson, G. B. (2009). "Archetypes as Action Patterns." *Journal of Analytical Psychology*, 54, 3, 325–339.

Jung, C. G. (1960). The transcendent function (R. F. C. Hull, Trans.; H. Read, M. Fordham, & G. Adler, Eds.). In *The collected works of C. G. Jung* (Vol. 8). Princeton University Press.

Jung, C. G. (1966). Two essays on analytical psychology (R. F. C. Hull, Trans.; H. Read, M. Fordham, & G. Adler, Eds.). In *The collected works of C. G. Jung* (Vol. 7). Princeton University Press.

Jung, C. G. (1971). Psychological types (R. F. C. Hull, Trans.; H. Read, M. Fordham, & G. Adler, Eds.). In *The collected works of C. G. Jung* (Vol. 6). Princeton University Press.

Kearney, R. (2003). *Strangers, Gods, and Monsters*. New York: Routledge.

Kinston, W. & Cohen, J. (1986). "Primal Repression: Clinical and Theoretical Aspects." *International Journal of Psycho-Analysis*, 67, 337–353.

Knox, J. (2004). "From Archetypes to Reflective Function." *Journal of Analytical Psychology*, 49, 1–19.

Knox, J. (2009). "Mirror Neurons and Embodied Simulation in the Development of Archetypes and Self-Agency." *Journal of Analytical Psychology*, 54, 3, 307–325.

Kristeva, J. (1989). *Black Sun: Depression and Melancholia*. New York: Columbia University Press.

Kritzman, L. D. (2006). *The Columbia History of Twentieth-Century French Thought*. New York: Columbia University Press.

Kugler, P. (2005). *Raids on the Unthinkable: Freudian and Jungian Psychoanalyses*. New Orleans: Spring Journal.

Kumar, M. (2009). "Recasting the Primal Scene of Seduction: Envisioning a Potential Encounter of Otherness in Jean Laplanche and Sudhir Kakar." *Psychoanalytic Review*, 96, 3, 485–513.

Lacan, J. (1977). *Écrits*. New York: W. W. Norton.

Lacan, J. (1981). *The Four Fundamental Concepts of Analysis*. New York: W. W. Norton.

Laplanche, J. (1989). *New Foundations for Psychoanalysis*. Cambridge, MA: Blackwell.

Laplanche, J. (1991). "Jean Laplanche Talks to Martin Stanton." *Free Associations*, 2C, 323–341.

Laplanche, J. (1997). "The Theory of Seduction and the Problem of the Other." *The International Journal of Psychoanalysis*, 78, 653–666.

Laplanche, J. (1999). *Essays on Otherness*. New York: Routledge.

Laplanche, J. (2002). "Sublimation and/or Inspiration." *New Formations*, 48, 30–53.

Lear, J. (1998). *Open Minded: Working Out the Logic of the Soul*. Cambridge, MA: Harvard University Press.

Levinas, E. (1998). *Otherwise Than Being or beyond Essence*. Pittsburg: Duquesne University Press.

Levinas, E. (2000). *Entre Nous*. New York: Columbia University Press.

Lyotard, F. (1979). *The Postmodern Condition*. Manchester, England: University Press.

Martin-Vallas, F. (2005). "Towards a Theory of the Integration of the Other in Representation." *Journal of Analytical Psychology*, 50, 285–293.

Miller, J. (2004). *The Transcendent Function: Jung's Model of Psychological Growth through Dialogue with the Unconscious*. Albany: State University of New York Press.

Pluth, E. (2007). *Signifiers and Acts: Freedom in Lacan's Theory of the Subject*. Albany: State University of New York Press.

Rotmann, M. (2002). "The Alienness of the Unconscious: On Laplanche's Theory of Seduction." *Journal of Analytical Psychology*, 47, 265–278.

Santner, E. (2006). *On Creaturely Life*. Chicago: University of Chicago Press.

Sartre, J.-P. (1943/1991). *L'être et le néant*. Saint-Amand: Gallimard.

Sartre, J.-P. (1956). *Being and Nothingness*. New York: Philosophical Library.

Solomon, H. (2002). "Reply to Michael Rotmann." *Journal of Analytical Psychology*, 47, 279–284.

Stack, A. (2005). "Culture, Cognition and Jean Laplanche's Enigmatic Signifier." *Theory, Culture and Society*, 22, 3, 63–80.

Stein, R. (2007). "Moments in Laplanche's Theory of Sexuality." *Studies in Gender and Sexuality*, 8, 2, 177–200.

Stein, R. (2008). "The Otherness of Sexuality: Excess." *Journal of the American Psychoanalytic Association*, 56, 43–71.

Tresan, D. (2007). "Thinking Individuation Forward." *Journal of Analytical Psychology*, 52, 1, 17–40.

Wall, T. C. (1999). *Radical Passivity: Levinas, Blanchot and Agamben*. Albany: State University of New York Press.

Zinkin, L. (1991/2008). "Your Self: Did You Find It or Did You Make It?." *Journal of Analytical Psychology*, 53, 3, 389–406.

Zizek, S. & Daly, G. (2004). *Conversations with Zizek*. Malden, MA: Polity Press.

Chapter 8

Unus Mundus – Transcendent Truth or Comforting Fiction?

Overwhelm and the Search for Meaning in a Fragmented World*

Fragmentation of the Unus Mundus

It's very special to be here with my sons, and to be able to share their thoughtfulness and creativity. My own task is to introduce our panel in this segment, entitled 'Fragmentation of the Unus Mundus'. I approach this task with a bit of trepidation! As we know, the Unus Mundus lies at the core of Jung's thought, and his privileging of this ideal reflects his longing to found an all-encompassing theory (Shamdasani, 2003; Samuels, 1985, p. 89ff.).

The search for universal ideas, often with utopian implications, has been a perennial quest for philosophy and psychology. We, too, as clinicians are tempted to 'reduce the universe to an originary and ultimate unity by way of panoramic overviews and dialectical syntheses' (Peperzak, 1997, p. 4). But Emmanuel Levinas, in a postmodernist mode, points out the negative ethical consequences that may ensue from such ways of conceiving the human condition. The 'Face of the Other,' including our patients in all their complexity and creativity, may be subsumed to an idea. My thesis is that Jung, for all his genius, falls prey to this very danger by privileging the Unus Mundus, and that this has had important implications for analytic theory and practice. But more about this later.

Jung describes the Unus Mundus as an experience where 'opposites' are transcended by unity, and an awareness of synchronicity becomes possible (Aziz, 1990; von Franz, 1975, p. 249). It serves as an implicit goal or telos, toward which a 'spiritus lector' (a spiritual guide in dreams or active imagination) leads the individual toward a 'unio mentalis' (a union of self and body/ matter). This eventuates in the union of the 'whole man' with a transcendent ground that is presumed to be foundational (1963/1970, paras. 759–775).

* Hinton L. (2011). Introduction: Fragmentation of the Unus Mundus. *The Journal of Analytical Psychology*, 56(3), 375–380. https://doi.org/10.1111/j.1468- 5922.2011.01915_1.x. Reprinted by Permission of John Wiley and Sons.

DOI: 10.4324/9781003641063-9

This telos or goal has often taken on the status of the '*constitutive myth*' of Jungian psychology (Gabriel & Žižek, 2009). That is, although one can cite many sides of Jung's writings, this particular set of assumptions tends to function, implicitly or explicitly, as the basic underpinning of Jungian thought and practice. It is his 'solution' to the ancient question of the ultimate truth of existence.

In the postmodern era, however, one can see how such foundationalism repeats a primal error of modern thought that can be very destructive in its unforeseen effects. My three sons will provide different examples of how the foundationalist search for truth and progress, for 'Enlightenment', has often had unpredictable and sometimes disastrous ethical consequences. Our hope is that these dramatic examples can help free us from our implicit biases toward a reified oneness or totality.

The primal dilemma can be traced back to the origins of Western thought, especially to interpretations of father Plato and his Allegory of the Cave (Plato, Book VII). As you may recall, this parable depicts humankind as fixed in place, staring at the wall of a cave. Some distance behind them, unseen, there is a large fire, and various objects are paraded in front of the fire. The shadows of the objects are visible on the wall of the cave, in front of the denizens emplaced there, and they take those shadows as 'reality'. Finally, one cave person is taken out into the light, where there is a different world and 'real' objects . . . not merely their shadows. When that person returns to the cave, however, his former compatriots will not believe him and go on staring at the shadows on the wall, believing that they are 'reality'.

The assumption of the parable is that the ideal foundations of life have always been there, but that a befuddled mankind has lost its way (Gibson, 2006, p. 159). From this point of view, 'Inside the cave' illustrates a view of humanity in error – an abject, 'fallen,' and 'lesser' humanity. No creative event of truth can happen there because the 'Truth' is depicted as a pre-existing ideal world, a thing outside in the light (Gibson, 2006, pp. 202–203). Such an ideal becomes the goal to be sought, the telos.

Plato's Allegory is reminiscent of some conventional views of the analytic situation! Like the cave dwellers, we are at first unaware of the illusionary state in which we exist. When we become aware of the degree of our lostness and blindness it terrifies us, and we search for foundational certainties that will provide an escape. The fantasy of a place 'outside' our condition, one that transcends our sense of helplessness and suffering, continually magnetises us (Carel, 2001, p. 2). This picture has largely dominated the course of Western theology and philosophy, and is related to Jung's conception of the Unus Mundus. Indeed, he specifically equates his viewpoint with Plato's Allegory (Jung, 1963/1970, para. 768), and describes it as restoring the 'potential world of the first day of Creation', the 'eternal Ground' of the empirical world 'before things were divided into a multiplicity' (Jung, 1963/1970, para. 760).

Such utopian views valorize the possibility of seeing from an 'objective' position 'outside the cave', which is impossible; from where could that position itself be observed and validated? In an attempt to solve this problem, Jung asserts the existence of an 'objective', Archimedean point by positing the concept of the 'psychoid', a 'non-psychic' structure that is 'neither mind nor matter' (Jung, 1960/1969, para. 417; para. 439, n. 130; para. 840). However, this merely shifts the illusion of objectivity and control to another level (Brooks, 2009). Like other utopian views, it ends in a tautology: *how does the eye see itself?* (Žižek, 2008). Jung himself sometimes raises the question of 'whether the soul could be known through itself', but this perspective usually becomes subsumed to his search for universals (1954, para 161 ff.; Shamdasani, 2003, p. 89; p. 94ff.).

Jung's theoretical construct, although it has inspired many practitioners as an ideal, in the end foundered. That may be due to his isolation from emerging perspectives that would have challenged the assumptions of the prevailing zeitgeist, and opened new dimensions in his work (Brooks, 2009).

A broader consequence of valorizing a 'larger, purer' totality is that it tends to minimise the raw particulars of human suffering. Seen through the lens of the utopian gaze, suffering is often depicted as an unfortunate but necessary dimension of the path toward an idealised unity (Levinas, 1998, pp. 91–102). Levinas repeatedly points out that such a totalizing point of view tends to obscure the ethical call of the singular Face of the Other and the stark reality of *useless* suffering (Levinas, 1969, pp. 21–30 & 194–219).

Contemporary postmodern thought offers a different view of the universe. It eschews utopian totalities that employ foundational principles. Based on speculations about an unknowable realm, such principles have no necessary relationship to the particulars of existence. In contrast, the postmodern ethos values particulars. In this view Being is always situated, and we are always-divided subjects in our 'worlds'. There is no experience of Being beyond all structure, beyond the situations in which we find ourselves (Gibson, 2006, p. 45).

In contrast to visions of totality, there is a fundamental incompleteness of reality itself that terrifies us (Johnston, 2008, p. 5). Things being *together* do not indicate that they constitute a *unity*; and what we tend to call 'opposites' are actually 'parallax views' that cannot be 'reconciled' (Žižek, 2006). Our knowledge is always condemned, in Lacanian terms, to be 'non-all', intrinsically lacking, invariably ending in enigma. This is an ontology of gaps and abysses, and the very structure of our subjectivity is a manifestation of such divisions. Jean Laplanche has carefully delineated this view, highlighting the prominence of enigmatic elements in the earliest formation of the subject (Laplanche, 1999; Hinton, 2009).

As a consequence, we are . . . 'constitutionally unable to keep things fixed and forever immune to disruption and change' (Lear, 2000, p. 112). However, the subject, when realizing this situation, may become a 'crack' in the very foundation of fundamental systems. Disruptiveness offers us something precious by opening up fields of possibilities (Carel, 2001, p. 6). Leaving the apparent comfort of life as a 'normal' automaton involves bearing the awareness of gaps or 'black holes' in consciousness; but such 'cracks' are also, paradoxically, the basis of human *freedom* (Žižek, 2006, pp. 25, 65, & 88–90).

This reverses Plato's journey. Consciousness or reflection indeed results in an awareness of what we creatures in the Cave lack; but a 'higher' unity or wholeness, a thing or substance that is the incarnation of ultimate Truth, always eludes our grasp like a phantom unicorn. The crucial point is that, in the process of descent into our cave-like depths, we may momentarily experience the *void* of an *always-missed encounter* with unity, with 'unprethinkable being'. It is such experiences that can open the *space of the subject* for poetry, new thoughts, images, and sometimes laughter (Bakhtin, 1984; Gabriel & Žižek, 2009, pp. 26–85; Gibson, 2006, pp. 54–55; Hinton, 2002; Johnston, 2008, p. 83).[1] This is the essence of the analytic task.

From this perspective psychoanalysis is not merely part of a necessary developmental unfolding, but rather it is a subversive influence involving our being in the world, a *break* [with given tradition, with 'totality'] that can open new horizons (Lear, 2000, p. 154). As Freud supposedly said to Jung as they were traveling to America to speak at Clark University, 'They don't know that we're bringing the *plague*!'.

Note

1 The void, as the constituting principle of experience, is the basis of the subject. It cannot itself appear as such but only in images such as the uncanny stranger. The self, the subject's manifest presence, is thus at root an appearance based upon an experience that can never itself be represented – although the inexhaustibility of aesthetic experience may touch upon this possibility (Gabriel & Žižek,

2009, pp. 79–80). This lends an uncanny quality to life (Gabriel & Žižek, 2009, pp. 20 & 31–32).

References

Aziz, R. (1990). *C. G. Jung's Psychology of Religion and Synchronicity*. Albany: State University of New York Press.

Bakhtin, M. (1984). *Rabelais and His World*. Trans. H. Iswolsky. Bloomington: Indiana University Press.

Brooks, R. M. (2009). *An Interpretation of Carl Jung's Use of Phenomenology and Hermeneutics*. Unpublished Monograph.

Carel, H. (2001). "Review of *Happiness, Death and the Remainder of Life* by Jonathan Lear." *Metapsychology Online Reviews*, 5, 10.

Gabriel, M. & Žižek, S. (2009). *Mythology, Madness and Laughter: Subjectivity in German Idealism*. New York: Continuum Books.

Gibson, A. (2006). *Beckett and Badiou: The Pathos of Intermittency*. Oxford: Oxford University Press.

Hinton, L. (2002). *Laughter, Humor and Transcendence*. Lecture Presented at the C. G. Jung Society of Seattle.

Hinton, L. (2009). "The Enigmatic Signifier and the Decentred Subject." *Journal of Analytical Psychology*, 54, 637–657.

Johnston, A. (2008). *Žižek's Ontology*. Evanston: Northwestern University Press.

Jung, C. G. (1954). *Development of Personality*. CW 17.

Jung, C. G. (1960/1969). *Structure & Dynamics of the Psyche*. CW 8.

Jung, C. G. (1963/1970). *Mysterium Coniunctionis*. CW 14.

Laplanche, J. (1999). *Essays on Otherness*. New York: Routledge.

Lear, J. (2000). *Happiness, Death, and the Remainder of Life*. Cambridge: Harvard University Press.

Levinas, E. (1969). *Totality and Infinity*. Pittsburgh: Duquesne University Press.

Levinas, E. (1998). "Useless Suffering." *Entre Nous: Thinking-of-the-Other*. New York: Columbia University Press.

Peperzak, A. T. (1997). *Beyond: The Philosophy of Emmanuel Levinas*. Evanston: Northwestern University Press.

Plato. *The Republic*. Trans. B. Jowett. Roslyn, NY: Walter J. Black, Inc.— corresponds to the 1942 edition published by Walter J. Black, Inc. in Roslyn, New York.

Samuels, A. (1985). *Jung and the Post-Jungians*. London: Routledge & Kegan Paul.

Shamdasani, S. (2003). *Jung and the Making of Modern Psychology: The Dream of a Science*. Cambridge: Cambridge University Press.

von Franz, M.-L. (1975). *C. G. Jung: His Myth in Our Time*. New York: C.G. Jung Foundation.

Žižek, S. (2006). *The Parallax View*. Cambridge: MIT Press.

Žižek, S. (2008). "The Ambiguity of the Utopian Gaze." *Umbr(a)*.

Chapter 9

Temporality and the Torments of Time*

Introduction

Our temporal nature is also our tormentor. Murky shades of the past and future haunt us. We could accurately dub the human being as *Homo Temporalis*. Everything that we experience has a temporal dimension, and temporality is at the core of subjectivity, especially the process of remembering. Time drives us, inspiring both our nobility of purpose and our destructiveness, and it is strangely elusive, appearing to vanish as soon as we try to describe it.

'Space contains [both] living and inert bodies; however, only the living human, hence the living psyche, is subjectively concerned with time' (Scarfone, 2006, p. 810). Entering into time involves loss of the illusion of safety and unity. We enter the world helpless, immersed in an enigmatic flood of messages, faced with the task of becoming subjects through the establishment of memories that anchor our sense of self. Thus, though entering time frequently involves an experience of disruption and loss, it also gives us substance and reality.

The cave art found in Southwest France powerfully evokes the potency of time. I was fascinated by it for years, and finally visited several sites during the 1980s. There are hand impressions on many of the cave walls, purposely done in realistic outline as if spray-painted. I had to restrain myself from touching my hand to theirs – alarming the guides when I made a gesture in that direction! The hands seemed to reach out directly to me, their visitor of the future. My feeling of kinship with those Cro-Magnons of 30,000 or more years ago was moving and powerful. These experiences increased my wonder about time and memory as the quintessential human concepts.

* Hinton L. (2015). Temporality and the Torments of Time. *The Journal of Analytical Psychology*, 60(3), 353–370. https://doi.org/10.1111/1468-5922.12155. Reprinted by Permission of John Wiley and Sons.

DOI: 10.4324/9781003641063-10

The vastness of the caves, sometimes narrowing into passages that force you to bend and squeeze through, invokes primal fear and fascination, an attitude of both anxiety and surrender. The surrounding pressure of the earth and the sense of an underworld, of another world, are pervasive. To create and then ritually return to such paintings deep in the caves, with only tiny lamps and handheld torches to provide light, required extraordinary motivation. A strong sense of spiritual and psychological renewal must have drawn these ancient people to these recollections that were so difficult to access (Leroi-Gourhan, 1967; Campbell, 1983). The artists and their comrades must have possessed an awareness of the future, imagining times when they would return to view their handiwork for ritual or other reasons. Like all artists, they probably envisioned others in an unknown future also regarding their works.[1]

One might speculate that ritual visits to such paintings manifested a drive to disrupt the grip of repetition (*agieren*), of circular action and reaction, the mere being of everyday life (Marucco, 2007; Scarfone, 2011). Remembering, continually re-creating the past, is the living ground of our subjectivity. Indeed, mind and memory are etymologically related (Loewald, 1972, p. 408). 'While repetition constitutes the basic level of mental functioning, remembering . . . [is] a fragile, pulsating, discontinuous, almost evanescent feature . . . [that involves] recomposing one's whole mind' (Scarfone, 2011, p. 71). In this view, remembering is an activity of differentiation, whereas uniformity and circular movement are typical of repetition, in which nothing happens but identical 'nows' (Merleau-Ponty, 2012, p. 167). Differentiation generates anxiety because it provokes a fear of fragmentation and consequent loss of an imaginary unity.

Temporality, then, is basic to reflective thought and the creation of culture, and, in particular, the theory and practice of psychoanalysis (Loewald, 1972, p. 401). Jung did not elaborate a theory of time in a single work, but some of his comments convey a multifaceted view that was somewhat innovative in its day. I have critiqued Jung's views on time elsewhere (Hinton, 2014).[2] His considerations about remembering ultimately depend on the assertion of an archetypal reality that 'transforms the past in the service of wholeness' (Jung, 1946, para. 54). However, reliance on 'archetypes' and a teleological view of experience can minimise concrete experiences of the past, including remembering, in all their substance. In fact, we are stuck with whatever our own time's images and gods happen to be, and we must always begin there (Giegerich, 2001, p. 77).

Most of the recent writings in the Jungian literature with regard to time focus on synchronicity. Von Franz made early efforts to explore the meaning of time, and Yiassemides recently did an excellent job of pulling together Jung's basic thoughts on the subject (von Franz, 1974; Yiassemides, 2014). In contrast to those works, my own concern is 'the time of our lives' and not the 'time of the universe'. I will use 'time' and 'temporality' somewhat interchangeably, although my basic concern is 'temporality' – the ordinary experience of our analytical work and our everyday existence. In my opinion, such temporal experience precedes the universal time of science or archetypal theory and not vice versa. We are present as temporal creatures in our own lives before we speculate about the cosmos (Hinton et al., 2011; Brooks, 2011; Hoy, 2012, pp. xiii–xiv & 92–93; Hinton, L. 2014).

From the ethical point of view, our personal and cultural pasts are written in time, and we are responsible for our acts, although we may interpret and reinterpret their meaning (Caruth, 1996). If one privileges the archetype as retranslating the past (i.e., via *Zurückphantasieren*), it would seem to diminish a feeling of concrete ethical responsibility; i.e. it lends itself to the view that 'it was archetypal', detracting from a sense of personal or collective accountability. In Levinasian terms, the concrete 'face of the other' can become obscured by abstraction (Lin, 2013). The practice of social ethics and justice are strongly affected by our views of temporality (Hinton, 2014).

After this brief introduction to the labyrinths of temporal horizons, I will relate a clinical case that provides a concrete sense of the workings of temporality in analytic work. That will provide the groundwork for further reflections. I will conclude by discussing some recent findings in the neuroscience of time that show a surprising degree of resonance with contemporary psychoanalytic views.

The following narrative chronicles the violent breakdown of a lifelong state of being partly 'frozen' in time, walled off from the flow of life. It describes how traumatic disruptions can open the possibility of a more dimensional sense of time, and conveys in depth the transition from a defensive state of iteration to one of alteration, and to a more open temporality.[3] I thank my patient 'Ralph' for being willing to share these experiences.

Ralph was in his mid-fifties when I first saw him. At our initial meeting, he was in anguish, almost to the point of panic, and quickly broke down in sobs. He had been without sleep and emotionally desperate for several days. Between eruptions of emotion, he began to tell his story.

His present turmoil had begun after the breakup of a brief love affair with a woman near his age. It had been the most intense and passionate experience of his life. As events evolved, he could not accept being separate from her, insisting that they be together constantly. 'All I can think about is her!', he said.

As time progressed, she had apparently found the situation to be overpowering and perhaps frightening, and had called a halt, refusing to see him. This rejection was a tremendous shock, and he was shattered and in despair, constantly beseeching her for contact-to no avail. She and his friends told him that he 'needed therapy'!

His wife of many years had died one and a half years previously, and this relationship was his first since her death. He described his former wife as a 'good' person to whom he had basically abdicated the raising of their three children and their interpersonal world. She 'ran their lives'.

Ralph was very talented in mathematics and science, and had been successful in biotechnology.

We began to meet three times per week, and quickly formed a distant though friendly working relationship. I noted that he increasingly watched me carefully to see the manner in which he was being perceived, but it also came through that he was very motivated to understand the state of his life. He did not come across as merely compliant, although that had often been one of his tendencies in the past. Occasionally, there were sparks of humour.

He began to discuss the pattern of his limited number of relationships with women. Most frequently, he had devoted his time and energy to any woman who appeared to provide acceptance and direction. 'I would give up my very being to be loved', he would later say. This type of relationship had largely been his experience of marriage, and he thought that he had remained emotionally 'frozen' as a husband and father, although he functioned well in his career.

I commented very little and primarily listened, asking occasional questions.

During the following weeks, the overwhelming emotions settled down with the containment of the analytic setting, and he appeared to progress with intellectual insights regarding his past and present situation, particularly his profound dependence on women. He had a scarcity of memories and, when he spoke of past events, I strained to visualise the interpersonal context. It was like hearing the report of a visiting social worker. When he visited his sister and her husband in another city, I had no sense of their or his presence or interaction. It had the quality of uncanny absence rather than mere coldness. This tendency was present with regard to most early memories, until the death of his wife and the recent affair.

The most typical focus in the past was his 'cold, disconnected' mother. She was a certified accountant, who maintained a busy practice during most of his childhood. He reported that he had no memory of her being affectionate with him or his sister. However, he vividly remembered photographs of his mother as a young woman who appeared to be happy and vivacious. These pictures haunted him. How could that be the mother whom he knew? Why had he never experienced such vivacity from her?

His childhood had been filled with a sense of lack and dread, a feeling that others had access to something he was denied. Gifted in mathematics and science, he took some pleasure in his academic achievements from an early age. He rarely spoke of everyday past events, or of 'chums' from his early years, and seldom mentioned friends from any era of his life. A tangible sense of pastness seemed almost absent.

After approximately two years, a new focus suddenly emerged. Ralph entered the room and sat down, intently staring at me with a fixed but expressionless gaze. I immediately experienced a powerful set of emotions. They were inchoate, 'other' – nearly impossible to capture in words. It was like a wave of dark blankness swirling in my mind, and I was stunned. After a few moments I looked at him quizzically; however, he was somewhere else in his mind and not really seeing me. It took all my fortitude to maintain my capacity for reverie. After several minutes, his visage shifted and he quickly continued with the details of his ongoing life as if nothing had happened. When I asked, 'What was that?' he just shook his head with a grimace of extreme discomfort, saying that it was a terrible feeling and that it was a horrible place he had 'always' known. He had no words to describe it. As we talked, he became extremely anxious and it was clearly torturous for him to say anything – to allow himself or me even a glimpse of what he had just experienced. However, it was apparent that something new and indefinable, a 'primitive agony', was now actually present in the field between us.

This feeling became a recurrent theme for approximately the next year, and the silent gaps occasionally extended to 10 or 15 minutes. I felt frozen out, just as he was frozen in. The absence of any psychic articulation sometimes felt like a death-like void. Occasionally, my mind swirled in near panic, and I would feel nauseated during and after the sessions. This embodied interplay evoked no interpretations in my mind, and I knew that I must refrain from inventing something clever to coat the experience more comfortably.

However, repetition is rarely pure. On one occasion, he glared at me angrily and accusingly, suddenly red-faced with emotion, and burst out with the words, 'I just can't figure out what you want!' The emotion quickly subsided, as if it had never happened. When I enquired further, he said he had no idea where that originated, and he did not remember his words. This experience was a clear example of that which Laplanche calls 'transfert en creu', to the empty pot, or the transference to the enigma to the analyst. This transference is frequently a harbinger of the opening of new dimensions. It likely reflects the question that Lacan noted as universal in human development: 'What does the other want'? (Johnston 2013, p. 28). It felt like the emergence in the transference of the question that had always mystified him. The past was becoming present in articulated form.

Finally, Ralph entered the room one day and lapsed into a painful silence that was different from before. For the first time he felt fully there, engaged with me in the room! With a piercing, angry look, he burst out loudly, 'What the hell are we doing here?!' With no hesitation, the words emerged from my mouth, 'Fuck if I know!'

I was totally startled by my words, as was he. We gazed at each other as if fixed in a momentary trance, and the room filled with anxiety and dread. Time seemed strangely suspended. Suddenly he flushed and I flushed, and we both broke down in peals of deep belly laughter!

We had both reddened in our mutual gaze, signalling shame in its full embodiment, but it was not the shame of denigration or humiliation. Shame can freeze or paralyse a person in time, alternatively, it can violently disrupt the frozen uniformity of things and open the temporal flow. Levinas connects shame, ethics, and temporality as experiences 'in which the Other does not block my future but rather opens it up' (Guenther, 2011, p. 25). That is, abrupt swerves of presence and absence may provoke shame, but that shame is often a marker of sudden shifts in experience rather than a merely negative symptom.

Bergson (2012) said that laughter removes the crust of the mechanical from the living. It opens the flow of time. André Green (2009, p. 17) called such moments of breakthrough of temporality, 'le temps éclaté' or 'exploded time'. In this view, linear structures and strictures of time are 'exploded', and a more 'open ensemble' of psychic life emerges (2009, p. 17). In Ralph's case, he was emerging from the frozenness of a past that had entered the present through the transference. Rather than endless repetitions, our experiences together had become his, and our 'history' through enactments of the previously unrepresentable (Marucco, 2007). The transference had slowly formed a new inner 'base' for him, enabling the dramatic eruption to occur without danger of complete disintegration.

He became more present in our relationship, as did I. There were fewer undertones of pleasing, and this attitude began to generalise to other dimensions of his life. His life felt more inwardly and outwardly populated. When I mentioned the shift in his demeanour and behaviour, he said that it was as if a big weight was off his back.

Events began to progress. He met a new woman, and their relationship appeared to be functioning well. He was much less inhibited and frozen in this relationship.

Approximately six months after the episode of laughter, he had the following series of dreams:

It is a surreal landscape, like a jungle area in Central America where I've done volunteer work. A young woman is walking along a trail on the side of a hill ahead of me, but suddenly disappears off to the side, like into a cave or something. I am alarmed, and plunge ahead, wanting to find her and help her. There is a wall of dry board covering the opening of the cave . . . I break through it, looking for the woman. There are some claw marks on the wall and I know there is an invisible monster in there. I feel absolutely terrified!

He stopped for a moment in his narration, appearing very apprehensive, and mentioned the following association: the young woman reminded him of the photos of his mother as a beautiful, lively young woman.

Slowly and seriously, he discussed his lifelong feelings of loss and loneliness and his ongoing terrors as a child – feelings that we had revisited many times. He had never been able to identify what terrified him. The fear had always seemed unknowable, and the more he had tried to contemplate it, the more mentally paralysed he had felt.

He continued the dream narrative:

Then I see some balls – large, blown up plastic balls like children play
with – and I think that I can distract the monster. I don't see it but it's
there. It seems like I can do it: distract it [with a ball].
Then it seems like the monster is different, like it has become playful.
The whole mood becomes different.

He said excitedly that it was the first time that he had been able to hold his
own and act in the face of such terror, whether in dreams or in everyday life.

These dreams remain remarkable to me. The jungle area is reminiscent
of Central America, where he had travelled for quasi-philanthropic reasons.
It had likely been his means of leaving the family environment and nourishing a spark of personal adventure. The jungle is nature, or whatever we
project as nature. He followed the woman as he has done his entire life,
but developed a more active concern when she disappeared. He crashed
through a barrier – which is unusual, as he is not an action-oriented person –
and found himself in a cave with the monster. This action was the revelation
of the manner in which his search for permanence and uniformity had kept
him frozen in time. It had had a monstrous effect on his life.

That is, the uniformity and unity that he had been pursuing all his life in
the form of the young woman in the photographs was in fact a type of trap.
By serving the monster, he had sought an atemporal Something that would
enable him to escape the flow of time and differentiation. The brief, intense
affair that had ended abruptly just before he entered analysis appeared to
offer that possibility. That loss felt as if he were losing access to the source
of life itself, and he was shattered. Such seductive illusions, like a Return
to the Garden, dominate much of human existence and frequently arrest us
in a type of prolonged childhood. The loss of these illusions creates shock
and disillusionment and occasionally a sense of subjective destitution. It is
such experiences that can result in major shifts in the temporal dimensions
of the soul (Giegerich, 2008; Žižek, 2014, p. 113).

Clawmarks are the only articulated presence in the cave, and conveys
figuration at its most elemental. As in Palaeolithic cave art, the most precious human creations are symbols. Symbolism is the emblem of human
participation in time. For Ralph, it signified entry into time at an entirely
new level, a transformative experience that affected him at the core (Cassorla, 2013).

Playing with the monster was his means of surmounting the terrifying encounter. The capacity for play and creative imagination is frequently crucial in surviving and transmuting the dark 'Things' that erupt in our lives during disturbing transitions (Bakhtin, 1981, 1984; Cassorla, 2013; Hinton, 2007; Huizinga, 1955; Kristeva, 1989; Parsons, 1999). Inchoate 'primitive agonies' can thus be translated into representation and memory, and an 'illumination' of the original traumatic scene can emerge, fostering a *re-creation of Time* (Scarfone, 2006; Winnicott, 1963; Stein, 2008; Marion, 2012). Ralph had been frozen in a state of iteration and sterile sameness, but the dialogical movement of temporality had been restored by the potent emergence of alteration.

The remaining 18 months of analysis continued in this vein, and more complex and articulate memories emerged. He made two extensive visits to his old hometown, and felt revitalised when he found classmates that he had forgotten. Now, when he visited his sister, I could feel the aliveness and visualise their interactions. Ralph's past was becoming present!

His sense of humour continued to evolve, and his general manner was less pleasing and more real. I typically hear from Ralph once a year. At the one-year anniversary of termination, he sent me a card picturing a Hindu fakir lying on a bed of nails; the fakir had a playful look and was almost laughing. This image appears to be a good summary of the best that one might achieve in analysis! Ralph has remarried and appears to be happy.

What contemporary psychoanalytic perspectives best contribute to understanding the psychological life of someone like Ralph, and for our patients and us? In my experience, most Jungians still tend to think of Freud as extremely reductionist, and deeply flawed in his understanding of the unfolding of the human personality. It is true that Freud had intended to create an analytic theory with solid foundational principles – principles that could be applied with a certainty that fit the science of his times; but, almost despite himself, he also laid the groundwork for later understandings that undermined his own intent. Based on some of his early writings, post-Freudian theory describes some very important ways of viewing the psyche.

Many of these new developments in psychoanalytic thought circulate around the nature of temporality, especially memory and remembering. From its foundations, an unresolved antinomy regarding time has plagued psychoanalysis, reflecting the two different sides of Freud's own thinking (Johnston, 2005, p. 21; Botella, 2014). On the one hand, there is Freud's better-known linear, developmental model, in which a fixed and identifiable past underlies the present and future in predictable ways, and another model demonstrating that the past is endlessly shaped and reshaped by future experiences, and that memory is a constant process of re-creation. This is dramatically visible in the case of Ralph, and lies at the heart of much contemporary theory, especially the French school.

Whatever his conscious intentions, Freud was an honest and keen observer. In 1895 (Freud, 1895/1950, pp. 348–359), he noticed the uncertain quality of time and memory when a young woman, Emma, who had a crippling fear of entering shops alone, remembered a disturbing event that had occurred just after she entered puberty. While shopping she had thought that two of the shop assistants were laughing at her clothes, and she left the shop in a panic. Subsequently she recalled that she had felt sexually excited by one of them. Later on, she remembered an incident at age 8 when an old shopkeeper had grabbed at her genitals through her clothes. However, notably, that original incident had not resulted in a fear of entering shops. Freud reasoned that the second event, which had occurred when Emma's sexual development was emerging, had enabled the first event to be retrospectively understood as a sexual assault. He saw that realization as the precipitant of the current symptoms.

Freud thereby discovered that the remembering of psychic life could be decisively influenced by an event that never occurred, a lost object that was never possessed, or a primal scene whose power was constituted retroactively (Boothby, 2001, p. 182). That is, he recognised that earlier experiences are subjected to revisions and alterations, and as a consequence, there is not a fixed past or an immutable time base. *Nachträglichkeit* was the term coined by Freud for these rearrangements of memory that endow the past with new meanings. The term was later translated as 'afterwardness' in English and 'après coup' in French. The nuances of the German word 'Nachträglichkeit' are difficult to translate. It means both going backwards and adding something, or a process of being 'drawn after' like pulling a wagon, with a hint of reluctance or even truculence. In psychoanalysis, it has to do with how later experiences may, in effect, retranscribe earlier ones. Such a view highlights remembering as an activity, not merely a recall of an identical datum (Loewald, 1972, p. 408).

Freud, as a scientist of his times, was always searching for foundational certainty in his theories. Nachträglichkeit seemed to undermine his quest for unchanging engrams of memory underlying, and therefore finally explaining, psychological experiences. He never provided a promised volume on memory, although he mentioned Nachträglichkeit from time to time, notably in a footnote in the case of the Wolf Man.

It was left to the next generation of analysts to further develop the concept of Nachträglichkeit. Lacan was the first to revise Freud's theory of memory, asserting that human experience always contains a remainder – a kernel of memory that defies signification. He named this enigmatic element 'the Thing' – 'das Ding' – a potent *something* at the core of experience that foments the process of Nachträglichkeit (Boothby, 2001, p. 162). This added a new dimension to Freud's concept by pointing to another and more terrifying significance of the old shopkeeper's desire that was beyond mere sexuality for the young girl's psyche. Because of her immaturity, the man's demand had defied representation in her memory. This was due to the gap between her perception of his desire and her capacity to represent this desire. At her level of development, his desire was an unrepresentable enigma. Such a gap in representation creates a remainder that cannot be symbolised, a potent 'Thing' that may feel like 'finding a hieroglyph in the desert' (Lacan, 1977, p. 194). For Lacan, it referred to an unknowable background of experience that lies at the core of the subject, a subject who is always asking the unanswerable question: 'What does the other want of me?' (Lacan, 1977, pp. 198–209). This lends a profound complexity to Freud's discussion, which emphasised only the development of sexual desire. It becomes not only a matter of a simple difference in sexual maturity between the child and the adolescent, but of something untranslatable and therefore more disturbing. From this point of view such memories have a core that can provoke endless translations, but can never be finally located in time. For Lacan this aspect of Nachträglichkeit assumed a primary significance.[4]

Laplanche later emphasised the intersubjective element of enigma, theorising that some memories are untranslatable because they are based on messages from parents to children that are communicated in ways and on levels – particularly sexual levels – that are unconscious. The adults transmit messages they themselves do not understand (Target, 2007). Such untranslatable messages are managed by means of what Freud called 'primal repression', in contrast to the everyday sort of 'secondary' repression that assumes a capacity for representation (Laplanche & Pontalis, 1973, pp. 333–334; Hinton, 2009). Laplanche emphasised the helplessness of children regarding such messages (*Hilflösigkeit*). Children are dependent on others for survival; they lack defences and do not understand all the levels of the adult communications directed toward them. The core of the primally repressed can never be fully articulated, and serves a role akin to drive (*Trieb*). That is, when such untranslatable memories of 'otherness' re-emerge later in life, they often disrupt repetition and sameness, violently thrusting the individual toward an unknown future requiring new understandings that in turn, create new memories.

Ralph's story describes such a process. Like the clawmark he discovered in the cave, such memories are impossible to finally translate, but provoke a process of remembering that is central to subjectivity, and is continuous throughout our lives (Laplanche, 1999, pp. 117–133). It is both a kind of freedom and limitation. There is no final 'knowing', except for lifelong translations and retranslations. This process can be lived playfully or tragically.

In conclusion, I want to relate the remarkable coincidence of recent discoveries in the neuroscience of memory and contemporary psychoanalytic theory. Such studies similarly describe a process that is never completed and is subject to revision each time a 'memory' is elicited (see, for example, Civitarese, 2010). Edelman calls memory the 'remembered present' (Edelman, 2004, p. 99). That is, past ideational traces can never be recovered in an unmodified form within the constraints of the present. These 'traces' are not similar to stable atomic units; they are moments caught in an ever-mobile Now (Johnston, 2005, p. 315).

We frequently fear that the 'ghosts' of the past will re-appear in the future, and the future might then encompass that which will have been remembered. In the future, we might remember and, thereby, produce a past. Such perspectives can seem a bit overwhelming and counter-intuitive at first glance, but they have strong grounding in neuroscience and metapsychology.

Endel Tulving of the University of Toronto, with others, has produced fascinating work in the area of memory and that which he half-humorously calls 'time travel'. His research indicates that human beings possess a specific form of memory involving the capacity to be consciously aware of one's continuing temporal existence. This type of memory is called *episodic* memory, in turn related to a form of consciousness known as *autonoetic* consciousness. No other animals seem to possess these characteristics (Szpunar & Tulving, 2011, p. 84). They are fundamentally different from a more general type of conscious awareness known as *semantic* consciousness (Ekstrom, 2014, pp. 37–38). 'The essential difference [between semantic consciousness and autonoetic consciousness] . . . is between knowing that something *is* such and such, or [*factually*] occurs so and so . . . [versus] remembering that *one had an . . . experience* (witnessed, felt or thought something) in a particular way at a particular time', within a particular human context (Tulving, 2005, p. 16; Ekstrom, 2014, pp. 34–36).

Episodic memory, the capacity for 'time travel', originates in semantic memory and adds the ability to travel in *time* to an already existing ability to mentally manoeuvre in *space*; it provides the capacity to 'travel' into the past and, more importantly, into the *future*. Thereby, *humans became able to create a world to fit them*, rather than live in one into which they had to fit (Tulving, 2005, p. 17; Suddendorf et al., 2009).

Many neuropsychological and developmental studies support the division between semantic time and a later-emerging episodic time, providing detailed evidence for this theory (Hsieh et al., 2014). One notable example is the case of a 30-year-old man, K.C. who suffered a brain injury that destroyed his capacity for episodic memory and, therefore, for travel into the past or future:

> However hard he tries, and however powerfully he is prompted, he cannot bring into his conscious awareness a single event, happening or situation that he witnessed or in which he participated. Nor is he capable of remembering anything ever having happened in the house where he has lived for [many] years. He knows that he owned a black Honda, but does not remember a single trip he ever took in it.
>
> (Tulving, 2005, p. 24)

It is particularly striking that K.C. has no thoughts regarding his future, which highlights his lack of autonoetic consciousness. He possesses many intact cognitive capacities regarding facts; however, he does not remember any episode from his life nor project himself into the future. When asked to do either, he states that his mind is 'blank, but a *blankness* only with regard to memories or prospective futures' (Szpunar & Tulving, 2011, p. 84).

Episodic memory is also largely missing in children under the age of four (Szpunar & Tulving, 2011, pp. 29–30). They do not remember personal contexts well, and the ability to remember interpersonal events comes after the emergence of knowledge regarding facts. Younger children lack the same types of episodic memory and autonoetic consciousness that appear to be absent in animals (Szpunar & Tulving, 2011, p. 31; Yim et al., 2013; Ekstrom, 2014, pp. 42–44).

Before around 18-months-old, children will pay attention to their mirror image but do not realise it is their own body, and will not use the mirror as a tool to think about themselves. However, passing the mirror test does not mean that they are aware of themselves as individuals with a past and a future. Episodic memory matures gradually, and it is difficult to pin down an exact age when it becomes fully functional. However, the general finding is that it is around 4 years of age (Tulving, 2005, p. 31; Yim et al., 2013).

The drawer test helps clarify the time of emergence of episodic memory. In one example 3- and 5-year-olds are told, shown, or given hints of the contents of a drawer. Within a short time they are asked what is in the drawer, and then how they knew what they knew. Most of the children in both age groups recalled the facts of what the contents were, but there was a large age difference regarding how they believed they had come by that knowledge. Most significantly, the 5-year-olds remembered that someone had just told them what was in the drawer. In contrast, the 3-year-olds mostly did not remember being told what was in the drawer (Tulving, 2005, p. 31; Yim et al., 2013). That is, the 5-year-olds recalled an event in the past in an interpersonal context, the essence of episodic memory, while the younger children recalled only the facts without a sense of past or context. It appears that young children cannot, or do not, represent their knowledge as deriving from a particular time in the personal past, but rather as detached, impersonal knowledge. For them, 'There are [just] crayons in the drawer' (Tulving, 2005, p. 32).

Such findings have been replicated in a number of ways. The growth of episodic memory apparently continues to increase with age, even into adulthood (Yim et al., 2013). 'The developmental findings not only emphasise the role that a fully developed human brain plays in episodic memory; they also underscore the fact that episodic memory is not necessary in a world in which one's needs can be and are satisfied without remembering autonoetically what happened in the past' (Yim et al., 2013, p. 35). The case of K.C. provides a similar perspective.

Recent MRI studies demonstrate that specific brain areas are connected to the experience of past and future, and that these areas are located together. Contemplating the prospective future and actively remembering the past result in activation of identical areas of the brain (Nyberg et al., 2010; Szpunar & Tulving, 2011). These findings reinforce concepts that I discussed earlier – Nachträglichkeit and the past as the 'remembered present'. Earlier, I pointed out the intimate and non-linear connection of past, present, and future. Derrida describes temporality as being more like a syncopated ensemble, or in Serres' words, resembling a folded and crumpled handkerchief! (Serres, 1997, p. 44; Pirovolakis, 2010, pp. 43–82).

Mental time travel is a source of cultural evolution as well as the origin of tragic aspects of the human condition. Human beings worry regarding the future, and we struggle to discern the threads of patterns that were or might be. This worry has clear adaptive aspects, and is the basis of culture and ethics. Ethics involves reflection upon the effects we might have had on others in the past and that we might have in the future. We have fears regarding future dangers, and we dwell on the past. Could certain troublesome others become dangerous to us or to our group? Should we eliminate them from the utopias we plan? Will the speed of technology entail a transcendence of human time? (Stiegler, 1998, p. 15; Fong, 2013).

At the core of all this is a view of analysis as a complex temporal process, a future that may alter the past, a past that may become the future, simultaneously existing along with an evanescent present as the pulsating intersection of past and future. This aspect of time is syncopated, multifaceted and non-linear. Shocks, disruptions, melancholy and enigma are at the heart of human experience and consciousness. However, embracing the perturbations inherent in temporality can open an element of freedom, and a sense of creative play in meeting the strange and tormenting, the delightful and ever-new vicissitudes of time (Parsons, 1999). This was what my patient Ralph discovered, to his great gain.

Notes

1 Laplanche speculates that what moves the 'Dichter' (poet) to 'Dicht' (poetise) is the desire to address another who is out of reach, or others 'scattered in the future' (Laplanche, 1999, pp. 223–224).
2 Many authors use Züruckphantasieren to describe Jung's theory of transforming memory. Strangely, this term does not appear in the Collected Works, but it does seem to convey Jung's perspective.
3 This case was discussed from a different perspective in *The Journal of Analytical Psychology*, 2009, 54, 637–657.
4 The concept of Nachträglichkeit strongly influenced Jacques Derrida, and was of importance in the formation of his basic concept of 'différance'. It was the impossibility of a foundational ground in memory and experience that caught Derrida's eye. Through him, Freud's early ideas strongly influenced postmodern philosophy (Derrida, 1998; Hodge, 2007, pp. 8–9).

References

Bakhtin, M. M. (1981). *The Dialogic Imagination*. Austin: University of Texas Press.

Bakhtin, M. M. (1984). *Rabelais and His World*. Bloomington: Indiana University Press.

Bergson, H. (2012). *Laughter: An Essay on the Meaning of the Comic*. CreateSpace Independent Publishing Platform.

Boothby, R. (2001). *Freud as Philosopher: Metapsychology after Lacan*. New York: Routledge.

Botella, C. (2014). "On Remembering: The Notion of Memory without Recollection." *International Journal of Psychoanalysis*, 95, 5, 911–936.

Brooks, R. M. (2011). "Un-Thought Out Metaphysics in Analytical Psychology: A Critique of Jung's Epistemological Basis for Psychic Reality." *Journal of Analytical Psychology*, 56, 492–513.

Campbell, J. (1983). *The Way of the Animal Powers*. Vol. 1. New York: Harper & Row.

Caruth, C. (1996). *Unclaimed Experience: Trauma, Narrative and History*. Baltimore: Johns Hopkins University Press.

Cassorla, R. M. S. (2013). "In Search of Symbolization: The Analyst's Task of Dreaming." In H. B. Levine (Ed.), *Unrepresented States and the Construction of Meaning* (pp. 202–219). London: Karnac Books.

Civitarese, G. (2010). "Nachträglichkeit." In *The Intimate Room*. New York: Routledge.

Derrida, J. (1998). *Archive Fever: A Freudian Impression*. Chicago: University of Chicago Press.

Edelman, G. (2004). *Wider Than the Sky: The Phenomenal Gift of Consciousness*. New Haven: Yale University Press.

Ekstrom, S. R. (2014). *Memory and Healing: Neurocognitive and Psychodynamic Perspectives on How Patients and Psychotherapists Remember*. London: Karnac.

Fong, B. Y. (2013). "Death Drive Sublimation: A Psychoanalytic Perspective on Technological Development." *Psychoanalysis, Culture and Society*, 18, 4, 352–367.

Freud, S. (1895/1950). *Project for a Scientific Psychology*. SE 1. London: Hogarth.

Giegerich, W. (2001). *The Soul's Logical Life*. Frankfurt: Peter Lang.

Giegerich, W. (2008). *Soul-Violence: Collected English Papers*. Vol. 3. New Orleans: Spring Publications.

Green, A. (2009). "From the Ignorance of Time to the Murder of Time: From the Murder of Time to the Misrecognition of Time in Psychoanalysis." In L. T. Fiorini & J. Canestri (Eds.), *The Experience of Time: Psychoanalytic Perspectives*. London: Karnac.

Guenther, L. (2011). "Shame and the Temporality of Social Life." *Continental Philosophy Review*, 44, 23–39.

Hinton, L. (2007). "Black Holes, Uncanny Spaces and Radical Shifts in Awareness." *Journal of Analytical Psychology*, 52, 433–447.

Hinton, L. (2009). "The Enigmatic Signifier and the Decentred Subject." *Journal of Analytical Psychology*, 54, 637–657.

Hinton, L. (2014). "Book Review Essay of Time and Timelessness: Temporality in the Theory of Carl Jung, by Angeliki Yiassemides." *Journal of Analytical Psychology*, 59, 3, 437–447.

Hinton, L. (2014). "Justice and Time at the Khmer Rouge Tribunal: In Memory of Vann Nath, Painter and S-21 Survivor." *Genocide Studies and Prevention: An International Journal*, 8, 2, Article 5, 7–17.

Hinton, L., III, Hinton, L., IV, Hinton, D. & Hinton, A. L. (2011). "Unus Mundus: Transcendent Truth or Comforting Fiction? Overwhelm and Search for Meaning in a Fragmented World." *Journal of Analytical Psychology*, 56, 375–396.

Hodge, J. (2007). *Derrida on Time*. New York: Routledge.

Hoy, D. C. (2012). *The Time of Our Lives: A Critical History of Temporality*. Boston: MIT Press.

Hsieh, L.-T., Gruber, M. J., Jenkins, L. J. & Ranganath, C. (2014). "Hippocampal Activity Patterns Carry Information about Objects in Temporal Context." *Neuron*, 81, 1165–1178.

Huizinga, J. (1955). *Homo Ludens: A Study of the Play-Element in Culture*. Boston: Beacon Press.

Johnston, A. (2005). *Time Driven: Metapsychology and the Splitting of the Drive*. Evanston: Northwestern University Press.

Johnston, A. (2013). "Jacques Lacan." In E. N. Zalta (Ed.), *Stanford Encyclopedia of Philosophy Archive* (Summer 2014 ed.). Retrieved from http://plato.stanford.edu/archives/sum2014/entries/lacan/.

Jung, C. G. (1946). *The Psychology of the Transference*. CW 16.

Kristeva, J. (1989). *The Black Sun*. New York: Columbia University Press.

Lacan, J. (1977). *Écrits: A Selection*. London: Tavistock/Routledge.

Laplanche, J. (1999). *Essays on Otherness*. New York: Routledge.

Laplanche, J. & Pontalis, J.-B. (1973). *The Language of Psychoanalysis*. New York: W.W. Norton.

Leroi-Gourhan, A. (1967). *Treasures of Prehistoric Art*. New York: Harry Abrams.

Lin, Y. (2013). *The Intersubjectivity of Time: Levinas and Infinite Responsibility*. Pittsburgh: Duquesne University Press.

Loewald, H. W. (1972). "The Experience of Time." *Psychoanalytic Study of the Child*, 27, 401–410.

Marion, P. (2012). "Some Reflections on the Unique Time of Nachträglichkeit in Theory and Clinical Practice." *International Journal of Psychoanalysis*, 3, 317–340.

Marucco, N. C. (2007). "Between Memory and Destiny: Repetition." *International Journal of Psychoanalysis*, 88, 309–328.

Merleau-Ponty, M. (2012/1945). *Phenomenology of Perception*. Trans. D. Landes. New York: Routledge.

Nyberg, L., Kim, A. S. N., Habib, R., Levine, B. & Tulving, E. (2010). "Consciousness of Subjective Time in the Brain." *Proceedings of the National Academy of Sciences*, 107, 51, 22356–22359.

Parsons, M. (1999). "The Logic of Play in Psychoanalysis." *The International Journal of Psychoanalysis*, 80, 871–884.

Pirovolakis, E. (2010). *Reading Derrida and Ricoeur*. Albany: SUNY Press.

Scarfone, D. (2006). "A Matter of Time: Actual Time and the Production of the Past." *Psychoanalytic Quarterly*, 75, 807–834.

Scarfone, D. (2011). "Repetition: Between Presence and Meaning." *Canadian Journal of Psychoanalysis*, 19, 70–86.

Serres, M. (1997). *The Troubadour of Knowledge*. Ann Arbor: University of Michigan Press.

Stein, R. (2008). "The Otherness of Sexuality: Excess." *Journal of the American Psychoanalytic Association*, 56, 43.

Stiegler, B. (1998). *Technics and Time*. Vol. 1: *The Fault of Epimetheus*. Stanford: Stanford University Press.

Suddendorf, T., Addis, D. R. & Corballis, M. C. (2009). "Mental Time Travel and the Shaping of Human Mind." *Philosophical Transactions of the Royal Society, B: Biological Sciences*, 364, 1317–1324.

Szpunar, K. K. & Tulving, E. (2011). "Varieties of Future Experience." In M. Bar (Ed.), *Predictions in the Brain: Using Our Past to Generate a Future* (pp. 83–94). New York: Oxford University Press.

Target, M. (2007). "Is Our Sexuality Our Own? A Developmental Model of Sexuality Based on Early Affective Mirroring." *British Journal of Psychotherapy*, 23, 4, 517–530.

Tulving, E. (2005). "Episodic Memory and Autonoesis: Uniquely Human?" In H. S. Terrace & J. Metcalf (Eds.), *The Missing Link in Cognition* (pp. 4–56). New York: Oxford University Press.

von Franz, M.-L. (1974). *Number and Time: Reflections Leading toward a Unification of Depth Psychology and Physics*. Evanston: Northwestern University Press.

Winnicott, D. W. (1963). "Fear of Breakdown." In C. Winnicott, R. Shepherd & M. Davis (Eds.), *Psychoanalytic Explorations*. Cambridge: Harvard University Press.

Yiassemides, A. (2014). *Time and Timelessness: Temporality in the Theory of C.G. Jung*. New York: Routledge.

Yim, H., Dennis, S. J. & Sloutsky, V. M. (2013). "The Development of Episodic Memory: Items, Contexts and Relations." *Psychological Science*, 24, 11, 2163–2172.

Žižek, S. (2014). *Event: Philosophy in Transit*. London: Penguin Books.

Chapter 10

Is Jung Existential or Not?
Reflections on Temporality and
Everydayness*

Introduction: Some Personal Reflections

Reflecting on the relationship of existential psychotherapy and Jungian
analytical psychology involves a return to the origins of my own lifelong
search for meaning and truth. Both traditions were crucial to me at different
times and in different ways, and I could not imagine my personal evolution
without both of them.

Existentialism in its different manifestations, as philosophy and as psychotherapy, was a pervasive early influence for me. I read Nietzsche's Beyond Good and Evil (1886/1961) and The Birth of Tragedy (1866/1999)
when I was a freshman in college, and never fully recovered! Some years
later, I completed a master's degree in philosophy, and wrote my thesis on
Husserl's concept of the transcendent – fascinated by the discovery of the
phenomenological epoché, the "suspension of judgement" that reveals both
phenomenal worlds and their presuppositions. Existential phenomenology
continued to influence me through medical school, and during my psychiatric
residency at Stanford University, I was fortunate that the now eminent existential therapist Irv Yalom was available for clinical supervision, pioneering
existential psychoanalyst Rollo May was still lecturing in the Bay Area, and
British existential psychiatrist R. D. Laing did a stint as a visiting professor.

Thomas Kirsch, a close friend during psychiatric training who went on
to become a prominent Jungian analyst himself, came from a distinguished
lineage of Jungians. I found his father, James, who had been in analysis
with Jung in Zürich, to be an intellectual delight. I became acquainted with
other analysts in the Jungian world in the San Francisco Bay Area and

* Hinton, L. (2018). Is Jung Existential or Not? Reflections on Temporality and Everydayness. *Journal
of Humanistic Psychology, 61*(5), 721–732. https://doi. org/10.1177/0022167818820464 (Original
work published 2021). Reprinted by Permission of SAGE Publications.

DOI: 10.4324/9781003641063-11

found them welcoming and open. The contrast between my experiences of the Freudian world and Jungian worlds of that time was stark. As I saw it then, semi-humorously, it was as if the Freudians held dogmatically to one single "archetype," one explanatory device – the Oedipal, the triangle, and so on. In contrast, Jungians seemed to have a lot of archetypes to choose from and that created an openness to broader realms of experience and ideas. Because of these positive experiences, I began my own analysis with a Jungian.

Eventually, I applied to the C. G. Jung Institute of San Francisco and completed my analytic training in 1975. Many of my teachers had been analyzed or supervised directly by Jung himself, and the atmosphere at the institute was generally warm and respectful. I learned a great deal clinically from interactions with my peers and teachers. However, from early on in analytic training, I began to harbour doubts about certain aspects of Jung's theories, and especially his foundational conception of archetypes. Seeing these so-called archetypes as the ultimate experience and ground of the human condition never felt quite right to me.

For some time – probably a period of years – I kept most of my doubts under wraps, perhaps hoping to become more "enlightened." I felt a bit of a failure for not "getting" archetypes. While there was not significant external pressure to accept Jung's view of human experience, critical thinking about Jung's ideas was uncommon. At that juncture, Jung had only recently died, and there was a strong sense of loyalty to his vision of the psyche.

During analytical training, the most common themes, clinically and theoretically, revolved around archetypes. That realm was seen as ultimate ground, underlying the process of analysis and individuation. Looking back, I think that my positive transference to my personal analyst and my genuine liking for my cohort and teachers, was a partial impediment to developing more of my own ideas. However, Sartre's existential adage, "Existence precedes essence" (1946/2007, p. vii), along with similar words from Heidegger (1953/2010), still strongly resonated at the core of my being. We never discussed such blasphemous things during analytic training, and few of my Jungian colleagues were familiar with the language or conceptions of existential phenomenology. However, that provocative worldview has creatively echoed in my thoughts these many years.

In discussing the question asked by my title, "Is Jung existential or not?," there is not adequate space here, nor do I have sufficient knowledge, to summarise the depth and breadth of existential thought. Therefore, I have chosen to use philosopher Martin Heidegger's work to illustrate the existential point of view, both because of the profound effect of his thinking on my own development and the general stature of his work in the existential literature. My personal reflections on Jung's life and work have continued over the decades, and I will discuss some of the concepts in his works that have continued to provoke questions in my mind, and that, in my estimation, strongly contrast with the existential approach to theory and therapy.

Jung, Heidegger, and the Time of Our Lives

Heidegger and Jung seem to have set out on a similar journey, a search for the origins of thought, the arché. They share a kind of nostalgia, a desire to restore, re-find, to connect with something timeless that had been lost to modern man (Jung, 1955/2001; Manoussakis, 2017). Jung continued to want to recapture what had been lost, to "re-enchant the world" by a return to an eternal world soul, a unity of archetypal elements under the medieval rubric of the Unus Mundus (Hinton et al., 2011). On the other hand, Heidegger later realised that *Being and Time* (1953/2010) was a relative failure, because it still contained vestiges of the foundational ideas and preconceptions derived from his earlier ways of thinking.

I would suggest, indeed, that, "The . . . desire for the beginning, the arché, this archeological desire constitutes at the same time an effort to escape time, to undo the catastrophe of history, to return to the nothing before creation, to the 'original state of non-existence'" (Manoussakis, 2017, p. 58). This return to an original state could be seen as related to Freud's "death drive" (Freud, 1915/1990, p. 45). As a result, Heidegger turned toward a hermeneutic, process-oriented approach that focused on historicity and everydayness (Guignon, 1983). Jung, however, always maintained his belief in foundational, timeless "archetypes." He seemed unwilling to abandon the structural elements of myth and history that he had inherited from his classical education and Swiss culture. Some researchers believe that such a holding-on engendered a significant and perhaps fatal flaw in Jungian thought, an intrinsic limitation that evokes, for them, the sense of a "requiem for analytical psychology" (Barreto, 2014).

In contrast to Jung, Heidegger built his theory on attunement to the deep anxiety stemming from the groundlessness of existence, believing that this could open future possibilities for the Being of beings (Heidegger, 1953/1977; Yanchar, 2018). To achieve such an openness to future possibility, "One is [first] left hanging without the firm ground of settled meaning, cultural ordinariness, or anything deeper for support" (Yanchar, 2018, p. 5).

On the other hand, although Jung often said that a symbol was dead as soon as it lost its enigmatic mystery and advised people to linger with the unknown; he almost invariably began to symbolise the unknown in concrete ways.

Another way of illustrating the contrasting positions of Heidegger and Jung is their different implicit and explicit relation to "existence" and "essence." Existence is the process of human being, of human experience in time. That is the basic meaning of the term, existential. This term has multiple dimensions and implications. To exist means immersion, our involuntary "thrownness" into temporality, into being-towards-death. One could more accurately call the human species homo temporalis, rather than homo sapiens (Hinton, 2015). With regard to human discourse, "Each field, approach or statement needs to rest against a temporal background, each uttered sentence assumes a temporal frame" (Yiassemides, 2014, p. xxxi).

In traditional philosophical thought, essence indicates certain qualities that are always present in an object or entity. One could call this the inherent "truth" of an entity. Aristotle defined the term as "what it is to be for a thing" (Smith, 2018, pp. 28–29.). This could be expressed in propositions: "All A are B, all B are C; therefore, all A are C." However, Heidegger questioned this view of truth as essence, often using metaphors of "seeing," of a process in time: aletheia. "Truth as aletheia is a form of disclosure, unconcealment, or uncoveredness that reveals itself through that which appears" (Mills, 2014, p. 11). When something emerges from hiddenness, something else is inevitably lost to view, and as a consequence truth can never be complete, is never a totality. Experience and memory can bring wisdom and ethics, over time and experience, but that is most often after the fact (Hinton, 2018). The story of Oedipus is a prime example of that truth (Manoussakis, 2009).

Edmund Husserl, Heidegger's mentor, developed an attitude of reflection that became the core of existential phenomenology. He called it the epoché, a suspension of judgement whose goal was a reflective description of world and self (Beyer, 2016). He developed a view of time, amplified by Stiegler, using music as an example of the flow of temporality (Stiegler, 1998, 2014). Beginning with Aristotle, many theories of temporality break the temporal process into bits or instances that, speaking somewhat simplistically, add up as the experience of time. However, Husserl points out how one cannot appreciate a piece of music without a memory of the tones that preceded the present ones and that anticipation of the notes to come are also intrinsic to the process. Thus, past, present, and future cannot be neatly separated, and temporal flow cannot be broken down into instances for counting (Husserl, 1966/1991).

Heidegger based his approach to temporality mainly on the theories of Husserl. The goal was description without presuppositions. Heidegger applied this method to everyday existence and thereby "existential phenomenology" came into being. Temporality was at the heart of that project. Existential anxiety, for Heidegger, had to do with an underlying awareness of human contingency, with being-towards-death. French philosopher Emmanuel Levinas later modified Heidegger's emphasis on the individual and focused more on the "loss of the other" as being at the core of temporal awareness (Levinas, 2000).

Again, speaking simplistically, for the existentialist, existence is the essence of human being, most basically including temporality. Dasein, "being-there," is temporal from the get-go. That is why Heidegger entitled his magnum opus Being and Time. Being, in that context, is temporality. He concluded that temporality is the à priori condition for there to be care – the sense-making and intelligibility that is Dasein's distinctive mode of being (Wheeler, 2015).

Applying his own version of Husserl's epoché to everyday life, Heidegger described such phenomena as moods, states of mind, debt to the past, the finitude of our knowledge of the future, everydayness, "fallenness," and authenticity. His life's work was based on this approach, and he looked to a hermeneutic process that could provide limited truth (Guignon, 1983). Truth is aletheia, an unveiling from hiddenness, a disclosing, and can never be complete. That is, the truth of an entity is not defined by an Aristotelian final cause (Horne et al., 2000).

One can divide philosophies by their attitudes toward "substance ontology," an ontological form which shapes, or doesn't shape, our existence (Guignon, 2011; Yanchar, 2018). That is, something that "stands under," that "sub-stands," that underlies the temporal, ever-changing properties of everyday reality. This is sometimes called the "metaphysics of presence." It encompasses Plato's notion of forms, Aristotle's primary substances, God the Creator of Christian belief, Descartes's Cogito, Kant's Noumenon, and the presuppositions of scientific naturalism. "Heidegger's goal [had been] to undercut the entire game by challenging the idea that reality must be thought of in terms of the idea of substance" (Guignon, 2011, p. 4). Rather than a theory of substance, he used a version of Husserl's phenomenological method and applied it to temporal existence. The lack of an ultimate foundation creates a basic anxiety, due to awareness of human contingency through loss, the enigmatic gaps and voids in knowledge, and death. This experience of groundlessness and loss of meaning would seem to be at the core of the existential position, both theoretically and therapeutically.

Jung, on the other hand, unlike Heidegger, never explicitly developed a full theory of temporality and employed a theory of "archetypes" that were atemporal or pre-temporal, underlying everyday reality. He contrasted arche-types with the "personal unconscious," the world of temporality. That is, in my view, he was ultimately a theoretician of substance.

Although Jung did not devote a single work to temporality per se, Jungian scholar Angeliki Yiassemides astutely discerned that a section of the Red Book (2009) clearly describes, in the form of a poetic-mythic work of the imagination, a quasi-Gnostic cosmology which clearly expresses his theory of time (Yiassemides, 2014). Jung named this work, written in 1916, the Septem Sermones Ad Mortuos (The Seven Sermons to the Dead). It was first officially published in 1961 as an appendix to one edition of Jung's "official" autobiography, Memories, Dreams, Reflections (1961). The entire Red Book, a private journal containing a panoply of poetic imagination and symbolic paintings describing Jung's protracted "confrontation with the unconscious," was not released by the Jung family until 2009, because they saw it as too personal a writing.

Some scholars regard the Seven Sermons as the heart of The Red Book: Liber Novus (Hoeller, 2017). Certainly, Jung gave it special treatment. In 1957, Jung reiterated that the Red Book itself represented the core of his theory:

> The years, of which I have spoken to you, when I pursued the inner images, were the most important time of my life . . . Everything later was merely the outer classification, the scientific elaboration, and the integration into life.
>
> (Jung, 2009, p. VII)

Jung's Red Book uses language that has a strange, archaic flavor, and I want to convey that quality here to help capture the full flavor of the work. In the Seven Sermons, Basilides is the Gnostic voice of the work. Creatura is the realm of the human. Pleroma is a state that cannot be grasped by humans and is unchanging, whereas Creatura is subject to change, to the vicissitudes of time (Yiassemides, 2014, p. 6). In the perspective of the narrative, humans must differentiate, or fall into dissolution or nothingness, and they project their inner reality onto the Pleroma (Yiassemides, 2014, p. 8). In this mythic view, the differentiated ego strives to return to the original wholeness of psychic reality (Yiassemides, 2014, p. 9). This ties into the Gnostic view of the universe – the Pleromatic state – which idealises a timeless dimension, in which *"the goal of salvation is to deliver us from the lie of time"* (italics added) (Yiassemides, 2014, p. 11).

In this classic work, Jung clearly conveys the view that the archetype is timeless, and that, for him, the everyday, temporal world is meaningful only when seen in the light of that "eternal reality." He depicts this personal unconscious as something lesser than a transcendent realm called the collective unconscious (Hinton, 2014). This perspective is evident throughout his life. The personal unconscious comes across as something rather inferior, in sharp contrast to the archetypal, timeless dimension of the collective unconscious. This strikes me as the antithesis of most traditional existential theory. It is important to examine some of Jung's writing closely and directly, to realise how much he tends to privilege a timeless, archetypal dimension of reality, underlying everyday temporal existence.

For instance,

I saw how the transpersonal control-point developed – I cannot call it anything else – a guiding function and step by step gathered to itself all the formal personal over-valuations; how, with this afflux of energy, it gained influence over the resisting conscious mind without the patient's consciously noticing what was happening. From this I realised these were not just fantasies, but self-representations of unconscious developments which allowed the psyche of the person to grow *out of a pointless personal tie* [italics added].

This change took place, as I showed, through the development of a transpersonal control point; a virtual goal, as it were, that expressed itself symbolically in a form that can only be described as *a vision of God* [italics added].

(Jung, 1943/1966b, pp. 134–135)

For Jung, there is clearly an underlying substrate that unconsciously guides or subsumes individual experience. In fact, he seems to consider the "personal," the sphere of the temporal, as "pointless." Finally, he describes the experience of the patient as something eternal and transcendental, a "vision of God."

To give another example:

> we are dealing here with an *a priori "type,"* an archetype which is inherent in the collective unconscious and thus beyond individual birth and death. The archetype is, so to speak, an "eternal" presence, and the only question is whether it is perceived by the conscious mind or not . . . the increase in the clarity and frequency of mandala motif is due to a more accurate description of *an already existing "type," rather than that it is generated in the course of a dream series* [italics added].
>
> In practice it is to be met with in a distinct form in relatively few cases, though this does not prevent it from functioning as a concealed pole around which everything else revolves.
>
> (Jung, 1944/1968, pp. 221–222)

Here, Jung asserts that there is a primary substrate in existence, seen or unseen, and that everyday life forms around that transcendent reality. He emphatically valorizes such a timeless guiding principle, underlying ordinary life and temporality. It seems to me that this starkly contrasts with Heidegger and the core existential view, and with the clinical emphasis in existential therapy, which focusses specifically on the anxiety of being temporal creatures, of being-towards-death. From the existential perspective, the concept of the archetype seems like a convenient, comforting escape hatch, a self-deluding defensive effort to avoid facing the groundlessness of existential reality: a deus ex machina.

Although throughout his writings Jung consistently and laudably asserts an ethical imperative to "have it out with the unconscious," he provides few examples of the blood, sweat, and tears side of a clinical encounter (Merkur, 2017, pp. 135–160). For instance, in his long essay on "The Psychology of the Transference" (1946/1966a), Jung delineates symbolic stages of analysis, but a sense of the everyday struggles of psychotherapy is absent. He provides only a symbolic description of "The Conjunction" (Jung, 1946/1966a) to convey the vicissitudes of the dyadic process. His emphasis is on the essence, not the gritty, mundane existential reality of life and therapy. Jungian analyst Betsy Cohen has thoroughly researched Jung's clinical writings and found 222 clinical cases mentioned in the 18 volumes of the Collected Works. She determined that Jung invariably emphasises the impersonal elements of the clinical process, mainly using the clinical material of his cases to corroborate his theory of timeless archetypal elements underlying the everyday (Cohen, 2015; Hinton, 2018).

In contradistinction to Jung's impersonal, timeless, archetypal approach to analysis, existential analysis, and my own existential orientation to psycho-analysis, emphasise the here-and-now everyday struggles we humans experience in dealing with and coming to terms with the vicissitudes of temporality, with its consequent impermanence, lack of final unity, and the evanescence of the body. This is our ordinary human reality. In my own clinical practice, I think of truth (little t) as the goal of the psychotherapeutic process, and am fundamentally guided by the idea of aletheia, of disclosedness as a temporal process from which all truly authentic being stems.

Conclusion

In conclusion, I gratefully acknowledge my profound debt to my Jungian mentors and their importance to my development as a psychoanalyst. The depth and breadth of the world of analytical psychology has been a great gift of wisdom and learning. However, from long and extensive study of his published writings, I cannot say that Jung was truly existential in his thinking. With regard to his clinical practice, it is unclear, since we only have anecdotal evidence. Jung was dogmatically wedded to his theory of archetypes, to the presence of preexisting structures, contrasting strongly with Heidegger's existential phenomenology, and with the general views of existential theory and practice. Colloquially speaking, Jung was dynamic and often "existentially" present as a man in the world, one who had a far-reaching impact on many people. He had a long and fruitful life. However, in my estimation, and that of most contemporary existential practitioners, he fell well short of a fully existential-phenomenological position in his writings. In my opinion, this significant shortcoming has proven to be a major obstacle to the creative development of post-Jungian theory. Authenticity always emerges from everydayness, and a dogmatic emphasis on timeless archetypes tends to cripple or abort the emergence of something truly new and different.

References

Barreto, M. H. (2014). "Requiem for Analytical Psychology: A Reflection on Jung's (Anti)catastrophic Psychology." *Journal of Analytical Psychology*, 59, 60–77. https://doi.org/10.1111/1468-5922.12055.

Beyer, C. (2016). "Edmund Husserl." In *Stanford Encyclopedia of Philosophy*. Stanford, CA: Stanford University. Retrieved from http://plato.stanford.edu/archives/win2016/entries/husserl/.

Cohen, B. (2015). "Dr. Jung and His Patients." *Jung Journal*, 9, 2, 34–49. https://doi.org/10.1080/19342039.2015.1021231.

Freud, S. (1915/1990). *Beyond the Pleasure Principle*. Trans. J. Strachey. New York, NY: W.W. Norton.

Guignon, C. B. (1983). *Heidegger and the Problem of Knowledge*. Indianapolis, IN: Hackett.

Guignon, C. B. (Ed.). (2011). *The Cambridge Companion to Heidegger*. New York, NY: Cambridge University Press.

Heidegger, M. (1953/1977). "What Is Metaphysics?" In D. F. Krell (Ed.), *Basic Writings* (pp. 95–112). San Francisco, CA: Harper.

Heidegger, M. (1953/2010). *Being and Time*. Trans. J. Stambaugh. Albany: State University of New York Press.

Hinton, L. (2014). "Book Review Essay of 'Time and Timelessness: Temporality in the Theory of Carl Jung,' by A. Yiassemides." *Journal of Analytical Psychology*, 59, 437–447. https://doi.org/10.1111/1468-5922.12090.

Hinton, L. (2015). "Temporality and the Torments of Time." *Journal of Analytical Psychology*, 60, 353–370.

Hinton, L. (2018). Jung, Time, and Ethics. In J. Mills (Ed.), *Philosophizing Jung*. New York, NY: Routledge.

Hinton, L. III, Hinton, L. IV, Hinton, D. & Hinton, A. (2011). "Panel: Unus Mundus – Transcendent Truth or Comforting Fiction? Overwhelm and the Search for Meaning in a Fragmented World." *Journal of Analytical Psychology*, 56, 375–396.

Hoeller, S. A. (2017). "Abraxas, Jung's Gnostic Demiurge in Liber Novus." In M. Stein & T. Arzt (Eds.), *Jung's Red Book for Our Time* (Vol. 1, pp. 85–102). Ashville, NC: Chiron.

Horne, M., Sowa, A. & Isenman, D. (2000). "Philosophical Assumptions in Freud, Jung and Bion: Questions of Causality." *Journal of Analytical Psychology*, 45, 109–121.

Husserl, E. (1966/1991). *On the Phenomenology of the Internal Consciousness of Time: 1893–1917*. Trans. J. B. Brough. Boston, MA: Kluwer Academic.

Jung, C. G. (1961). *Memories, Dreams, Reflections*. Ed. A. Jaffé, Trans. R. Winston & C. Winston. New York, NY: Random House.

Jung, C. G. (1946/1966a). "The Psychology of the Transference." In R. F. C. Hull (Trans.), H. Read, M. Fordham, G. Adler & W. McGuire (Eds.), *The Collected Works of C.G. Jung* (Vol. 16, 2nd ed., pp. 163–323). Princeton, NJ: Princeton University Press.

Jung, C. G. (1943/1966b). "Two Essays on Analytical Psychology." In R. F. C. Hull (Trans.), H. Read, M. Fordham, G. Adler & W. McGuire (Eds.), *The Collected Works of C.G. Jung* (Vol. 7, 2nd ed.). Princeton, NJ: Princeton University Press.

Jung, C. G. (1944/1968). "The Symbolism of the Mandala." In R. F. C. Hull (Trans.), H. Read, M. Fordham, G. Adler & W. McGuire (Eds.), *The Collected*

Works of C.G. Jung (Vol. 12, 2nd ed., pp. 95–223). Princeton, NJ: Princeton University Press.

Jung, C. G. (1955/2001). *Modern Man in Search of a Soul*. Trans. W. S. Dell & C. F. Baynes. New York, NY: Routledge.

Jung, C. G. (2009). *The Red Book: Liber Novus*. Trans. S. Shamdasani, M. Kyburz & J. Peck. New York, NY: W. W. Norton.

Levinas, E. (2000). *God, Death, and Time*. Trans. B. Bergo, Foreword by Jacques Rolland. Stanford, CA: Stanford University Press.

Manoussakis, J. P. (2009). "Thebes Revisited: Theodicy and the Temporality of Evil." *Research in Phenomenology*, 39, 292–306.

Manoussakis, J.P. (2017). "Cracked: The black Theology of Anatheism." In M. Clemente & R. Kearney (Eds.), *The Art of Anatheism* (pp. 49–64). London, England: Rowman & Littlefield.

Merkur, D. (2017). *Jung's Ethics: Moral Psychology and the Cure of Souls*. Ed. J. Mills. New York, NY: Routledge.

Mills, J. (2014). "Truth." *Journal of the American Psychoanalytic Association*, 62, 267–293.

Nietzsche, F. (1886/1961). *Beyond Good and Evil*. New York, NY: Penguin Classics.

Nietzsche, F. (1866/1999). *The Birth of Tragedy and Other Writings*. Cambridge, England: Cambridge University Press.

Sartre, J.-P. (1946/2007). *Existentialism is a Humanism*. Trans. C. Macomber. New Haven, CT: Yale University Press.

Smith, R. (2018). "Aristotle's Logic." In *Stanford Encyclopedia of Philosophy*. Stanford, CA: Stanford University. Retrieved from https://plato.stanford.edu/entries/aristotle-logic/.

Stiegler, B. (1998). *Technics and Time*. Vol. 1: *The Fault of Epimetheus*. Stanford, CA: Stanford University Press.

Stiegler, B. (2014). *Symbolic Misery*. Vol. 1: *The Hyperindustrial Epoch*. Malden, MA: Polity Press.

Wheeler, D. (2015). "Martin Heidegger." In *Stanford Encyclopedia of Philosophy* (Fall ed.). Stanford, CA: Stanford University. Retrieved from https://plato.stanford.edu/entries/heidegger/.

Yanchar, S. C. (2018). "Agency, World, and the Ontological Ground of Possibility." *Journal of Theoretical and Philosophical Psychology*, 38, 1–14.

Yiassemides, A. (2014). *Time and Timelessness: Temporality in the Theory of Carl Jung*. New York, NY: Routledge.

Chapter 11

Trauma, Shame and Enigma

Reflections on Joseph Conrad's
Lord Jim

Engaging works of literature, such as Joseph Conrad's novel, *Lord Jim*, are helpful in providing some reflective distance from the frantic hubbub of our times (1992). It is a tale of trauma, shame, and the monstrous, a portrayal of a man's search for an ethical stance in an enigmatic world. It was published in 1900, the same year as Freud's *Interpretation of Dreams*. That millennial passage was a significant turning point, and the novel seems well-suited for reflection on historical shifts, moral confusion, and shamelessness.

****

We first see the idealistic young Jim in maritime training to become a ship's officer. He was noted to be 'very smart aloft', looking down on others from above. When down below with the other trainees, he immersed himself in light literature, keeping separate imagining himself as a hero in romantic-heroic dramas. However, when there was a real chance to participate in a heroic rescue, he failed to act in time. The author raised questions about the romantic view of life, wondering whether Jim was trapped in a childlike idealism that could never come to fruition and was foredoomed to fail at crucial moments the rest of his life.

****

After completing his training, Jim took a berth as first officer of the *Patna*.

The *Patna* was a steamer "as old as the hills", engaged by 800 pilgrims to take them to Mecca. As the pilgrims streamed aboard over three gangways . . . "urged by faith and the hope of paradise", the German captain's initial comment to Jim, his new first mate, was, "Look at dese cattle" (pp. 16–17). His visage conveyed another, underlying dimension of life on the *Patna*.

DOI: 10.4324/9781003641063-12

"There was something obscene in the sight of his naked flesh . . . the odious and fleshy figure . . . fixed itself in . . . [Jim's] memory for ever as an incarnation of everything vile and base that lurks in the world we love . . ." (pp. 2–23). The contrast between Jim's idyllic imaginations and the reality of the rusting ship and the men around him was stark.

A few days into the voyage, the engineer was drunkenly arguing with the captain when there was a gigantic jolt that pitched him down headfirst. A faint sound like remote thunder came and went, and the whole ship quivered. The sharp hull . . . seemed to rise a few inches in succession through its full length . . . and then settle rigidly. They had evidently run into an old hulk lying half-submerged in the water.

Jim saw that the rusty iron bulkhead was bulging, apparently ready to give way, and the rest of the crew were hurriedly launching one of the few lifeboats to abandon the ship and the pilgrims.

One of the fleeing crew clutched at the air with raised arms, tottered and fell dead, but the others didn't know that. As they escaped in the lifeboat, they cried out to the fallen man to join them: "Jump! Geo-o-o-orge! . . . Jump!" (p. 101).

Later, Jim blurted out to Marlow, who had become his interlocutor,
    [Instead of George] *I had jumped . . . I knew nothing about it until I looked up* . . . and saw the hull of the ship rising above [me] (p. 101) . . . It was as if *I had jumped into a black well – into an everlasting deep hole* (p. 102).

Indeed, in some sense, he had. The enigma of his act became the shame-ridden core of the rest of his life, a horror that his mind endlessly struggled to assimilate.

******

Jim's trauma lies at the basis of the rest of this discussion, and it is useful to consider the meaning of that term.

A *trauma* [is] . . . an event without necessity; a cause for the subject as an accidental, contingent event; an event without immediate purpose; an event that does not make sense, or rather a senseless event that has to be made sense of, an event that hereafter will be made the foundation of sense.
                                            (Hyldgaard, 2000, p. 235)

At first, Jim mostly took his traumatic 'failure' as his *personal* shame and wanted to ameliorate that experience; but, over time, his search became more enigmatic and all-consuming, a search that had to do with his singular presence in the world.

******

Jim was deeply ashamed to find himself in the lifeboat, in the company of the monstrous captain and the other crew. They were soon picked up by another ship and taken to port, where they learned that the *Patna* did *not* sink but was towed to the harbor by a French gunboat. The crew's original cover story of a romantic tragedy now seemed like a shameful farce, and Jim and his fellows on the lifeboat now looked like irresponsible clowns.

There was to be an official hearing, a sort of trial, with much at stake for the crew of the *Patna*. At this point, Marlow became the narrator of the story. He was an experienced ship's captain himself and somewhat senior to Jim.

Jim first met Marlow during a break in the proceedings, and they almost came to blows. Outside the courtroom a feral, yellow dog was running loose, and someone stumbled over him, saying with a laugh, "Look at that wretched cur!". Jim heard those words and spun around, stopped Marlow, and asked in a low, intense voice, "Did you speak to *me*?" He felt ashamed and angry because he thought that Marlow had called him a cur (p. 65).

Marlow grasped the source of his anger and simply pointed at the nearby dog. Jim's shame response was intense.

The red of [his] fair sunburnt complexion deepened suddenly . . . [and] spread to the roots of his curly hair. His ears became intensely crimson, and even the clear blue of his eyes was darkened . . . by the rush of blood to his head (p. 69).

However, Marlow sensed something special in Jim and became his friend and benefactor, as well as his main narrator.

****

The other officers of the *Patna* skipped town, avoiding the board of inquiry. Jim will have none of that and confronted the hearing determinedly, but with little satisfaction. He explained to Marlow, "They wanted facts, facts! They demanded facts . . ., as if facts could explain anything" (p. 28). The intent of the hearing focused on guilt and logical explanation, delineating formal wrongs and possible reparations, but shame brings into question one's deeper, enigmatic relation to those happenings. Shame experiences range from the most primitive to a subjective destitution that provokes questions about the individual's very place in the universe (Hegel, p. 19).

****

The board found Jim guilty, and he lost his certificate as a ship's officer. Deeply distraught, he went to see Marlow, who offered him money and a letter of recommendation for a job and a fresh start.

His new work involved meeting ships just as they arrived in harbours, and people saw him as daring, sometimes even showing disregard for his survival. He was very successful and well-liked at a series of jobs and was even offered the lure of a substantial fortune. However, he continually fled the scene whenever a person or rumour from the past surfaced. His shame was still too personal to endure.

******

In the light of Jim's repetitive pattern of success and flight, Marlow decided to consult a man named Stein, a wealthy and respected merchant who was noted for his wisdom and his avocation of entomology (p. 183).

Upon arriving at Stein's home, Marlow found him inside, contemplating the beauty of one of his butterflies. Greeting Marlowe, he exclaimed, "Marvelous . . . this is Nature – the balance of colossal forces. Every star is so . . . and the mighty Kosmos in perfect equilibrium produces this . . . masterpiece . . ." (p. 187).

Marlow replied cheerfully, "Masterpiece! And what of man?"

Stein responded,
Man is amazing, but he is not a masterpiece. Perhaps the [Divine] artist was a little mad, eh? Sometimes it seems to me that man has come to where he is not wanted, where there is no place for him; for if not, why should [he always want something more]?

Marlow told Stein that he had come with a specimen, Jim, and told him the story. Stein responded, "I understand very well. He is *romantic*".

Marlow questioned further, "What's good for it?" . . . and Stein expanded:

"A man that is born falls into a dream like a man who falls into the sea. If he tries to climb out into the <u>air</u> as inexperienced people attempt to do, he drowns – *nicht war?* No! I tell you! *The way is to the destructive element submit yourself,* and with the exertions of your hands and feet in the water make the deep, deep sea keep you up . . . *In the destructive element immerse . . . That [is] the way . . .".*

(pp. 192–193 & 195)

******

Stein had personal connections in a small, isolated island named Patusan, and planned to appoint Jim as his new agent there. Jim could finally "Slam the door" on the past (p. 212). Freed of his past, he could perhaps create his life anew. When Marlow asked whether he would ever return to the world he had known, he exclaimed, "Never!".

Stein gave Jim a ring that was a symbol of friendship with Doramin, a significant traditional leader in Patusan. They had been old war comrades, and it was a symbol of eternal friendship, and Stein had once saved Doramin's life. Thus, Jim became a kind of heir to a history of courage, honor and friendship that endured. The ring seemed to embody virtues that transcended time, race, or culture.

Jim thereby entered a new phase of his life, now on land.

****

Two years later, Marlow came to Patusan to visit Jim. After he landed, he quickly discovered that the local people now called him 'Tuan Jim', or 'Lord Jim', and spoke of him with awe.

Jim told Marlow his story. After landing in Patusan, a crowd of armed men had swarmed around him as soon as he arrived. They had kept him prisoner in a filthy shed in the courtyard for three days when a sudden awareness of his peril came upon him. "[Then, all] at once, *without any mental process* . . ., without any stir of emotion, he set about his escape as if executing a plan that had matured for a month".

Jim left the shed and ran past a dignitary with armed guards coming to question him again and scaled the palisade surrounding the compound. However, there was a very muddy creek separating the compound from the town that was his goal, and he became stuck in a deep pit of soft and sticky mud, although there was higher and drier ground a few feet above him.

He reached and grabbed desperately with his hands, and only succeeded in gathering a horrible cold shiny heap of slime against his breast – up to the very chin. It seemed to him that he was burying himself alive, and then he struck out madly, scattering the mud with his fists. It fell on his head, on his face, over his eyes, and into his mouth.

(p. 228)

Finally, with a desperate effort he reached the other side and fled toward the centre of town, "beplastered with filth out of all semblance to a human being". Finally, he ran into a group of several startled men, and had barely enough breath to gasp out, "Doramin! Doramin!" (p. 228).

The men half carried him to the top of the hill and took him into a large enclosure full of palms and fruit trees, where he saw a massive man with a great dignity of bearing sitting quietly amidst the hubbub. Doramin was a respected chief, and for him, Stein's ring was an ancient talisman of friendship. "His impassive repose . . . was like a display of dignity . . . [and] his ponderous movements were like manifestations of a mighty deliberate force" (p. 233). His bearing and hospitality for Jim conjured a picture of primal virtue during barbarous times.

As things evolved in Patusan, Jim, and Dane Waris, Doramin's only child, became close friends, and later war comrades, when Jim devised a means of taking the fort of a renegade in the hills, freeing the people from his raids and barbaric acts. Afterward, Jim became the virtual ruler of Patusan, even appointing the headmen in conjunction with Dane Waris.

******

Cornelius was the man whom Jim had replaced as Stein's agent, and Jewel was his stepdaughter. He was a man filled with envy and resentment, but Jim and Jewel fell in love and became inseparable. She watched over him carefully, gave him advice, and on occasion warned of assassination plots against him.

Marlow returned to the outside world, convinced that Jim had mastered his fate (p. 292).

******

The story continued some time later, narrated by a bundle of letters that Marlow had written to an unknown recipient. It concerned a man called Brown or, more sarcastically, "Gentleman Brown". The son of an English baronet, he seemed to be the moral antipode to Jim. Marlow had been able to interview him on his deathbed, and his letter described the encounter in detail.

Brown was a buccaneer, but he was distinguished from his fellows by the "arrogant temper of his misdeeds and a vehement scorn for mankind at large and for his victims in particular". He would bring to the shooting or maiming of some quiet, unoffending stranger a savage and vengeful earnestness. This was the man who sail[ed] into Jim's history.

Brown and his small crew had gone upriver to Patusan town in search of supplies and plunder. Jim was away on a mission at the time. When the motley crew reached the town, there was an uproar, and they were confronted by defenders, mustered by Dane Waris and Jewel. Seeing they were outnumbered, the pirates retreated to a knoll nearby and set up a defense. There was an impasse.

Then Jim returned, and the situation confronted him.

****

Marlow's letter continued. Brown was nearing death, and his character and emotions emerged with a primal rawness. He had hated and envied Jim from first sight. They confronted each other at the very spot, the divide where Jim had taken the second desperate leap of his life – the leap into the 'destructive element', the muddy struggle that had landed him in the midst of the life of Patusan, into the trust and love of the people.

Marlow described Brown:

He was terrible – relating this to me – this tortured skeleton of a man drawn up together with his face over his knees, upon a miserable bed in that wretched hovel, and lifting his head to look at me with malignant glee . . . I knew [just] what to say, Brown gloated (p. 343).

He was indeed extremely cunning about finding the soft and vulnerable places in people's character, and he partly accomplished that with Jim. He first tried to convince Jim that they were birds of a feather. When Jim asked him, "What made you come here?", Brown responded, ". . . Hunger. And what made *you*?" (p. 343). Jim responded by becoming very red in the face. Then Brown cunningly and intuitively asserted that Jim must understand that when it came to saving one's life . . ., one "didn't care [how many others [perished], three, thirty, three hundred . . .", cleverly reminding Jim of the shame of the *Patna*.

Brown finally agreed to leave Patusan but would not give up his weapons (p. 350). Dane Waris had led a group to guard the river route to the sea, and

Jim sent him his ring as assurance that there was an agreement with the pirates and that they should be allowed to continue downriver.

However, Cornelius, possessed by envy, treacherously told Brown of an alternate route down the river that would pass behind Dane Waris' encampment and agreed to guide the pirates' boat down the little-known passage. Seizing the chance for revenge, they made a surprise attack. Dane Waris was shot in the forehead. Then the pirates escaped to their ship at the mouth of the river. One of the survivors frantically returned to Patusan town to break the news.

****

When he reached the town, he shouted out: "They have killed Dane Waris and many more"! (p. 366). Jim immediately understood that he was, in some sense, the one to blame. He had retreated from one world, and now the other, the work of his own hands, had fallen in ruins around him.

As Jim stood looking at the river, Jewel was staring at him in a state of anguish. She cried out, "Will you fight?" and he answered, "There is nothing to fight for". Then she cried out again, "Will you fl[ee]?" He replied, "There is no escape" (p. 371).

She could not understand that "[Jim] was going to prove his power in another way and conquer the fatal destiny itself . . . 'Open the gates!' he ordered" (p. 368–369).

****

When Dane Waris' body was brought back to Doramin's place of residence, the grieving father sat staring at it for a long time. Someone took the well-known ring from his dead son's hand and held it up, and there was a murmur from the crowd. Doramin stared at it,

> . . . and suddenly let out one great fierce cry, deep from the chest, a roar of pain and fury, as strong as a wounded bull, bringing great fear . . . by the magnitude of his anger and his sorrow . . . (p. 370).

When Jim reached Doramin's area, the venerable patriarch sat in his armchair, immense and desolate, with a pair of flintlock pistols on his knees, surrounded by an armed throng. Jim stood silently before him for a time, then came up, looked at his dead friend, lifted the sheet, and then dropped it.

"He came! He came!" ran from lip to lip . . . "He hath taken it upon his own head" (p. 373).

Jim heard those words and responded, "Yes. Upon my head". After a few moments, he said gently to Doramin, "I am come in sorrow . . . I come ready and unarmed". From the throat of the unwieldy old man came gurgling, choking, inhuman sounds, and his two attendants helped him stand from behind. The ring, the talisman that had opened so many doors . . ., reportedly dropped from Doramin's lap and rolled to Jim's foot.

> . . . Then, while Jim stood stiffened and with bared head in the light of the torches, looking [Doramin] straight in the face . . . [the older man] lifted his arm deliberately, [and] shot his son's friend through the chest (p. 373).

"They say that the white man sent [a proud and unflinching glance] right and left at all those faces. Then, with his hand over his lips he fell forward, dead" (p. 373).

****

What are we to make of this story and Jim's death? It comes across as an ultimate act of fidelity, a creative act 'out of nowhere' so to speak. At a time in history when faith in duties prescribed from on high was collapsing, the story hints of an ethos beyond mere duty (Caputo, 2004, p. 127).

The stark contrast between Jim's original failure and this last test stands out. A life of languid ease as a ship's officer in 'exotic' shores had seemed in his future, a moral cesspool of expat decadence and childish romantic fantasies. Then, without conscious intent, he had jumped into a 'black hole' of shame and enigma (Hinton, 2007). Rather than fleeing or being destroyed by despair, this trauma became a rending passage of transformation. It made his life worth living (Stiegler, 2013, pp. 59–78).

At the hearing, hints of the emergence of an unusual destiny became evident. Jim wanted something more than facts and formal guilt. It required that he bear and acknowledge his shame. He initially feared that he had become like a mongrel, a 'cur', to others.

Jim increasingly embraced his shame and the haunting enigma of his act . . . "in the destructive element immerse", as Stein had put it. Hegel described this process as, "Tarrying with the negative" (Mogensen, 2017, p. 11). In his view, the life of the spirit is such that it, ". . . wins its truth only when, in utter dismemberment, it finds itself" (Hegel, 1977, p. 19; Mogensen, 2016, p. 11). The basic structure of Jim's world shifted, and his deep personal shame evolved into an *ontological shame*.

At the end, Jim refused to escape with Jewel; he did not fight, he did not commit suicide, and he did not run back to England. He embraced the penumbra of the unknown, tarrying with the negative. In that process, something different emerged for him, something that was highly ethical but inexpressible in terms of mere duty. It was not cold and indifferent, or based on lofty romantic imaginations, but immersed in the dense human surround of Patusan (Barreto, 2013, pp. 230 & 236).

Doramin seemed to be the incarnation of a reservoir of primal human virtue, and Jim's death felt like an affirmation of an almost knightly honoring of friendship and keeping faith (Appiah, 2010; Watt, 1987, p. 99).

In my view, he didn't *know* what the outcome would be when he went to meet Doramin, but he died in a free and honorable act that resulted in preserving the community. He seemed to have had awareness of what *not* to do, *not* pretending to know the future. This opened a different kind of space, a singular space. Freedom stems from a hole in being that often feels shaming, even monstrous. We are not perfect butterflies going along a preplanned course, and we do not control the future. Jim had been an apprentice to shame and not-knowing for many years, and in my view, his death should be seen from that perspective. It was an ethical act with true honor, performed in creative freedom.

References

Appiah, K. A. (2010). *The Honor Code: How Moral Revolutions Happen.* New York: W. W. Norton & Co.

Barreto, M. H. (2013). "The Unity of the Ethical and the Religious in Jung's Thought." *International Journal of Jungian Studies*, 5, 3, 226–242.

Caputo, J. (2004). *Against Ethics.* Evansville: Indiana University Press.

Conrad. J. (1992). *Lord Jim: A Tale.* New York: Penguin Random House.

Hegel, G. W. F. (1977). *Hegel's Phenomenology of Spirit.* Trans. A. V. Miller. New York: Oxford University Press.

Berkeley: North Atlantic Books.

Hinton, L. (2007). "Black Holes, Uncanny Spaces, and Radical Shifts in Awareness." *Journal of Analytical Psychology*, 52, 433–447.

Hyldgaard, K. (2000). "The Cause of the Subject as an Ill-Timed Accident: Lacan, Sartre and Aristotle." *Umbr(a): A Journal of the Unconscious*, Fall Issue, 67–80.

Mogensen, G. (2017). "Dereliction of Duty and the Rise of Psychology: PDI in the Light of Conrad's *Lord Jim*." ISPDI Website.

Stiegler, B. (2013). *What Makes Life Worth Living: On Pharmacology.* Trans. Dan Ross. Malden, MA: Polity Press.

Watt, I. P. (1987). "The Ending of *Lord Jim*." In Ted Billy (Ed.), *Critical Essays on Joseph Conrad* (pp. 85–102). Boston: G. K. Hall & Co.

Chapter 12

Shame and Temporality in the Streets*

Consumerism, Technology, Truth and Raw Life

The cask of ages past is spent:
it's final.
The plight of Anima Mundi's song is
fatal.
We want to hear it sing again;
we try,
Refusing to believe that voice
did die.
We urge it to return;
we cry!
But nothing comes and nothing will –
the end seems nigh.
And mourning speaks as mourning must,
we sigh.

The Vanishing of the World Soul[1]
Ladson Hinton, 2015

Introduction

Indeed, we sigh! No longer do we experience a world soul, an Anima Mundi that contains and connects all things. The view that there is an underlying unity between the world and all the entities of the world has tended to dominate Western thought since the time of Plato (Plato, 2000, p. 16). The alchemists attempted to revivify this idea with the concept

* Hinton, L. (2018). Shame and Temporality in the Streets: Consumerism, Technology, Truth and Raw Life. In: Ladson Hinton & Hessel Willemsen (eds.). *Temporality and Shame*. London: Routledge. Reprinted by permission of the publisher (Taylor & Francis Ltd, http://www.tandfonline.com).

DOI: 10.4324/9781003641063-13

of the *Unus Mundus*, a unified world, with a Self that is a carrier of the unity of the individual (Jung, 1970, pp. 537–539). At this time in history, we have lost confidence in such an 'enchanted', interconnected world sustained by the regularity of the heavens circulating around us. In the face of this loss, we feel troubled and bewildered (Hinton et al., 2011).

Freud wrote of the threefold narcissistic wounds suffered by humanity in recent centuries, namely the Copernican, the Darwinian and the psychoanalytic revolutions. In other words, an awareness that the earth revolves around the sun, and not vice versa; an awareness that humankind is descended from apelike creatures and an awareness that reason itself is dubiously based and often blindly irrational (Freud, 1917/1955). Today, we would certainly add the terrible events of the Holocaust, the Khmer Rouge and Rwanda genocides, slavery, apartheid and colonialism. Such histories of profound evil further shook our faith in human progress. Following upon these shattering blows, potent technologies, evolving at the speed of light in the 21st century, have far surpassed ordinary human capacities. This crescendo of happenings has created a state of shame and disorientation (Ross, 2006; Stiegler, 2008, pp. 64–96).

Time is speeded up, and our sense of continuity with the past and with our ancestors is tenuous. The world seems to be in a state of violent transition, and raw life greets us daily on the streets as we hurry about equipped with our many electronic and smart devices, or technics. We have become addicted to spectacles of wonderment and terror, and each morning we glance at the news to see what disaster has transpired. Indeed, Virilio calls the contemporary world a Museum of Accidents (Virilio, 2003, pp. 40–57). When our containing traditions are stripped away, we search for ways to endure the screams and cries that run through us (Eigen, 2005, p. 51).[2] We wonder whether this is, indeed, the end of the Anthropocene, also known as the time when the human no longer dominates, the end of the era of *Homo sapiens* (Ross, 2016). What cyborg or other technologised creature might replace us?

At such a time in history, we need, above all, a capacity for reflection. However, the relentless promotion of consumption promises access to immediate gratification and an escape from the truth of the present. Tempting spectacles are endlessly offered with all of the sophisticated attractions of advanced technics, 'short-circuiting' the deferral of pleasure that sublimates our desires for individual and communal goods (Stiegler, 2013b, pp. 102–108). As a result, there is an increasing 'proletarianization of the mind', a deficiency in the capacity for long-term thought due to the automation of memory and a general loss of '*savoir-faire*' (Stiegler, 2013b, pp. 37–38 &

123–126). We have become addicted to short-term fixes and are left with a psyche that is uncontained and unformed, in fact dangerous, because a surplus of unsublimated is the truth of the frighteningly 'raw life' that is emerging post *anima mundi* (Stiegler, 2013a, pp. 80–102; 2014, pp. 1–13).

Sequence of Discussion

Shame and temporality, along with truth, provide crucial lenses for reflecting upon our present condition, and I will begin by briefly delineating these basic concepts. Following this, I will describe a provocative encounter on the streets of Seattle that provides insight into undercurrents that are visibly emerging in contemporary life. My hope is that this detailed example, along with a few others, will contribute to a deepened understanding of the contemporary scene, enhance the reader's knowledge of shame and temporality and offer space to reflect upon these basic experiences. In the concluding part of the chapter, I amplify those reflections from the perspectives of several philosophers and psychoanalysts who share a deep concern about the future of the human being.

Shame, Truth and Temporality

The experiences of shame, truth and temporality are interrelated. In psychoanalytic work, it is difficult to discuss one without the others. The many levels of memory are deeply interconnected with temporality and lie at the core of the analytic process. Individual versions of the ghost of Hamlet's father appear in their several voices, emerging from the past, making their claim to truth and shaming those who survive into deep reflection about the future. In psychoanalysis, the analyst's interpretations are intended to enhance awareness of unconscious truths, past and present, opening frozen dimensions of the patient's world and allowing fuller participation in the flow of time. Such insights often provoke turbulent evolution and shame, along with potential new openings towards the future; thus, a brief summary of some salient aspects of shame and temporality and their interrelationship with truth is necessary.

First, shame often involves the question, 'What kind of person am I?' It makes us wonder, sometimes with horror, 'How could I have done such and such a thing?' It stops us cold and makes us want to disappear. Its etymology has to do with covering or hiding. At times, shame seems to combine a sense of the immediate and the particular with questions about the very structure of being (Hultberg, 1986). Furthermore, it can open up further dimensions of temporality because it slows us down from the mad pace of our culture, and when we slow down, we can 'see' more.

As shame often has a very social dimension, we flush with shame when we are seen, or see ourselves, violating our concept of an ideal self (Seidler, 2000, pp. 47–97). 'Skin shame' can be superficial and connected with self-conscious conformity, but deeper shame can motivate us to question our deepest core and most primal sense of meaning. This seems to be true across cultures, and there is evidence that it is biologically innate (Sznycer et al., 2016; Tracy & Matsumoto, 2008). It seems to involve both emotional and metaphysical stirrings, often inciting us not only to acknowledge a factual wrongdoing but to engage with the question of the very nature of our humanity (Heidegger, 1956, p. 27).

The shamelessness of our times is alarming, but shame often goes unacknowledged and ignored (Giegerich, 2001, p. 34; Morrison, 1989, pp. 121–123). Indeed, Stiegler believes that shame is not lacking but rather that it is present in a pervasive, although unarticulated, form as 'symbolic misery', that is 'the shame of being human' (Stiegler, 2013a, pp. 105–106). In his view, the contemporary deficit of selfhood is a dimension of late-stage capitalism, and we are living through a decadence of industrial democracy. These feelings of shame, very often bypassed and unconscious, result in a 'symbolic misery' (Stiegler, 2013a, p. 5) that is expressed by apathy, disaffection and social collapse. It is, in many ways, a product of mass media and the technologies of consumerism to which we have become addicted.[3]

While we can often delineate guilt and obtain a pardon, it is much more difficult to atone for shame. It requires a full, total examination of self. However, throughout the history of psychoanalysis, shame has been perceived as an inferior emotion that is typical of women, cultural and racial minorities and colonised others (Aron & Starr, 2013, pp. 51–64; Bewes, 2011). Western cultures are often portrayed as guilt cultures and, therefore, supposedly superior. However, guilt may actually be an evasion of shame, a focus on something that appears to be specific and 'solvable' in lieu of facing the more intractable and searching questions that shame poses. Indeed, guilt can be a seductive way to explain and dismiss one's deeper sense of responsibility (Stiegler, 2013a, p. 24).

Shame and truth are closely interconnected. I am not speaking of Truth as an absolute or foundational Truth, but truth with a small t. It is truth as a process, which the ancient Greeks called *aletheia*.

Truth is related to temporality, '[and] we should view truth not as an absolute category that discloses itself in its entirety but rather as a contextual process that reveals itself a bit at a time and from many different perspectives' (Stiegler, 2013a, p. 9). That is it unfolds in time. 'Authentic truth . . . seems to be a matter not of what one knows, but instead of how one lives' (Guignon, 1983, p. 348). As new elements of truth are disclosed, others may fade into hiddenness or obscurity.

Giegerich discussed the importance of remembering that truth often has a violent effect on the psyche (2008, pp. 4–8). He employs the story of Actaion and the Hounds as an illustration. In this story, Prince Actaion was out hunting, and by chance, he found the goddess Artemis naked, bathing in a pool with her acolytes. When she realised that he was spying on them, she turned him into a stag, and he was then dismembered by his own hounds (Giegerich, 2001, pp. 105–111, 203ff).

The story of Actaion dramatically illustrates how we may unexpectedly come across a naked truth about ourselves, thereby creating a dire sense of psychic disruption and inner crumbling that may provoke deep shame. In the longer run, such experiences can open the space for reflection and profound shifts in awareness. It is also the universal tale of the 'otherness' of time unfolding, impacting a psyche that tends to reflexively maintain continuity and an illusion of safety (Giegerich, 2001, p. 28).

This leads to my last theme, temporality, which is the experience of lived time, the time of our lives (Hoy, 2012, pp. xii–xiii). Temporality is uniquely human and is the basis of culture. Awareness of time drives us, inspiring both the nobility of our future purpose and our destructive paranoias (Johnston, 2005, pp. 300–332). However, time is strangely elusive, appearing to vanish as soon as we attempt to describe it: 'Space contains both living and inert bodies, but *only the living human – hence the living psyche – is subjectively concerned with time*' (Scarfone, 2006, p. 810, emphasis added).

Nothing occurs except in the context of temporality. In a profound sense, temporality is *Homo sapiens*.[4] Our temporal being is also our tormentor, driving us on into an unknown future, evoking both shame and truth, which in turn can radically alter the experience of time.

Memory and our sense of the past disrupt us, and we can endlessly dwell on our memories. However, memory is always subject to revision, and its truth is never final. Our identity has changing levels with no final foundation. Due to the effects of *Nachträglichkeit*, or 'afterwardness', there is a constant reconfiguration of memory, a factor that comprises much of the work of psychoanalysis. This process not only shifts the meaning of the past but also alters the qualities of the future that we envisage (Civitarese, 2010, pp. 96–108).[5] A fear of the future and the projection of unassimilated traumas may result in a kind of frozenness in time (Hinton, 2015, p. 355). Temporality is uniquely human, and it denies us the peaceful complacency of the other animals on the planet as we anticipate our death and the death of others. Such awareness of the truth of our finitude may create deep shame.

'The Man in the Street'

New perspectives often come from the raw, disowned elements of our world. In that spirit, I will describe an experience that I had last year on a street in Seattle, near our home. This incident highlights shame, truth and temporality in a specific context, and it touches upon many questions about contemporary life and the state of psychoanalysis.

We live in the Capitol Hill area, a large neighbourhood adjacent to the urban core that is filled with old family residences in the north half, and apartment buildings, restaurants, bars, coffee houses and occasional halfway houses in the south half.

One day I stopped for bread at my favourite bakery, which is, more or less, in the centre of the Hill. When I returned to my car, I found a mildly dishevelled man, probably 30 years old, lounging against it with a large cup of coffee sitting on the hood. Vaguely wondering if there would be some sort of messy encounter, I started to unlock my door, saying quietly, 'Sorry to disturb'. The man suddenly sprang up to his full height – he was tall and solidly built – and his face dramatically reddened. His eyes became wide and wild, and he began to shout loudly at the surroundings and at me, 'Do you know about what's happening?! Do you know about what's happening?!' There was a sense of panic, almost terror, in the air, as if he suddenly felt shattered.

With hardly a pause, I looked directly at him in a friendly way and said calmly and succinctly, 'I don't have a clue about what's happening'. Those words had come directly to mind and were the direct truth of what I felt. The man's visage changed within seconds, lost its red-faced wildness and he looked almost happy. Nodding slightly to me with the hint of a smile, he took his coffee and strolled off quietly down the street. The flow of life was restored.

Reflections on the Encounter

My response to him was truly without conscious thought. Indeed, in that moment, I felt a sort of kinship with him. The change in his demeanour was dramatic and memorable. That I did not 'know' or pretend to 'know about' what was happening was somehow profoundly reassuring to him. It was a special 'moment of meeting', something unforgettable.

Life is often difficult for individuals whose usual lens of experience is from a 'vertex' that differs from the cultural norm, resulting in a painful sense of being an outsider. This kind of awareness may also evoke a different sense of temporality from that of the average person. Frequently, and very uncomfortably, it seems to them that everyone else knows 'about what is happening' except them. Such experiences are disconcerting, even terrifying and are also endlessly shame-inducing.

The Man in the Street flushed dramatically when he reacted to my intrusion, but it felt much more like shame than anger. If it had been anger, my own visceral response would have been different. I had violently startled him by my appearance, disrupting his peaceful interlude with his coffee and my car.

My sense is that he had been in a fantasy/reverie state in which he was a 'normal person', a somebody who, for a moment, 'belonged'. He was in a place where he 'had a place', and that was what I had disrupted in a way that probably felt violent to him (Giegerich, 2008, pp. 4–8). It is also what was made okay by my response, the message that, on some level, I too did not really have a place. That made our relationship more symmetrical. As a result, his shame dissolved. He was no longer reduced to being a defective object in the eye of the surroundings.

I had suddenly disrupted the Man in the Street during a fantasy of access to the vast power of technics, of cars and coffee and commerce, along with their extensive cultural memories.[6] He had been momentarily entranced by the seductions of the consumer society. I had disrupted his simulation of power and connection, throwing him into a state of psychic disequilibrium. My presence was an existential truth. The car belonged to me. The disruption of his reverie was acutely shaming, thrusting him back into the sense of being an outsider, a social outcast, a crazy piece of trash on the street who existed outside cultural time.

In his panic, the man seemed to be appealing to me and the surrounding surprised people on the sidewalks – appealing, in a sense, to the world as a witness, looking for some kind of justice. Without some hope for justice, cultures cannot hold together, although justice is never final but is always in process, as ethics and law. Shame and justice are deeply interconnected (Stiegler, 2013a, p. 18). They are basic cultural elements that hold people together and make possible a sense of future and hope. A lack of hope lays the foundation for violence, terrorism and shameless acts (Stiegler, 2013a, pp. 8–9, 19).

The question posed by the Man in the Street about what was happening expressed his anguished uncertainty about whether there was any coherent order left in the world, something that included him. Appealing to the collective surround, to 'society', he beseechingly asked if, indeed, anyone knew 'about' what was happening in a way that went beyond merely literal facts. He had immersed himself in the emblems of 'belonging', which provided a fragile sense of gratification and proof that life was worth living. I had shattered that fantasy. Was there anyone who could affirm a world in which there was any consistent hope of 'belonging', any possible future?

At some level, he was also posing the 'God is dead' question that seems so overtly and covertly present at this time in history. What do we do when there seems to be no coherent discourse to keep things in place so that we can think about them and lead meaningful lives beyond our driven consumerism? In that none of us really knows what is happening, and we feel lost in the frantic pace of things, we are not unlike the Man in the Street. He is us, and we are him.

When I told him that I did not have a clue, he immediately exhibited a profound sense of relief. This acknowledgment that we shared a common human plight evoked a dramatic shift that seemed dialectical. One could surmise there were several levels involved. First, my sudden appearance had shattered his reverie of ownership and his sense of belonging in the cultural present and thrown him into shame and panic.[7] Second, I responded to his frantic, screaming questions with a negative assertion, rather than with scorn or irritation. The raw truth was that I did not have a clue![8]

In a dialectical movement, these two negations opened up an expanded sense of space and time.[9] I would call this a dimension of soul, of interiority (Giegerich, 2008, p. 3). Indeed, it was as if we shared a secret, some glimmering of a different truth. This seemed to dissolve the shame he had experienced. As he strolled down the street, back into the everyday flow of time, there was a wink of kinship, almost of complicity, that was fascinating and special, a secret that we shared. We both knew that the world is not as it pretends to be. This contributed an undercurrent of freedom and humour. We had glimpsed another dimension of reality together, and this involved interconnected shifts in the experience of shame, truth and temporality (Civitarese, 2016, pp. 485 & 490–493).

This experience has continued to reverberate in my mind. Sociological and psychiatric explanations seem not merely less than adequate but almost unethical in their reductionism. Several theoretical perspectives have helped me understand the dimensions of my experience with the Man in the Street.

Wilfred Bion

I begin with Wilfred Bion. In 1954, he discussed the case of a psychotic man, whom he described as having a severe phobia about wearing socks with holes. At that time, his interpretation was that the man experienced the holes as a symbol of castration, turning the socks into terrifying, attacking objects that could sever his leg. The socks became persecutory objects (Bion, 1954, pp. 113–218; 1967, pp. 27–29).

Twenty years later, Bion returned to the case, saying, 'I suggest that the patient did not have a phobia of socks but could see that what . . . [seemed to be] socks . . . [were actually] a lot of holes knitted together' (Bion, 1973/ 1990, pp. 21–22; Rhode, 1998, pp. 23–26). That is the man saw the holes as the primary phenomenon, not the socks as intact and unified objects that were penetrated (Hinton, 2007). Bion called this latter medical-rational point of view the 'medical vertex', which assumes a primal unity and wholeness of the body along with the assumption that signification proceeds from there in a rational chain.

In contrast, viewed from within another perspective that Bion called the 'religious vertex', the patient could see the holes as barely contained voids opening into an infinite abyss into which everything might disappear, or as openings into an infinite enigma or an inexpressible truth. This awareness was the source of the patient's terror, not the fear of castration that he had originally postulated (Rhode, 1998, pp. 19–20).

This example has remained with me for many years as a wonderful example of the capacity to see the infinite in the ordinary and a potential dimension of interiority of all things (Giegerich, 2007, p. 3). I personally think of 'interiority' as being like the experience of repeatedly reading a good poem and experiencing how more and more dimensions manifest themselves. Indeed, one could call this perspective a poetics of everyday life, as opposed to, for example, the view of medical psychopathology, which only sees validity in that which is immediately visible.

There is a depth of experience in the everyday that we tend to miss because of the ego's fear of losing control in the face of enigma, of that which we endlessly attempt to grasp or know, but which defies any final knowing. It challenges and torments us. However, for the person subsumed by a pervasive madness, the problem is often being unable to perceive anything that does *not* seem enigmatic. The challenge is being able to live at all in such a state of being. Artists and theologians often have the ability to 'see' creatively from that perspective, and Bion felt that psychoanalysts also needed to perceive such dimensions of truth. For that to happen, Bion often repeated that one must come from a place that is without memory or desire, a place that does not privilege goals based on a causal understanding from the patient's past or from culturally or personally contrived future goals. That perspective has helped me to understand the Man in the Street, and his shifts vis-à-vis shame, truth and temporality.

Wolfgang Giegerich

Bion's perspective resembles that of Wolfgang Giegerich, although Giegerich's theory is broader because it underlines historical and cultural factors that Bion does not include. Giegerich calls his approach the discipline of interiority (Giegerich, 2012b, p. 206; 2008, pp. 3–4). That is it does not rely on the external material characteristics of a phenomenon any more than one could rely on dictionary definitions of the words of a poem to deeply understand the poem. 'Interiority' is a depth of experience that may be revealed by ongoing reflection. This does not mean the inside of things in a literal sense but a quality of interiority, or soul that is potentially present in all experiences.[10] From his perspective, 'If psychology wants to establish itself as a discipline of interiority, it must [also] show that it is capable of accounting for external reality, for the "world" *in terms of its own standpoint of* interiority' (Giegerich, 2012a, p. 1; 2012b, p. 43). Giegerich emphasises a process of 'the negation of a positive, tangible, demonstrable reality, [and] a taking off into the interiority of the phenomenon itself' (Casement, 2011, p. 52). Such a profound shift into the experience at hand is vastly different from viewing or imagining things from the outside as positively given objects. This is similar to Bion's religious vertex, which is very different from the medical vertex of unity, positivity and linear cause and effect.

According to Giegerich, classical Jungian analysis has become problematic because the time of myth is in the past. We are no longer contained on the inside of such signifying structures. Now, what passes as myth, symbol and archetype are often simulacra of a bygone age (Whan, 2015). Thus, Giegerich asserts that an analytic practice relying on dead concepts can, itself, be a form of neurosis because it privileges an illusory quest. In other words, symbolic realisation as Jung conceived it, a dialogue of ego and archetype guided by the Self, is no longer possible because those concepts were dependent on myths such as the *anima mundi* that have lost their meaning, and we cannot replace them (Giegerich, 2001, pp. 84–85).

One can view the singular experiences of people such as the Man in the Street as manifestations of the larger movements of consciousness, of the truths of an age.[11] That is soul truth 'wants to be embodied . . . as a personal reality in people' (Barreto, 2015, p. 16). To become modern adults, we must arrive at where we already are in a reflective way (Barreto, 2015, p. 17). That is the purpose of the discussion of the Man in the Street. In some way, he loudly broadcast the truth of where we already are, helping us know more about that, reflectively and consciously. Without such an authentic point of departure, there is no journey.

Tanaka's Empirical Observations

In his clinical studies, Yasuhiro Tanaka creatively and empirically grounds Giegerich's perspective, revealing our cultural situation in stark relief. Tanaka describes a contemporary phenomenon that he calls 'unborn-ness' (Tanaka, 2014). To move on from mere biological birth and become a psychical entity, an infant needs a frame of reference, a matrix of signification and a 'grammar' for articulating inner and outer experience. Perhaps due to cultural and historical changes and the consequent loss of guiding frameworks, Tanaka observes that psychological birth, the capacity for deeper reflection and soulfulness, has become only a distant possibility (Tanaka, 2014, pp. 6–8).

His studies of the patient population in Kyoto over many years reveal a steady diminishing of dissociation or inner conflict. In his view, this is due to a failure of development rather than repression. As a result, there has been an evident decline in the presence of an internal frame of reference or sense of what is going on inside the person (Tanaka, 2013, pp. 3–4; 2014, pp. 13–17). Shame, an important dimension of insidedness, is often lacking, and he speculates that this shift means that individuals increasingly lack the psychological infrastructure for classic analytic approaches (Tanaka, 2013, pp. 7–11).

One could view this as a consequence of the 'God is dead' phenomenon. Shame, as well as the shock of truth and temporality, is necessary to develop the capacity for psychological reflection. If there is a deficiency of a signifying structure, that is a lack of containment in family and culture, there can be no subsequent experience of leaving the Garden with all its tension, torment and psychological awakening.

Tanaka sees this state of unborn-ness as related to the autism spectrum disorder and feels that it may be a *Merkmal* of our times – a German word for an indicator that is a harbinger of the future (Tanaka, 2014, pp. 5–6). Psychoanalysis originated from the study of the dissociation of personality, that is the divided, hysterical selves that Janet and Charcot studied at the Salpêtrière in the 19th century. This sense of tormenting self-division motivated the kind of reflection that was at the core of clinical work from its beginnings (Ghazal & Hinton, 2016; Tanaka, 2008). Self-division evokes a sense of self that is other than itself and is therefore motivated to reflect on itself. Psychoanalytic thought and practice are based on this fertile ground of anxious self-doubt and self-reflection. However, in the case of a gross deficiency of self-structures, there is nothing to be divided, thus making the transference and dialogue difficult or impossible. Accordingly, for many patients, the classic psychoanalytic quest for truth may be inconceivable.

Tanaka quotes empirical studies of Japanese students over several decades that show an increasing shift from inner-focused anxieties accompanied by emotions, such as shame, towards complaints regarding the 'out there'. The students became increasingly more concrete in their thinking, with fewer psychological complaints that convey self-consciousness (Tanaka, 2013, p. 6). His work indicates a clear decline of inner structure over decades, along with related deficits in the experiences of shame, truth and temporality.

Similar to Giegerich, Tanaka's startling conclusion is, 'the 20th century, which was called 'the century of psychology', both temporally and psychologically, has already ended, and its process of decline . . . [can] easily be observed in the history of psychotherapy' (Tanaka, 2014, p. 3). He reflects on possible approaches to patients who lack psychological infrastructure, contending that the new approach will differ significantly from the more 'classical' forms. Indeed, he questions whether psychoanalysis will survive at all!

Conclusion

We no longer feel contained by a world soul. The thrust of temporality inexorably drives us towards an uncertain future, still haunted by historical traumas that we cannot assimilate. The ghosts of the past and the uncanny dimensions of the future, the strange new world to come, disrupt individuals and societies in multiple ways. This disruption makes us prone to raw emotions that strip us bare, and we feel increasing shame at the truth of our helplessness, or we flee into alarming, shameless acts of violence.

The encounter with the Man in the Street summarises some of the profound dilemmas we face. Similar to an Old Testament prophet, the Man in the Street provokes anguished speculations about shame, temporality and the raw truth of our times.

The works of Bion, Stiegler and Giegerich usefully amplify the dimensions and questions of our contemporary situation, and Tanaka's research provides an important empirical grounding.

One indeed wonders whether a deeper psychological birth is still possible in our time. Who are we? Where are we going? What are we? Is this the end of the human age, the end of the Anthropocene? Feeling naked and vulnerable as we face the unknown future, we mourn the loss of the comforting *anima mundi*.

Notes

1 'We must say that divine providence brought our world into being as a truly living thing, endowed with soul and intelligence. Let us lay it down that the world resembles more closely than anything else that Living Thing of which all other living things are parts, both individually and by kinds. For that Living Thing comprehends within itself all intelligible living things, just as our world is made up of us and all the other visible creatures. Since the god wanted nothing more than to make the world like the best of the intelligible things, complete in every way, he made it a single visible living thing, which contains within itself all the living things whose nature it is to share its kind' (Plato, 2000, p. 16).

2 'Variations of a scream run through life. We are that scream and much more. But when the smile comes, the scream does not stop. The smile that grows out of the scream is not the same as the seamless smile, one that makes us believe that no scream is there' (Eigen, 2005, p. 51).

3 Technological memory, or 'mnemotechnics', the exteriorisation of memory into technical objects and automation, the 'industrialisation of memory', has radically decreased the value of workers' *savoir faire*. This has contributed to a profound loss of a sense of individuation. They become more and more servants of the machine and subject to the spirit of calculation (Roberts, 2012). This contributes to the shame of being human, with a sense of deep discontent and a propensity for violence.

4 The emergence of endogenous attention, which comprises a rudimentary sense of temporality in infants, may create the scaffolding for more complex language

development (de Diego-Balanguer et al., 2016). One may speculate that this is related to the view of Stiegler and Leroi-Gourhan that the development of bi-pedal posture, freeing the hands for the use of tools and the mouth for speech, preceded and accelerated brain development in *Homo sapiens*. The discovery of *Homo naledi* in 2014 in South Africa, an ancestor from a million or more years ago with modern feet and evolving hands but a brain the size of an or-ange, lends credence to this theory (Shreeve, 2015). That is the emergence of technics, the use of tools and the anticipations of their future use over millennia stimulated the emergence of a larger brain with a capacity for temporality and also enabled a richer scaffolding for language (Stiegler, 1998, pp. 134–179).

5 The past is always alive, never completed. In this sense, it is like an ever-changing dance floor on which the dance of everyday life takes place. Perhaps this is most apparent when we view Palaeolithic cave art, which clearly reflects the 'dance floors' of ancient peoples, now largely indecipherable to us. Stiegler, in his rich development of Husserl's theory of memory, describes this phenom-enon with precision. He calls the intricate compositions of memory, perception and protension (anticipation) a kind of archi-cinema (Stiegler, 2014).

6 For Stiegler, technics refers to the technical domain or to technical practice as a whole. It includes things from primitive tools and weapons to systems of writing. It is the very condition of culture. It is necessary to distinguish this from technol-ogy or the technological. Technics indicates the basic human need for prosthetics, the fact that the human is not simply a biological being (Roberts, 2011).

Stiegler elaborates his point of view in a discussion on the fault of Epimetheus, the creator-god who forgot to save a special survival attribute for human beings when they were created. Prometheus, his brother, took pity on them and stole fire and other things from the gods and gave these to humans. In mythic form, this expresses Stiegler's view that humankind, from its begin-nings, was defined by the 'prosthetic' devices of technics. That is technics fills a basic default intrinsic to the human (Stiegler, 1998, pp. 85–203).

The control of fire was certainly a crucial human achievement, and with a bit of imagination, one could create a genealogy of the automobile as a fire chariot stemming from the evolution of the mastery of fire. Of course, technics clearly has a downside as well as an upside, considering its present-day effects on the natural and cultural historical environment. However, to understand technics, Stiegler feels that it is also essential to understand that humans and technics are, in a sense, one. That is technics is not something encrusted on human beings who had originally been in some paradisiacal 'state of nature' (Stiegler, 1998, pp. 82–133).

7 Reverie refers to a capacity to set aside everyday concerns of the ego and to tune in to the interiority of people and things. Within the psychoanalytic world, it is most frequently associated with the work of Wilfred Bion. It requires the capacity to set aside memory and desire, by which he meant a setting aside of fantasies of goals or affect-laden memories that would prejudice our thoughts or behaviour. It is related to the capacity of a mother to tune in to her infant.

8 I had extensive experience conducting verbal therapy with schizophrenic patients during the 1960s and 1970s. Don Jackson, who was trained by Sullivan, was an early supervisor at Stanford (Jackson, 1964). I heard R. D. Laing
speak in 1963 and was impressed by his work with psychotic patients at the
Tavistock Institute (Laing, 1960). During the 1960s and 1970s, I had extensive contact with John Weir Perry, a Jungian analyst who was a pioneer in
the understanding and treatment of psychotic patients (Perry, 1974). Most of
these experiences with psychotic patients involved little or no medication and
convinced me that psychotic communications have meanings that may be very
profound, both personally and culturally. During this period of my clinical
work, we often spoke about 'speaking schizophrenese'. This experience has
also made me more aware of the value of the insane parts of sane people over
the years (Hinton, 2007; Leader, 2012). Therefore, when I encountered the
Man in the Street, I was startled, but his language felt instinctively familiar to
me, and I did not have to contrive a reply. The words were there immediately,
without thought.

9 I am implying, of course, a dialectical shift in this everyday encounter in the
midst of life.

   In his essay on sublation, 'Conflict/Resolution', 'Opposites/Creative Union'
versus 'Dialectics and The Climb up the Slippery Slope', Giegerich beauti-
fully elaborates the process of dialectical movement and sublation. He makes
clear the difference between the concept of conflict resolution and a dialectical
movement to a different level, a *sublation*. With the former, the perspective
is exterior, while the dialectical view opens up the interiority of persons and
events (Giegerich, 2005).

10 Soul, for Giegerich, is a negative concept (Giegerich, 2012b, pp. 22–23 & 52–
56). I take this to indicate a quality in the object that exceeds any positivity.
This seems akin to Stiegler's description of Winnicott's transitional object as
that '[whose] virtue [is that] it does not exist', but is also what makes life worth
living. When that quality is not preserved by family and culture, the result is
symbolic misery (Stiegler, 2013b, pp. 1–5). There is no sense of the future.

   In a similar vein, Laplanche discusses an enigmatic quality of life that
hermeneutics endlessly attempts to translate but cannot reduce to positivity
(Laplanche, 1999, pp. 138–165). This quality is also highly temporal in its horizon. To quote Laplanche (1999, p. 224): 'the cultural [itself] is an address to
another who is out of reach, to others "scattered in the future" as the poet says',
and he further asks, 'why does the Dichter Dicht – why does the poet poetise –
except in response to an enigmatic other?' That is a crucial temporal element is
intrinsic to the experience of the enigmatic signifier or the transitional object. In
a similar fashion, Giegerich speaks of 'The Soul's Logical Life' as an historical
(i.e. temporal) process (Giegerich, 2001, pp. 76–78).

11 As an example *The Scream*, as well as other works by Edvard Munch, illustrates
the emergence of panic and agoraphobia in the late 19th century. In the great cities of Europe during the early 1870s, the terror of raw life emerged in the form of
agoraphobia and panic. The main symptoms were dizziness, buzzing in the ears,

dyspepsia, palpitations and a wax-like quality in the legs. The malady was viewed as generated by the draining chaos of crowds due to the increasing population of cities and the destruction of intimate containing plazas, along with the creation of vast circular spaces, such as the Place de la Concorde in Paris, which were bustling with traffic and the hubbub of pedestrians. One could easily become disoriented by the cacophony of sound and motion within these large, impersonal spaces.

The sufferer felt as a normal person would when looking down from atop Niagara Falls or when peering into a large abyss. This was an evolution of modernity and was the first time in the history of psychiatry that *anxiety* figured as a primary factor shaping the configuration of symptoms. It is not too far a reach to read this as a movement of the *opus magnum*, as Giegerich and Barreto discuss (Barreto, 2015; Ghazal & Hinton, 2016; Giegerich, 2001; Hinton, 2002).

References

Aron, L. & Starr, K. (2013). *A Psychotherapy for the People: Toward a Progressive Psychoanalysis*. New York: Routledge.

Barreto, M. H. (2015). *End of Man in the Modern Form of Consciousness*. Unpublished Paper, Faculdade Jesuíta de Filosofia e Teologia Belo Horizonte, Brazil.

Bewes, T. (2011). *The Event of Postcolonial Shame*. Princeton, NJ: Princeton University Press.

Bion, W. R. (1954). "Notes on a Theory of Schizophrenia." *International Journal of Psychoanalysis*, 35, 113–118.

Bion, W. R. (1967). *Second Thoughts: Selected Papers on Psycho-Analysis*. London: Heinemann.

Bion, W. R. (1973/1990). *Brazilian Lectures*. London: Karnac Books.

Casement, A. (2011). "The Interiorizing Movement of Logical Life: Reflections on Wolfgang Giegerich." *Journal of Analytical Psychology*, 56, 532–549. https://doi.org/10.1111/j.1468-5922.2010.01927.x.

Civitarese, G. (2010). "Nachträglichkeit." In *The Intimate Room: Theory and Technique of the Analytic Field* (pp. 96–108). New York: Routledge.

Civitarese, G. (2016). "Truth as Immediacy and Unison: A New Common Ground in Psychoanalysis? Commentary on Essays Addressing 'Is Truth Relevant?'" *The Psychoanalyltic Quarterly*, 88, 2, 449–501.

de Diego-Balaguer, R., Martinez-Alvarez, A. & Pons, F. (2016). "Temporal Attention as a Scaffold for Language Development." *Frontiers in Psychology*, 7, 44. https://doi.org/10.3389/fpsyg.2016.00044.

Eigen, M. (2005). *Emotional Storm*. Middletown, CT: Wesleyan University Press.

Freud, S. (1917/1955). "A Difficulty in the Path of Psychoanalysis." In *The Complete Psychological Works of Sigmund Freud* (Vol. 17, pp. 139–144). London: The Hogarth Press.

Ghazal, Y. A. & Hinton, D. E. (2016). "Platzschwindel, Agoraphobia, and Their Influence on Theories of Anxiety at the End of the Nineteenth Century: Theories of the Role of Biology and 'Representations' (Vorstellungen)." *History of Psychiatry*, 27, 4, 425–442.

Giegerich, W. (2001). *The Soul's Logical Life.* Frankfurt: Peter Lang Publishing House.

Giegerich, W. (2005). "'Conflict/Resolution', 'Opposites/Creative Union', Versus Dialectics, and the Climb up the Slippery Slope." In *Dialectics and Analytical Psychology: The El Capitan Canyon Seminar* (pp. 1–24). New Orleans, LA: Spring Journals.

Giegerich, W. (2007). *Technology and the Soul.* New Orleans, LA: Spring Publications.

Giegerich, W. (2008). *Soul Violence, Collected English Papers.* New Orleans, LA: Spring Journal Books.

Giegerich, W. (2012a). *Soul and World.* Paper Presented at the Meeting of the International Society for Psychology as the Discipline of Interiority, Berlin.

Giegerich, W. (2012b). *What Is Soul?* New Orleans, LA: Spring Journal Books.

Guignon, C. B. (1983). *Heidegger and the Problem of Knowledge.* Indianapolis, IN: Hackett Publishing.

Heidegger, M. (1956). *What is Philosophy?* Lanham, MD: Rowman & Littlefield.

Hinton, D. (2002). "Munch, Agoraphobia, and the Terrors of the Modernizing Urban Landscape." In L. J. Schmidt & B. Warner (Eds.), *Panic, Origins and Treatment* (pp. 229–252). Berkeley, CA: North Atlantic Books.

Hinton, L. (2007). "Black Holes, Uncanny Spaces and Radical Shifts in Awareness." *Journal of Analytical Psychology*, 52, 433–447. https://doi.org/10.1111/j.1468-5922.2007.00675.x.

Hinton, L. (2015). "Temporality and the Torments of Time." *Journal of Analytical Psychology*, 60, 353–370. https://doi.org/10.1111/1468-5922.12155.

Hinton, L. III, Hinton, L. IV, Hinton, D. & Hinton, A. (2011). "Panel: Unus Mundus – Transcendent Truth or Comforting Fiction? Overwhelm and the Search for Meaning in a Fragmented World." *Journal of Analytical Psychology*, 56, 375–396.

Hoy, D. C. (2012). *The Time of Our Lives: A Critical History of Temporality.* Boston, MA: MIT Press.

Hultberg, P. (1986). "Shame: An Overshadowed Emotion." In M. A. Mattoon (Ed.), *The Archetype of Shadow in a Split World.* Zurich: Daimon Publications.

Jackson, D. (1964). *Myths of Mindness: New Facts for Old Fallacies.* New York: Macmillan Publishing.

Johnston, A. (2005). *Time Driven: Metapsychology and the Splitting of the Drive.* Evanston, IL: Northwestern University Press.

Jung, C. G. (1970). *Mysterium Coniunctionis.* Trans. R. F. C. Hull. Princeton, NJ: Princeton University Press.

Laing, R. D. (1960). *The Divided Self: An Existential Study in Sanity and Madness.* Harinondsworth: Penguin.

Laplanche, J. (1999). *Essays on Otherness.* New York: Routledge.

Leader, D. (2012). *What Is Madness?* London: Penguin Books.

Morrison, A. P. (1989). *Shame: The Underside of Narcissism.* Hillsdale: The Analytic Press.

Perry, J. W. (1974). *The Far Side of Madness.* Upper Saddle River, NJ: Prentice Hall.

Plato. (2000). *Timaeus*. Trans. Donald J. Zeyl. Indianapolis, IN: Hackett Publishing Company.

Rhode, E. (1998). *On Hallucination, Intuition, and the Becoming of "O"*. Binghampton, NY: ESF Publishers.

Roberts, B. (2012). "Technics, Individuation and Tertiary Memory: Bernard Stiegler's Challenge to Media Theory." *New Formations*, 77, 8–20. https://doi.org/10.3898/NEWF.77.01.2012.

Ross, D. (2006). "Democracy, Authority, Narcissism: From Agamben to Stiegler." *Contretemps*, 6, 74–85.

Ross, D. (2016). "The Question Concerning the Anthropocene: Yachay Tech." www.academia.edu/22810427/The_Question_Concerning_the_Anthropocene.

Scarfone, D. (2006). "A Matter of Time: Actual Time and the Production of the Past." *Psychoanalytic Quarterly*, 75, 807–834. https://doi.org/10.1002/j.2167-4086.2006. ib00058.x.

Seidler, G. H. (2000). *In Others' Eyes: An Analysis of Shame*. Madison, CT: International Universities Press.

Shreeve, J. (2015, September 10). "This face changes the human story. But how? Photographs by Robert Clark." *National Geographic*. Retrieved from http://news. nationalgeographic.com/2015/09/150910-human-evolution-change.

Stiegler, B. (1998). *Technics and Time*. Vol. 1: *The Fault of Epimetheus*. Palo Alto, CA: Stanford University Press.

Stiegler, B. (2008). *Technics anal Time*. Vol. 2: *Disorientation*. Palo Alto, CA: Stanford University Press.

Stiegler, B. (2013a). *Uncontrollable Societies of Disaffected Individuals: Disbelief and Discredit*. Vol. 2. Malden, MA: Polity Press.

Stiegler, B. (2013b). *What Makes Life Worth Living: On Pharmacology*. Trans. D. Ross. Malden, MA: Polity Press.

Stiegler, B. (2014). "Organology of Dreams and Archi-Cinema." *Nordic Journal of Aesthetics*, 47, 7–37.

Sznycer, D., Tooby, J., Cosmides, L., Porat, R., Shalvi, S. & Halperin, E. (2016). "Shame Closely Tracks the Threat of Devaluation by Others, Even across Cultures." *Proceedings of the National Academy of Sciences of the United States of America*, 113, 2625–2630. https://doi.org/10.1073/pnas.1514699113.

Tanaka, Y. (2008). "On Dissociation as a Psychological Phenomenon." *Psychologia*, 51, 239–257. https://doi.org/10.2117/psysoc.2008.239.

Tanaka, Y. (2013). *Anthropophobia: An Old and Typical Japanese Neurosis, Its Conceptual Transition and Clinical Disappearance*. Paper Presented at the International Jungian Conference, Taipei.

Tanaka, Y. (2014). *What is Born in the Analytic Practice for Patients with the Problem of 'Un-born-ness'?* Paper Presented at the 2014 Conference of the Journal of Analytical Psychology, Berlin.

Tracy, J. L. & Matsumoto, D. (2008). The Spontaneous Expression of Pride and Shame: Evidence for Biologically Innate Nonverbal Displays." *Proceedings of the*

National Academy of Sciences of the United States of America, 105, 11655–11660. https://doi.org/10.1073/pnas.0802686105.

Virilio, P. (2003). *Unknown Quantity*. New York: Thames & Hudson.

Whan, M. (2015, April). "The Logic of Image: Simulating 'Mythic Image'." In Anselm Kiefer's 'Parsifal II': *The International Society for Psychology as the Discipline of Interiority Newsletter*. Retrieved from http://ispdi.org/index.php/en/newsletter/ispdi-newsletter-april-2015.

Chapter 13

Jung, Time and Ethics*

Introduction and Genealogy

The connection of time and ethics is ancient but not familiar to most contemporary thinkers. A reflection on Jung and time and ethics is even less
common. I will begin with some perspectives on temporality in order to ori-
ent the reader and then focus on Jung's theories in that context. I will begin
in our beginnings, with a brief genealogy of temporality and the emergence
of the human.

It is temporality that most clearly distinguishes *Homo sapiens* from the
higher primates. Leroi-Gourhan points out that the great break between our
human ancestors and other mammals came with bipedalism – erect posture (Audouze, 2002, p. 298). This freed the hand and mouth, and opened
room in the braincase for more complex motor structures, including areas
involving language and memory. Recent studies have shown the crucial
importance of diet in the increase of hominids' brain size. Bipedal posture
and tools and weapons facilitated a richer, meatier diet that stimulated brain
development (DeCasien et al., 2017).

Bernard Stiegler describes technics as a process of *exteriorisation*: the
pursuit of life by means other than pure biological life (Stiegler, 1998,
pp. 16–17).[1] *Anticipation* and the stimulation of foresight are embodied by
tools, which function like mirrors of memory. Stiegler asserts that the relation of being and time only developed within the horizon of technics (Stiegler, 1998, pp. 134–135). 'Internal' and 'external' were comingled from the
beginning of culture.

The first clear sign of awareness of temporality was the appearance of
intentional burial practice in the Middle Palaeolithic (Lieberman, 1991,

* Hinton, L. (2019). Jung, Time and Ethics. In: Jon Mils (ed.). *Jung and Philosophy*. London: Routledge. Reprinted by permission of the publisher (Taylor & Francis Ltd, http://www.tandfonline.com).

DOI: 10.4324/9781003641063-14

pp. 162–164). The corpses were coated with red ochre, which was strongly connected with pregnancy in the later cave art. The trauma and mystery of death and the hope for a future were evident.

Cave art began to appear around 40,000 BC. It was clear that there was a *future* expectation of return to the scene for rituals of some kind – clearly a horizon of temporality. In that sense, creative imagination was directed towards an unknown future, employing a potent collaboration of tools and images. Technology and cave art were highly interrelated. The various pigments, the lamps and torches used for working deep into caves and the technique used by the artists showed a sophistication that would have taken a long time to develop – gifts and memories from an unknown past of unknown ancestors.

Time and space are crucial to the organisation of who we are (Blommaert & De Fina, 2016, p. 1). Culture stems largely from the awareness of future times with all their possible dangers and opportunities, along with the need for creating provisions for the safety and well-being of the group. It is difficult to know when spoken language developed, but written language developed during the Neolithic period of settled farming around 8,000 years ago. A form of exteriorised memory emerged for cataloguing stored items and then expanded. This was a mode of taking care of the future, of planning for a rainy day! Written memory was basic in cultural development, and our growing dependence on technology for memory is part of the crisis of our times (Audouze, 2002, p. 293).

Developmental psychology lends credence to a view that time sense is basic to both speech and interpersonal memory. The development of speech may be dependent on the emergence of a rudimentary temporal sense (Diego-Balaguer et al., 2016). In addition, it has been consistently found that the capacity to retain past events as interpersonal and specifically temporal seems to emerge around 4–5 years of age. Before that consciousness is mainly spatial (Tulving, 2005, p. 32).

An increasing capacity to remember interpersonal events is crucial to the development of ethical awareness – the effect of our actions upon others, the capacity to recall and take responsibility for what we have done and how we have been – our traumas and triumphs. One would assume that this developed on the grounds of preexisting practical habits of care and survival, such as one sees in other animal species that lack a developed sense of time (Cortina, 2017).

After a slow development over 2–3 million years, there was a profound acceleration of culture and technics in the Upper Palaeolithic. It is important to note that *technics evolves more quickly than culture* (Stiegler, 1998, p. 15). Upon such a basis, Stiegler has developed a theory of *epiphylogenesis*, which is the idea that increasing retention of the past by means of early technics had the effect of strongly accelerating the process of technological and cultural evolution. That is such 'retentions' became, in turn, a reflexive stimulus for evolution, constituting a dramatic break from the simpler manifestations of mere biological and cultural evolution (Stiegler, 1998, pp. 139–140 & 175–177).

Both neuroscience and psychoanalysis have demonstrated the constant augmentations and revisions of memory that are part of expanding human identity (Edelman, 2005, p. 99; Green, 2017, pp. 77–82). A sense of conscience, of debt to unknown ancestors, is part of the human condition, a part of our thrownness into the world (Stiegler, 1998, pp. 258–259). We emerge into the world in debt to those on whose shoulders we ride. This contributes to a sense of care for our world, the basic ethical stance for being-in-the-world (Stiegler, 1998, pp. 46–47; Heidegger, 1967, p. 274). If we evade our debt to our ancient heritage, we suffer the fate of Narcissus, who could only survive if he never knew himself, only took from life and never immersed himself in time, never accumulated memories. He could only be echoed in the present.

Phronesis: The Ethic of 'Practical Wisdom'

In this reflection on Jung and ethics, I will favour the lens of 'virtue ethics', an approach that emphasises personal character and that tends to become more apparent with time (Hursthouse & Pettigrove, 2016).[2]

The most common way that one falls short of virtue is through lacking *phronesis*, or practical judgment (Colman, 2013). One may reflect on Jung's life and ideas in multiple ways, and those ways often seem contradictory. However, the practical effect he had on people's lives, and the inspiration he provided for both individuals and the broader culture, make his life and ethos significant. Early on, he advocated immersion in experience along with a deeply ethical dedication to the quest for consciousness, and he maintained that stance throughout his life. A temporal perspective is most useful in reflecting upon how all the dimensions of his ethos emerged.

For Plato, speaking through the words of Socrates, it often comes across that, to live well ethically, one should base one's decisions on *epistêmê*, or 'scientific' knowledge, grounding one's actions on an intellectual grasp of the Idea of the Good itself (Kirkland, 2007, p. 127). This provoked Aristotle to bring a charge of intellectualism against Platonic ethics (Kirkland, 2007, p. 127). The implication of that approach to ethics could be a preference for the Good above existence itself, including the life of the body; at the extreme, one could see that as an apprenticeship for death (Goodchild, 2010, p. 24)! Aristotle attacks not only Plato's view of the role of the abstract and general idea of the Good but also what he sees as an attempt to ground ethical judgment solely in *epistêmê*. He systematically distinguishes the *practical* region of human understanding from the *theoretical*.

According to Aristotle, character, not intellect, is the core of ethical virtue. It is a matter of prudence or practical wisdom, not knowledge (*epistêmê*), for it is concerned with the particular, the singular character of the thing having to be done in any situation. In contemporary terms, one would say that the life of the mind and body escapes representation (Goodchild, 2010, p. 25). For Aristotle, *epistêmê* is a way of conceiving universals – *absolutes that are actually everywhere and always the same*, and thus atemporal (Kirkland, 2007, p. 128). He tells us that *phronesis* attends principally to the particular available means, which are *within time*, the basis being provided by the agent's quality of character. Phronesis derives its enigmatic power from its complete immersion in time, in the past, present and future (Kirkland, 2007, p. 130). This complexity lends a basic imprecision to ethics.

In the ethical context, Aristotle asserts, one must look to the *kairos*, 'the right or opportune moment'. This is *the good that manifests in time*. However, the *kairos* in any situation cannot be judged with absolute precision because it reflects the desire to bring about this or that result *in the future*. However, the future is hidden from us.

> *Phronesis* must therefore be understood as a power by which one looks properly toward *what does not appear*, toward what remains hidden because [it is] in the future, and makes good ethical decisions precisely by doing so.
>
> (Kirkland, 2007, p. 131)

Ethics and life itself both have a strongly future-oriented quality.

Temporality is a kind of intrinsic limitation, emphasising the finitude of ethical judgment, situated between a past that can never be totally known and a future that can't be predicted. That is one cannot overcome these temporal limits because we must acknowledge that *phronesis* is bound both to a particular past and particular future possibilities that we can only partly know (Kirkland, 2007, p. 134).

Deliberation with others is crucial in the process of 'looking to the *kairos*'. Thinking in itself is a virtuous act, in Aristotle's view (Goodchild, 2010, p. 30). This process would be endless, except that *kairos* appears in a fleeting moment that cannot be anticipated, but when action must be taken. To await that moment requires courage (Kirkland, 2007, p. 136). One could, with Deleuze, call this a 'transcendence in immanence' or a kind of 'transcendental empiricism' (Smith, 2012, p. 153). To attain the necessary virtue requires grounding in everyday life (Kirkland, 2007, p. 137).

On the one hand, *Phronesis* seems to describe an intensely dialogical process, and that is sometimes present in Jung's approach. On the other hand, he often seems to value *epistêmê*, the archetype or archetypal. Sometimes that attitude is pronounced and comes across in an authoritative pronouncement of 'truth', the archetype as 'truth', in contrast to the murkiness of everyday life. Jung had a great curiosity about ideas and cultures, and he often conveyed a generous and dialogical spirit. That seemed to increase with age, as manifested in his interest in alchemy. This dichotomy in his thinking between *epistêmê* as archetype and *phronesis* with its richly dialogical spirit can be confusing, and this confusion often seems to derail Jungian discourse and its underlying ethos.

The Emergence of Jung's Ethical Orientation

Given the above contexts, I want to focus more specifically on some dimensions of the ethical perspective that the human being, Carl Gustav Jung, developed within his own time, experience and reflection. I will provide some lengthy quotes because I think that is crucial in gaining a real sense of his presence and ideas. From early on in his career, he foregrounded the 'moral factor' in his thought, and that strongly differentiated his approach from Freud's. In fact, he held that the moral factor was innate (Merkur, 2017, p. 17). Whatever Jung's vicissitudes, his commitment to self-understanding was profoundly ethical, and one could call it religious in the broader sense of the word (Barreto, 2013). He was determined to live and to think about his experience.

In 1910, the 35-year-old Jung wrote a letter to Freud, expounding critically about the possibility of supporting a new 'International Fraternity for Ethics and Culture' (Jung, 1973, pp. 17–18):

I cannot muster a grain of courage to promote ethics in public, let alone from the psychoanalytic standpoint! At present, I am sitting so

precariously on the fence between the Dionysian and the Apollonian . . .
The ethical problem of sexual freedom really is enormous and worth
the sweat of all noble souls. But 2000 years of Christianity have to be
replaced by something equivalent. An ethical fraternity, with its mythical Nothing, not infused by any archaic-infantile driving force, is a pure
vacuum and can never evoke in man the slightest trace of that age-old
animal power that drives the migrating bird across the sea . . . I think
we must give it time to infiltrate into people from many centers . . . ever
so gently to transform Christ back into the soothsaying god of the vine,
which he was, and in this way absorb those ecstatic, instinctual forces
of Christianity for the *one* purpose of making the cult and sacred myth
what they once were – a drunken feast of joy where man regained the
ethos and holiness of an animal. That indeed was the beauty and purpose
of classical religion, which from God knows what temporary biological
needs has turned into a Misery Institute! Yet how infinitely much rapture
and wantonness lie dormant in our religion, waiting to be led back to
their true destination!

Just prior to the time of this youthful, exuberant, iconoclastic letter, Jung
had been involved in a 'mutual analysis' with Otto Gross, a creative and
troubled pioneer in psychoanalysis who was an admirer of both Nietzsche
and Freud. He was an advocate of 'free love' and felt that psychological
problems were due to sexual repression. At times, Jung referred to Gross as
his 'twin brother' (Heuer, 2001). This early letter is an example of Jung's
experimental attitude towards life and practice as a young analyst. It was
also a precursor to his later involvement with female patients.

Fifty years later, a young student studied the letter to Freud and wrote to
Jung, questioning him about his remarks. Jung reflected (Jung, 1973, p. 19):

Best thanks for the quotation from that accursed correspondence. For me
it is an unfortunately inexpungable reminder of the incredible folly that
filled the days of my youth. The journey from cloud-cuckoo land back to
reality lasted a long time. In my case, Pilgrim's Progress consisted in my
having to climb down a thousand ladders until I could reach out my hand
to the little clod of earth that I am.

There are many things one could consider here about this thoughtful and
honest reply, but the crucial thing to me is the ethical perspective gained

through time and memory, 'The better part of a lifetime'. The profound subjective tension with which Jung had lived, and his fierce commitment to reflect and create amidst that turbulence, was remarkable. Whatever his vicissitudes, a sense of ethical commitment to consciousness seemed to always be there: 'where Kant insists on the consciousness of duty, Jung emphasises rather the duty to be conscious' (Colacicchi, 2015, p. 43).

Jung's 'Seven Sermons' and Temporality

I will now focus on some of the specific fluctuations and evolutions of Jung's ideas over a broad length of time, the process that emerged in the decades between his sojourn in 'cloud-cuckoo land' and the moving letter he wrote towards the end of his life, embracing that 'clod of earth' that he was.

Jung himself did not construct a focused analysis of temporality, but Angeliki Yiassemides (2014) has written a valuable elaboration of his views, employing the text, *Septem Sermones Ad Mortuos* (The Seven Sermons to the Dead). This was a philosophical poem written in 1916, but not published until 1961, when it appeared as an appendix to some editions of *Memories, Dreams, Reflections* (Jung, 1963, pp. 378–390). It was later found in the closing pages of *The Red Book* and was the only part of that work published during Jung's lifetime. He employs several voices in this work, and they can seem a bit strange and esoteric if you are not accustomed to that mode of expression. I will use them because it seems important to capture the intensity and uncanniness of his process.

In the *Seven Sermons*, the Gnostic 'Basilides' is the narrative voice of the poem. The distinction between 'Pleroma' and 'Creatura' is a core element of the text. Pleroma indicates the totality of the divine, a *timeless* dimension which cannot be grasped by humans, whereas Creatura is the realm of the human (Yiassemides, 2014, p. 6). Creatura has qualities and is subject to change, whereas in Pleroma there are no distinctions; that is Creatura is *embedded in temporality*.

This is the first emergence of the temporal perspective in Jung's work (Yiassemides, 2014, p. 10). A division, more like a chasm, lies between time and timelessness. According to the text, Creatura foments differentiation in the universe by projecting its (temporal) inner reality on (timeless) Pleroma. One can see how this sets the stage for the development of Jung's major ideas. There are hints of the Kantian division of phenomenon and noumenon, or Platonic Ideas versus being a prisoner in the Cave (Plato, 380 B.C./1992, paras. 514–541).

It would seem that the Pleroma was later expressed by the idea of the Self, or more abstractly, even metaphysically, as the Unus Mundus, whereas Creatura encompassed everyday, time-bound consciousness, ego, etc. (Yiassemides, 2014, p. 10). In Yiassemides' view, 'Jung provided a detailed account regarding the process by which the differentiated ego strives to *return to the original wholeness of psychic reality*' (Yiassemides, 2014, p. 10, italics added). This 'original wholeness' was timeless. Creatura must accept its time-bound nature and, in addition, seek 'participation in the . . . eternal reality of the universe' and 'return to [its] true nature' (Yiassemides, 2014, p. 10). This is a process of individuation, seen as the *interplay of time and timelessness*. In this view, there is an Eternal, timeless ground to which Creatura may return: an ultimate, underlying foundation. In the view of Barreto (2014), such vestiges of timeless bastions ultimately undermined the integrity of Jung's process, as well as analytical psychology in general, because such bastions constitute a means of 'escape' from an ultimate kenosis, a deeply dialectical emptying that could lead to a new level of life.

Another Gnostic entity named 'Abraxas' appears later in the poem. This is 'The deity that rules over the totality of time and in whose power time is both made and unmade' and is thus

> the sum of and the liberator from the cycle of necessity, freeing man from the cycle of time and in whose power time is made and unmade . . . freeing man from the cycle of necessity . . . [Abraxas] is the eternally available timeless moment, the eternal now . . . which brings freedom from time in both its linear and its cyclic aspects. That is, for the Gnostics, the ultimate goal is the return to the Pleromatic state, which is timeless. '*The object of salvation is to deliver us from the lie of time.*'
>
> (Yiassemides, 2014, p. 11, italics added)

In this view, liberation from time is a repeatable event in the present.

The atemporal and eternal power of Abraxas is the key to the soul's deliverance, which can be obtained repetitively at the present moment. This seems to imply that the 'atemporal' can dominate the flow of temporality: *When time is tamed and subdued*, psychic salvation is attainable.

(Yiassemides, 2014, p. 11, italics added)

This privileging of the 'timeless' had a powerful effect on Jung's theorising, especially during the middle period of his life. The 'personal unconscious' became a lesser thing, deserving only moderate interest that Jung often looked upon with a somewhat condescending tone. He often mentioned disparagingly that Freud and Freudians found their meaning only in the everyday and in the personal past. When the ground of existence is timeless, everyday life – the personal unconscious – comes across as inferior, as opposed to the 'eternal' archetypes or the collective unconscious. Strangely, there are only two chapters in the *Journal of Analytical Psychology* that seem to specifically address this question, although it is touched upon throughout the Jungian literature (Williams, 1953; Zinkin, 1979). The most common Jungian theorising has concerned various relationships, dimensions and manifestations of archetypes, or the adoption of an object-relations perspective that largely bypasses these issues.

Wolfgang Giegerich and Michael Whan speak of the Jungian focus on myth and symbol as the 'Neurosis of Psychology' (Giegerich, 2005, pp. 1–17; Whan, 2015, pp. 3–7; 2017, pp. 242–260). They hold that the myths of the past are largely dead, while pointing out that Jung wanted to 're-mythologise' the world, and that many Jungians still have hope for a return to a mythical, timeless place. However, they see this desire to reverse history creates a neurosis of its own, due to the strain of sustaining a simulated reality. Ascribing this simulation to a defensive denial, Giegerich says that our childish dependency on dead myths must die for us to be fully present in the everyday, to have a kenotic attitude, an openness to the temporal processes of our own times – as opposed to a defensive quest to recreate the past, to escape, like a child wanting to return to a fantasy of eternal delight (Giegerich, 1986/2008; Mogenson, 2010).

The tormenting richness of our everyday trauma and turmoil, the endless process of elaborating the enigmatic core of our memories through *Nachträglichkeit*, tends to get lost in an assumed teleology that privileges the timeless as the goal. A more complex view of temporality is required:

> The past is not the passive container of things bygone. The past, indeed, is our very being, and it can stay alive and evolve; the present is the passage where the retranscription and recontextualization of our past continually occur, in line with Freud's (1895) concept of *Nachträglichkeit*.[3]
>
> (Scarfone, 2006, p. 814)

It is memory and reflection on the past that make ethical reflection possible. Jung's memories of being in 'cloud-cuckoo land' had enabled him to reflect in depth on his past and reply so authentically to the student who wrote to him. It is reflection upon what we have done, and what we have thought, that provokes ethical awareness. The past is not static and does not imply a reductionistic approach to the psyche. It lies at the heart of ethical awareness. If clinical work has ethics at its core, as Jung was wont to say, then the past is also at the core – and not 'archetypal' potentials.

This contradiction pervades much of Jung's writing but evolves somewhat after he became involved in alchemy, which seems to privilege process more than concept. In some respects, he begins to more closely approach the mode of *phronesis*, a processual view that seems closer to phenomenology. This process may begin with the most basic primal stuff (*prima materia*) of life: excrement (Jung, 1956, para. 276.)!

The Personal Unconscious and the Collective Unconscious

Warren Colman powerfully and critically describes the impact of Jung's disownment of everyday reality and temporality as a Kantian/Cartesian view of a mind '"shut up in its own sphere", apart from the living world' (Colman, 2017, p. 36). What was left to Jungian psychology was a view of the world

> as the expression of archetypal forces, somehow apart from the realities of geography, climate, competition for resources, and social and political conflict . . . [that] not only fails to address the complex interrelation between states of mind and the state of the social world but reduces the latter to a kind of ghost-life as if it is merely a screen for psychic projections.
>
> (Colman, 2017, p. 37)

In a convincing way, Colman's ethical purview of Jung's theory describes how privileging a set of 'archetypes' that seem 'inner', and are 'timeless', can deeply undermine ethical concerns about everyday human needs and activities, as well as larger temporal/historical/cultural contexts and events. Exposition of alchemical process still retains some sense of a mind isolated in its own subjectivity, as Colman elaborates.

To elaborate upon these thoughts, reviewing some of Jung's specific remarks about time and the 'timeless' is very useful. In speaking about the progression of a case, Jung describes the emergence of a 'transpersonal control point' (Jung, 1966, paras. 216–217):

> I saw how the transpersonal control-point developed – I cannot call it anything else – *a guiding function* (sic) and step by step gathered to itself all the formal personal overvaluations; how, with this afflux of energy, it gained influence over the resisting conscious mind without the patient's consciously noticing what was happening. From this I realised that the dreams were not just fantasies, but self-representations of unconscious developments which allowed the psyche of the patient gradually to grow out of a *pointless personal tie* (italics added).[4]
>
> This change took place, as I showed, through the unconscious development of a transpersonal control point; a virtual goal, as it were, that expressed itself symbolically in a form that can only be described as a vision of God.

What is notable to me here is how quickly Jung attributes 'guidance' or change to the transpersonal. The personal is deemed 'pointless', and any meaningful subjective fantasies are deemed self-representations of 'deeper' unconscious developments, via the 'transcendent function', 'the Self' or 'God'.

That perspective would seem to undermine a sense of ethical agency or personal responsibility, of change born from the sweat and toil of everyday life. It is as if only something 'special' can save us, and that is a preexisting religious or transpersonal factor, not immanent in the everyday.

Later, he gives a similar description of psychological life (Jung, 1944/1968, paras. 329–330):

> we are dealing here with an a priori 'type,' an archetype which is inherent in the collective unconscious and thus *beyond individual birth and death. The archetype is, so to speak, an 'eternal' presence, and the only question is whether it is perceived by the conscious mind or not* . . . the increase in the clarity and frequency of the mandala motif is due to a more accurate *description of an already existing 'type', rather than that it is generated in the course of a dream series.* In practice . . . it is met with in distinct form in a few cases, though this does not prevent it from functioning *as a concealed pole around which everything else revolves* (italics added).

Again, the 'archetype' is behind the scenes at all times, seemingly directing the action. It is 'eternal', that is timeless, not 'generated' from experience, but on a different plane from temporality and the everyday. It does not seem too much of a leap to imply, with regard to ethical perspectives, that 'the archetype did it'. This would seem to reflect and even encourage an abdication of personal responsibility.

Jung mentions an affinity for Platonic ideas (*epistêmê*) in other writings (Jung, 1960, paras. 274–275):

> Just as it may be asked whether man possesses many instincts or only a few, so we must also raise the still unbroached question of whether he possesses many or a few primordial forms, or archetypes, of psychic reaction . . . In Plato, however, an extraordinarily high value is set on the archetypes as metaphysical ideas, as 'paradigms' or models, while real things are held to be only copies of these model ideas . . . St. Augustine, from whom I have borrowed the idea of the archetype . . . still stands on a Platonic footing in that respect.

Here, Jung references archetypes as resembling Platonic entities, leaving 'real things' as only copies, or perhaps simulacra (Whan, 2015). These seem set apart from time and *phronesis*. The 'personal unconscious', the everyday, our temporal life, is then only a copy of these eternal forms. Archetypes begin to sound almost classificatory, like a mythological version of *Psychological Types* (Jung, 1936).

Further (Jung, 1959, paras. 3–5):

> *A more or less superficial layer of the unconscious* is undoubtedly personal. I call it the *personal unconscious* . . . But this personal unconscious rests upon a deeper layer, *which does not derive from personal experience but is inborn*. I call this the *collective unconscious* . . . 'Archetype' *is an explanatory paraphrase* of the Platonic *eidos* . . . it tells us that so far as the collective contents are concerned we are dealing with archaic or – I would say – primordial types, that is, with *universal images that have existed since remotest times* (italics added).

The reference to Plato is repeated, and the 'personal unconscious' is obviously viewed as inferior by comparison (see pages 5–6 of this writing). That would seem to be the position of the inmates of Plato's Cave! Archetypes are the 'deeper' part of psychological life. Again, the real action is not in the realm of personal experience.

And, finally (Jung, 1968, para. 81): 'This "personal unconscious" must always be dealt with first, that is, made conscious, otherwise the gateway to the collective unconscious cannot be opened'. Here, the 'personal unconscious' is an apprentice piece at best, only a preliminary gateway on the path to the 'real stuff' behind the scenes. Everyday life, to repeat Colman's rich description, becomes a sort of ghostly presence, an inferior sort of reality. From this perspective, *temporality*, the realm of the human, pales in comparison to the timeless archetypal dimension. The everyday world of temporality, in its messy fascination, its wars and its loves and hates, is not the true scene of action. This negates the ethical point of view.

Jung sometimes discussed archetypes as hypothetical, 'irrepresentable' factors that were also, perhaps, elements of brain structure (Jung, 1960, para. 29). However, many of his pronouncements carried the ring of an authority that 'knew' when those elements were present in psychological life. A notable – and regrettable – instance of this attitude was his essay, 'Wotan', published in 1936. In this essay, he portrayed the phenomenon of Nazism as a manifestation of the 'Wotan archetype' (Jung, 1936, paras. 385 & 389). This seems to undermine consideration of real-time historical events and responsibilities (Colman, 2017, p. 36). His views appear especially poignant in the face of the sufferings that the Nazis were, as Jung to some degree notes, already inflicting on Jews and other minorities in nearby Germany. Even more alarmingly, he also stated that those evil excesses, though dangerous and regrettable, might actually represent a *reculer pour mieux sauter*, a sort of cultural regression in the service of cultural evolution.

I don't think that Jung was a Nazi sympathiser, but I do believe that 'archetypal' thinking can at times result in a dulling of ethical vision. How can an 'archetype' express the reality of a concentration camp? Such a view all too easily serves as a lofty resistance to the very necessary 'thick description' of the brute reality of personal and historical suffering – the torments of everyday life, whatever the setting (Hinton, 2015, 2016).

Oedipus and Time

Sophocles' *Oedipus Rex*, probably the best-known story in the psychoanalytic world, is a moving and multidimensional depiction of the connection between ethical awareness and time. John Manoussakis (2017) has written a thought-provoking set of reflections on Oedipus (see pp. 68–75). In his view, ethical stories are clearly based on the intricacies of time, but he points out that, in most discussions, interpretations are modified to sound as if they are simple before-and-after events. The substance of the everyday is redacted. Manoussakis' perspective on Oedipus reveals the many layers of ethical situations that require time to unfold, time for the reflection on the past that is necessary in revealing their truth.

In the opening of the play, there is an awful plague affecting the city of Thebes, where Oedipus has become the ruler. Sophocles implies that it is a political disease, a moral disease. Something is rotten in the city of Thebes. The city is sick, and the spectator of the play knows that, beneath appearances, Oedipus is also sick. The devastating crisis is the result of a history of multiple expulsions of otherness, of enigma: first, Oedipus himself as an infant, due to the dire prophecy that he will murder his father and marry his mother, his accidental killing of his father and finally the expulsion of the Sphinx through Oedipus' clever use of reason. Oedipus strongly identifies with his role as the man who vanquished the Sphinx and had thereby become the ruler of the city. He publicly preens himself for his exploit.

Very insightfully, Jung pointed out in 1916 (Jung, 1956, para. 264), 'Little did he know that the riddle of the Sphinx can never be solved directly by the wit of man'. However, he then seems to adopt a rationalistic view of Oedipus' dilemma.[5] Jung speculates that, '*those tragic consequences . . . could easily have been avoided* if only Oedipus had been sufficiently intimidated by the frightening appearance of the "terrible" or "devouring" Mother whom the Sphinx personified' (Jung, 1956, p. 181, italics added). He discusses the symbolism of the Sphinx, usefully differentiating his own theories from what he saw as Freud's emphasis on the narrower dimensions of sexuality and the incest taboo (Jung, 1961, para. 565).

In 1958, Jung returned to the question of the Sphinx, pointing out that

> Oedipus did not use his intelligence to see through the uncanny nature of this childishly simple and all too facile riddle, and therefore fell victim to his tragic fate, because he felt he had answered the question. It was the Sphinx itself that he ought to have answered and not its façade.
>
> (Jung, 1936, para. 714)

This was a profound insight into the enigma of the Sphinx, but he then proceeds to connect it to the 'anima', a 'mediatrix between the unconscious and the conscious'. The goal of justifying his theory overrides the raw truth and necessity of the process of time and the humility of realising that hindsight is not foresight. There is even a hint of arrogance in Jung's depiction when he criticises Oedipus' naïveté vis-à-vis the Sphinx. As is so common with Jung, he describes an enigmatic dimension of life but then obscures its impact with a profusion of amplifications, which seems to privilege 'knowing'.[6]

To continue the story: Oedipus had ostensibly liberated the city from the Sphinx's enigmatic presence, from her otherness. This is ironic because he had himself been a terrifying enigma that had to be extruded from the city because of the dire prophecy that he would kill his father and marry his mother. He had been put out to die as an infant – but he only comes to know that with time. The expulsion of otherness, out of fear of chaos, dominated the history of Thebes. Typically fearing instability, the chorus begs Oedipus, their ruler, to always remain the same, apart from time and change.

Clinging to recurring sameness, otherness is excluded, and there is no diachrony that could disrupt but renew life. Within synchrony, time does not flow – there is stagnation and pollution in the form of a plague. Ethical taint creates a mood of miasma. The past cannot be past without truth and reflection. As a result, there is only a recurring present, and a mood of monotonous, deathlike synchrony pervades the city.[7]

The Sphinx, in her enigmatic presence, had been a reminder of the uncanny nature of transitions, which usually involve acknowledgment of primal loss as well as new and unknown horizons. What is crucial for the Oedipal drama is ethical re-reflection on the past that is not past, that has remained an 'Unpast' polluting the present and future (Scarfone, 2006, pp. 807–834).[8] Vanquishing the Sphinx's enigmatic reality resulted, paradoxically, in the re-emergence of the massive, unacknowledged 'dim past' of Oedipus and Thebes in the form of a plague, mightily disrupting and terrifying the city (Manoussakis, 2017, p. 71).

The sage, Teresias, enters the stage exactly where Oedipus will later exit it. He is blind, led by a child and knows the truth. As this thread to the future appears, Oedipus asks the terrifying question about his past and about his parentage: 'Who are my parents?' Tiresias answers, 'This day shall be your parent and your destroyer' (Sophocles, 429 B.C./1994, p. 367). The crucial, diachronic question could not be articulated until Teresias had appeared in the present as the harbinger of a possible future (Sophocles, 429 B.C./1994, p. 72). The question about Oedipus' beginnings signals the traumatic end to his imaginary, narcissistic self. At first, he violently rejects Teresias, banishing him from the city. But the seed of truth has been planted, and the progression towards knowing terrible truths soon follows.

Oedipus had been a rationalist, a man who could think the enigma but not live it. His illusion had been to believe that thinking the enigma would solve it: *Cogito ergo sum*. The truth of time proves otherwise. It is only after he has fulfilled the original Delphic prophecy that he can know his criminality, through time and reflection (Sophocles, 429 B.C./1994, p. 74). The Unpast can then become truly past, and wisdom can emerge, born out of terrible truth.

The Oedipus story is a dramatic instance of how living an engaged life can enable a recollection of the self from the Unpast, through time and narrative memory (Manoussakis, 2017, p. 83). We lack foreknowledge, and that fact is intrinsic to the human condition. Our dearly won wisdom comes through *phronesis*, not only through clever logic and reason. Oedipus is not merely a man who killed his father and married his mother but something more profound that penetrates to the core of the human condition. It requires time to reveal the nuances and multidimensional truth of human actions. The good is a temporal process, a complex process that is never complete (Manoussakis, 2017, n. 25, p. 181).

Some Later Thoughts: Alchemy

At age 79, Jung still held firmly to the idea that the unconscious is timeless, although his attitude had mellowed to some degree, and there is less of a sense of a tormenting division between archetype and everyday (Jung, 1976b, para. 1572):

Through the progressive integration of the unconscious we have a reasonable chance to make experiences of an archetypal nature providing us with the feeling of continuity before and after our existence. The better we understand the archetype, the more we participate in its life and the more we realise its eternity or timelessness.

Alchemy grew in importance for him. In 1954, he describes a transition from the 'personal unconscious' to archetypal symbols, but he described the relationship between the personal and the collective unconscious as a dissociation, more fluid and seemingly closer to a relationship of equals (Jung, 1967, paras. 480–481):

> *the symbol is not reduced . . . but is amplified by means of the context which the dreamer supplies* . . . the unconscious can be integrated and the dissociation overcome . . . [through] an experience of a special kind, namely, the recognition of an alien 'other' in oneself, or the objective presence of another will. The alchemists, with astounding accuracy, called this barely understandable thing Mercurius . . . he is God, daemon, person, thing and the innermost secret in man; *psychic as well as somatic. He is himself the source of all opposites, since he is utriusque capax* ('capable of both').

'Mercurius' describes a general process, involving not merely an 'archetypal' realm but seemingly involving embodiment. In any case, he seemed to shift away from the perspective of an overexciting, somewhat inflated, 'archetypal' realm that contrasted with the seemingly lesser dimension of the everyday, the personal. Edinger notes that the spirit Mercurius is a 'peacemaker, the mediator between the warring elements and the producer of unity' (Edinger, 1995, p. 31).

In mythology, Mercury was unique among the gods because he could transit between the worlds of divinities and men, and was concerned with everyday shopkeepers as well as gods (*Oxford Classical Dictionary*, p. 962). The end stage of the alchemical process is most often depicted in everyday, 'chop wood and carry water' terms, not some dramatic transcendence (Henderson & Sherwood, 2003, pp. 159–169).

Jung saw the Unicorn as a symbol of Mercurius, and the end plate of the Unicorn Tapestries at the Cloisters in Manhattan clearly shows, in the background, a symbolic 'royal couple' in jail, even as a lively marital festivity takes place. Perhaps this is a warning that there is danger in a too confident view of 'unity' (Cavallo, 2010, p. 70). In the hands of the 'Spirit Mercurius', the thread of life is always on the move!

This presents a view of a process that is experimental and inventive, in endless movement, yet remaining the same. 'Mercurius is a psychological concept [that] contains both reality and our subjectivity within itself'

(Giegerich, 2008, p. 137). This is an evolution beyond an excited discovery of 'the archetype' and represents a process that cannot be bottled up in the form of static mythic entities and symbols. Now, 'the history of the soul has entered a stage with which the stage of mythology is once and for all super-seded' (Giegerich, 2008, p. 137).

'Mercurius' has a strongly temporal sense of life flowing endlessly in all its strangeness and variations, its past, present and future. Each time and place has its own symbolic realm, its own temporal 'realities', and this is our fate, our 'thrownness'. We are stuck with whatever our time's real images and temporalities happen to be, and we are stuck with death at the end. It is part of ethics to know this, and to also know that life is change, and the future tends to appear in unexpected, even reviled forms. To disown or obstruct this temporal process is to disown life itself, and that is the essence of evil. This is what Jung seems to have learnt from being tossed about, but not fleeing from, the strange and stormy vicissitudes of his many-sided life.

A 1957 letter to Eric Neumann reflects many of his later thoughts, com-menting upon how limited we are in our capacity to foretell the effects of our actions: we can only know about it with time (my italics) (Jung, 1976a, p. 365):

> I know that I do not want to do evil and yet I do it just the same, not by my own choice but because it overpowers me. As a man I am a weakling and fallible, so that evil overpowers me. I know that I do it and know what I have done and know all my life long I shall stand in the torment of the contradiction. *I shall avoid evil whenever I can but shall always fall into this hole* . . . I am therefore like a man who feels hellishly afraid in a dangerous situation and would have run for his life had he not pulled himself together on account of others, feigning courage in his own eyes and theirs in order to save the situation . . . for anyone who passes off his shadow as a passing inconvenience or, lacking all scruple and moral responsibility, brushes it off as irrelevant, they offer dangerous oppor-tunities for aberrations in moral judgment, *such as are characteristic of people with a moral defect who consequently suffer from an intellectual inflation.*

This powerfully conveys the perspective of the aging Jung, reflecting on his rich and extensive memories, having been deeply engaged in all the dimensions of temporal existence. It feels very personal and everyday rather than 'archetypal'. He takes no refuge in transpersonal justifications or speculations. His profound honesty conveys a rare depth, an almost excruciatingly painful awareness of the raw truth of experience and of the human condition. This is the sort of ethical awareness that only comes with time. His profound declaration certainly approaches the Oedipal level of tragic recollection and the perspective of *phronesis*. It provides a moving summation of the ethical life of an extraordinary man, Carl Jung.

Notes

1 'Technics', refers here to technical practices as a whole; 'technology' refers to the amalgamation of technics and modern sciences.

2 As an example a virtuous person would be someone who is kind across many situations over a lifetime because of their character and not because they want to maximise utility or gain favours or simply do their duty. 'Virtue ethics' deals with wider questions such as how one should live, what is the good life and what are proper family and social obligations (Athanassoulis, 2017). In this writing, I will view 'morals' as normative social customs and practices, and 'ethics' as the philosophy of that realm of human experience, including the broader dimensions of good and evil. In practice, morality and ethics are often not clearly separable.

3 Nachträglichkeit refers to the continual revision of memory due to new experiences, as well as the discovery of enigmatic dimensions of pastness that influence – and open up – reconstructions of memory (Boothby, 2001, pp. 198–208). This concept has been developed especially by Lacan and the French school (Green, 2017). In Wider Than the Sky, Gerald Edelman has written of a similar process in the neuroscience of memory (2005, p. 99ff). The point here is that the dimensions of memory and the 'personal unconscious', are, potentially, almost limitless.

4 There is a footnote here referring to the 'transcendent function' in Psychological Types, Def. 51, 'Symbol'.

5 Jung has a deep insight here but then seems unable to stay with the idea that there is an enigmatic core of life that lies at the heart of human existence and is ultimately untranslatable (Hinton, 2009).

6 In many ways, Jung was a man of his times. 'For the philosophical tradition of the West, all spirituality lies in consciousness, thematic experiences of being, knowing' (Levinas, 1998, p. 99).

7 I use 'synchrony' here to describe a unified, unchanging self or culture – something timeless. In the early part of Oedipus Rex, both Oedipus and the Chorus equate the stability of his health with the stability and health of Thebes. They ask him to be unchanged, and he reassures them. 'Diachrony' is the intrusion of

otherness, of new truth, into the same, offering the possibility of a restoration of the flow of time. The initial picture is of a mood of dread and fear, trapped in a lifeless synchrony, anticipating the diachronic, disruptive events to come – in time. One could call synchrony pre-ethical because, without a temporal horizon, there is no way to ascribe an ethical value to an act (Manoussakis, 2017, p. 69).

8 By 'Unpast', Scarfone indicates experiences that have not acquired a quality of pastness but are not 'timeless' (Zeitlos).

References

Athanassoulis, N. (2017). "Virtue Ethics." *Internet Encyclopedia of Philosophy*. www.iep.utm.edu/virtue/.

Audouze, F. (2002). Leroi-Gourhan, a Philosopher of Technique and Evolution. *Journal of Anthropological Research*, 10, 4, 277–306.

Barreto, M. H. (2013). "The Unity of the Ethical and the Religious in Jung's Thought." *International Journal of Jungian Studies*, 5, 3, 226–242.

Barreto, M. H. (2014). "Requiem for Analytical Psychology: A Reflection on Jung's (Anti)Catastrophic Psychology." *Journal of Analytical Psychology*, 59, 1, 60–77.

Blommaert, J. & De Fina, A. (2016). "Chronotopic Identities: On the Timespace Organization of Who We Are." *Tilburg Papers in Culture Studies*, Paper 153. www.tilburguniversity.edu/upload/ba249987-6ece-44d2-b96b-3fc329713d59_TPCS_153_Blommaert-DeFina.pdf.

Boothby, R. (2001). *Freud as Philosopher: Metapsychology after Lacan*. New York: Routledge.

Cavallo, A. S. (2010). *The Unicorn Tapestries*. New York: The Metropolitan Museum of Art; New Haven & London: Yale University Press.

Colacicchi, G. (2015). *Jung and Ethics: A Conceptual Exploration*. Doctoral Thesis, Centre for Psychoanalytic Studies, University of Essex.

Colman, W. (2013). "Reflections on Knowledge and Experience." *Journal of Analytical Psychology*, 58, 2, 200–218.

Colman, W. (2017). "Soul in the World: Symbolic Culture as the Medium for Psyche." *Journal of Analytical Psychology*, 62, 1, 32–49.

Cortina, M. (2017). "Adaptive Flexibility, Cooperation, and Prosocial Motivations: The Emotional Foundations of Becoming Human." *Psychoanalytic Inquiry*, 37, 7, 436–454. https://doi.org/10.1080/07351690.2017.1362920.

DeCasien, A. R., Williams, S. A. & Higham, J. P. (2017). "Primate Brain Size Is Predicted by Diet But Not by Sociality." *Nature Ecology & Evolution*, 1, Article 112. https://doi.org/10.1038/s41559-017-0112.

Diego-Balaguer, R., de Martinez-Alvarez, A. & Pons, F. (2016). "Temporal Attention as a Scaffold for Language Development." *Frontiers in Psychology*, 7, 44. https://doi.org/10.3389/fpsyg.2016.00044.

Edelman, G. M. (2005). *Wider Than the Sky: The Phenomenal Gift of Conscious-ness*. New Haven: Yale University Press.

Edinger, E. (1995). *The Mysterium Lectures*. Toronto: Inner City Books.

Freud, S. (1895). *Studies on Hysteria (with J. Breuer). S. E., 2: 19–312*. London: Hogarth.

Giegerich, W. (2005). "Introduction." In *Collected English Papers*. Vol. 1: *The Neurosis of Psychology* (pp. 1–17). New Orleans: Spring Publications.

Giegerich, W. (2008). *The Soul's Logical Life*. Frankfurt: Peter Lang.

Giegerich, W. (1986/2008). "The Rescued Child, or the Misappropriation of Time: On the Search for Meaning." In *Collected English Papers*. Vol. 3: *Soul-Violence* (pp. 45–75). New Orleans: Spring Publications.

Goodchild, P. (2010). "Philosophy as a Way of Life: Deleuze on Thinking and Money." *SubStance #121*, 39, 1.

Green, S. (2017). "Lacan: Nachträglichkeit, Shame, and Ethical Time." In L. Hin-ton & H. Willemsen (Eds.), *Temporality and Shame: Perspectives from Psy-choanalysis and Philosophy* (pp. 74–100). New York & Milton Park, Abingdon, Oxon: Routledge.

Heidegger, M. (1967/1927). *Being and Time*. Trans. J. Macquarrie & E. Robinson. Oxford: Blackwell.

Henderson, J. L. & Sherwood, D. N. (2003). *Transformation of the Psy-che: The Symbolic Alchemy of the Splendor Solis*. East Sussex & New York: Brunner-Routledge.

Heuer, G. (2001). "Jung's Twin Brother: Otto Gross and Carl Gustav Jung." *Jour-nal of Analytical Psychology*, 46, 4, 655–688.

Hinton, L. (2009). "The Enigmatic Signifier and the Decentred Subject." *Journal of Analytical Psychology*, 54, 5, 637–657.

Hinton, L. (2015). "Temporality and the Torments of Time." *Journal of Analytical Psychology*, 60, 353–370.

Hinton, A. (2016). *Man or Monster? The Trial of a Khmer Rouge Torturer*. Dur-ham: Duke University Press.

Hursthouse, R. & Pettigrove, G. (2016). "Virtue Ethics." In *Stanford Encyclopedia of Philosophy* (pp. 1–43). Stanford: Stanford University Press.

Jung, C. G. (1936). *Wotan*. CW 10, paras. 371–399. Trans. R. F. C. Hull. New York: Bollingen Foundation.

Jung, C. G. (1944/1968). *The Symbolism of the Mandala*. CW 12, paras. 329–330. Princeton: Princeton University Press.

Jung, C. G. (1956). *Symbols of Transformation*. CW 5. Princeton: Princeton Uni-versity Press.

Jung, C. G. (1959). *The Archetypes of the Collective Unconscious*. CW 9i. Prince-ton: Princeton University Press.

Jung, C. G. (1960). *The Structure and Dynamics of the Psyche*. CW 8. Princeton: Princeton University Press.

Jung, C. G. (1961). *Freud and Psychoanalysis*. CW 4. Princeton: Princeton University Press.

Jung, C. G. (1963). *Memories, Dreams, Reflections*. Ed. A. Jaffé. New York: Vintage Books.

Jung, C. G. (1966). *Two Essays on Analytical Psychology*. CW 7. Princeton: Princeton University Press.

Jung, C. G. (1967). *Alchemical Studies*. CW 12. Princeton: Princeton University Press.

Jung, C. G. (1968). *The Unicorn in Alchemy*. CW 12, paras. 518–519. Princeton: Princeton University Press.

Jung, C. G. (1973). *Letters I: 1906–1950*. Eds. G. Adler & A. Jaffé. Trans. R. F. C. Hull. Princeton: Princeton University Press.

Jung, C. G. (1976a). *Letters II: 1951–1961*. Eds. G. Adler & A. Jaffé. Trans. R. F. C. Hull. Princeton: Princeton University Press.

Jung, C. G. (1976b). *The Symbolic Life*. CW 18. Princeton: Princeton University Press.

Kirkland, S. D. (2007). "The Temporality of Phronesis in the Nicomachean Ethics." *Ancient Philosophy*, 27, 127–140.

Levinas, E. (1998). *Otherwise than Being or beyond Essence*. Trans. A. Lingis. Pittsburgh, PN: Duquesne University Press.

Lieberman, P. (1991). *Uniquely Human*. Cambridge, MA: Harvard University Press.

Manoussakis, J. P. (2017). *The Ethics of Time: A Phenomenology and Hermeneutics of Change*. New York: Bloomsbury Publishing.

Merkur, D. (2017). *Jung's Ethics: Moral Psychology and His Cure of Souls*. Ed. J. Mills. New York: Routledge.

Mogenson, G. (2010). "Post Mortem Dei Jungian Analysis." *Spring 84: A Journal of Archetype and Culture* (pp. 207–270). New Orleans: Spring Publications.

Plato. (380 B.C./1992). *Republic*. Trans. G. M. A. Grube. Indianapolis, IN: Hackett Publishing.

Scarfone, D. (2006). "A Matter of Time: Actual Time and the Production of the Past." *Psychoanalytic Quarterly*, 75, 807–834.

Smith, D. W. (2012). *Essays on Deleuze*. Edinburgh: Edinburgh University Press.

Sophocles. (429 B.C./1994). *Oedipus Tyrannus*. Ed. & Trans. H. L. Jones. Cambridge, MA: Harvard University Press.

Stiegler, B. (1998). *Technics and Time, 1*. Stanford: Stanford University Press.

Tulving, E. (2005). "Episodic Memory and Autonoesis: Uniquely Human?" In H. S. Terrace & J. Metcalfe (Eds.), *The Missing Link in Cognition* (pp. 4–56). New York: Oxford University Press.

Whan, M. (2015, April). "The Logic of Image: Simulating 'Mythic Image': In Anselm Kiefer's 'Parsifal II'." *ISPDI Newsletter*. http://ispdi.org/index.php/en/newsletter/ispdi-newsletter-april-2015.

Whan, M. (2017). "Disavowal in Jungian Psychology: A Case Study of Disenchantment and the Timing of Shame." In *Temporality and Shame: Perspectives from Psychoanalysis and Philosophy* (pp. 242–261). London & New York: Routledge.

Williams, M. (1953). "The Indivisibility of the Personal and Collective Unconscious." *Journal of Analytical Psychology*, 8, 1, 45–50.

Yiassemides, A. (2014). *Time and Timelessness: Temporality in the Theory of Carl Jung*. New York: Routledge.

Zinkin, L. (1979). "The Collective and the Personal." *Journal of Analytical Psychology*, 24, 3, 227–250.

Chapter 14

The Unsilencing of Oedipus
Time, Monstrousness, Truth and Shame

Evil is, then, nothing more than the denial of life's trauma and as such, the nostalgia for non-existence, that is, the nostalgia for a timeless existence, which, since it was never given or experienced, means nothing else but the nostalgia for nothing itself.

– John Manoussakis, *The Ethics of Time*

Introduction

The rubric of IFPE's 2018 conference, 'Unsilencing,' denotes that something has gone unseen, but is starting to become visible. There is a mood of anxious hope in unsilencing, of a freeing from the structures of domination. It involves something that was concealed or lost becoming more visible, and emerging from a forgotten or frozen state, into the flow of *time*.

Unsilencing may evoke violent emotions that threaten the fabric of who we are, both personally and culturally (Caruth, 1996; LaCapra, 2000). Perhaps most, if not all, transformative action has its source in unsilencing (Vattimo, 2016). A turbulent remembrance of *monstrous acts and emotions* may rend our illusions of a neatly unified self or society.

At its best, psychoanalytic ethos involves voicing the *truth* of the hidden dramas that human beings must somehow face (Scarfone, 2016). *Shame* often appears amidst the terror of such exposure. The Oedipus complex is a profound depiction of unsilencing, and, is one of the core constructs that Freud used to convey his view of the human condition. This conception was a work of genius, emphasizing the father principle, the triangle of mother-father-and-child, and especially the development of the civilizing function of the superego. However, it evolved within the milieu of Freud's

DOI: 10.4324/9781003641063-15

Originally published in IFPE's online journal, "Other/Wise," Issue 1: Spring 2020: "UNSILENCING" www.IFPE.org

cultural and historical surround, when there was a greater sense of patriar-
chal 'knowing.' At present, it seems to have lost its pre-eminence in psychoanalytic theory, often occupying a side room rather than being the main
show (Fritsch, 2018; Perelberg, 2015).

Ironically, Freud never gave a systematic account of the Oedipus complex,
even though it lay at the heart of his approach from early on (Laplanche &
Pontalis, 1973). Over and over, he focused on the profoundly ethical truth
that there is a violence in human interaction that needs to be acknowledged
and sublimated, so that culture may exist (Fritsch, 2018; Perelberg, 2015).
By looking at some relatively Silenced aspects of the more comprehensive
myth of Oedipus, I hope to 'unsilence' Freud in ways that will better expand his relevance for our times. In this chapter, I will first summarise the
basic Oedipal story, using the play trilogy by Sophocles, as well as supple-
mentary sources, and then enlarge more specifically upon the four central
dimensions of *time, monstrousness, truth* and *shame*.

Oedipus: The Introductory Narrative

The Athenian audience was well-steeped in its own history and lore, the
wars with Persia and Sparta, the changing alliances between the Greek city-
states, and the advances in culture, including the mythic tales of Oedipus
and his family of origin. There was a strong, trans-generational aspect of the
myth. Laius, Oedipus' father, had been the perpetrator of a terrible crime.
According to Greek mythology, while entrusted with the care of Chrysip-
pus, the young son of King Pelops, he fell in love with him and raped him.
In his shame and anguish, the boy committed suicide. His father cursed
Laius, dooming him to the fate that, someday, his own son will kill him
and marry his mother, Laius's wife. It was also told that the goddess Hera
was so incensed by Laius' crime that she created the Sphinx to torment
Thebes, where Laius was king. Not all these details of the myth were fully
explicated in the Sophocles' plays – and perhaps the lapse is indicative of a
mythological inter-generational silencing (Priel, 2002).

The play goes on to show that because of the prophecy, Laius was determined not to have children, but one night when he was drunk, he conceived
a child with his wife, Jocasta. The child, of course, was Oedipus. To thwart
the curse, Laius pierced the nameless baby's ankles, and gave him over to
a servant, with instructions that he be left to die on Mount Cithaeron. However, he was saved by a passing Corinthian shepherd who took pity on him

Originally published in IFPE's online journal, "Other/Wise," Issue 1: Spring 2020:
"UNSILENCING" www.IFPE.org

and gave him over to the childless King and Queen of Corinth for adoption. Growing up, Oedipus was never told that he was adopted, however, his name, "Oedipus," means "swollen foot" – clearly hinting at his unusual origin. However, he became enraged when anyone enquired about his name. Like his father Laius, he was known for his rashness and irritability. Finally, he received a personal prophecy from an oracle, foretelling that he would murder his father and marry his mother. Thinking that this prophecy referred to his adoptive parents, he did not reflect, and instead left Corinth in an attempt to avoid that fate. Along the road to Thebes, the actual city of his birth, he met a group of men at an intersection, and the two parties attempted to pass simultaneously. There was an altercation, and King Laius, his father, was killed.

Oedipus: The Middle Narrative

Continuing on to Thebes – unknown to him that it was the city of his birth and the place of memories – he met the Sphinx at the portal of entry. This was a *monstrous* being with the head and breast of a woman, wings of an eagle, body of a lion, and a serpent's tail, who stood as a barrier. The creature challenged him with a riddle, which he had to answer at peril of his life. The riddle was: "Which creature has one voice and yet becomes four-footed and two-footed, and three-footed?" He answered quickly, "Man – who crawls on all fours as a baby, then walks on two feet as an adult, and then uses a walking stick in old age." The Sphinx vanished, and he assumed it had been destroyed by his cleverness. Oedipus gloried in his victory, flaunting his deed to the people of Thebes, and taking on an identity as the saviour of the city. Of course, he and they were totally unaware that he had already committed the monstrous crime of killing his father, Laius, the previous Ruler of Thebes.

Failing to reflect upon his encounter with monstrousness, Oedipus' rationalistic illusions hurled him further into its depths (Goux, 1993, p. 155). In the more ancient Egyptian culture, the Sphinx was the keeper of the most profound knowledge. Due to his shame and reactive disposition, he did not see that the riddle that referenced feet, might refer to him, the man named "swollen foot," who could never walk normally, due to the wounds of infancy, and whose progression through the stages of life had been violently disrupted from the beginning. Oedipus continually evaded the *truth*

Originally published in IFPE's online journal, "Other/Wise," Issue 1: Spring 2020: "UNSILENCING" www.IFPE.org

of his origins and had no curiosity about unsilencing his memories. On the surface, in his own eyes and in the eyes of the people of Thebes, he was the man who had vanquished the terrifying barrier to their city, the paradigm of the rational philosopher, and, the hero who could always keep memories and monstrousness at bay.

The city lacked a ruler because Oedipus had killed Laius during the incident on the road. In celebration of his apparent victory over the Sphinx, Oedipus was declared the new sovereign of Thebes, and married Laius' widow, his mother, Jocasta. Their four children, one of them Antigone, later had challenging fates as well.

Oedipus: The Culminating Narrative

The plays reveal that, after some years, a devastating plague arose in Thebes, and the populace was terrified. One imagines a cityscape littered with corpses. An oracle declared that the cause of the calamity was the continuing presence in Thebes of King Laius' murderers. Their discovery and banishment was ordered by Apollo, in order to end the moral pollution that caused the affliction. No one except the blind sage, Tiresias, realised that the plague was actually the return of the Sphinx/enigma in a new form. There was a cultural belief that the state of the ruler was synonymous with the state of the city. Therefore, the populace, in their anxious unknowing, pleaded with Oedipus to never change, clinging to the illusion that sameness, synchrony, resisting the flow of time, could insure well-being. Instead, sameness escalated ethical disaster and monstrous suffering. Ironically, following the oracle's commanding message from the gods to discover and banish Laius' murderer, Oedipus took it upon himself to find the killer. This quest for memory rapidly led to a violent eruption of truth, guilt, shame and horror.

Events culminated in the appearance of a Corinthian messenger with the news of the death of Oedipus' adoptive father, and eventually disclosed the facts of his biological parentage. The truth then emerged that, indeed, Oedipus was his father's killer, and his wife, Jocasta, was, in fact, his mother. Shame and horror overwhelmed him. His wife-mother hung herself, and he violently blinded himself. The 'unsilencing' of Oedipus to himself and to his world shattered that world, but his *eyepits* might then embody a different kind of vision, a different relation to being (Civitarese, 2008). In a later play in the trilogy by Sophocles, *Oedipus at Colonus*, Oedipus became a blind outcast who was more open to the world, finally immortalizing his life

Originally published in IFPE's online journal, "Other/Wise," Issue 1: Spring 2020: "UNSILENCING" www.IFPE.org

in a sudden disappearance in a sacred grove (Zupančič, 2000). The King of Athens then declared that place a shrine to be honored by the people of Athens.

Elaboration of Basic Themes

Now, I will elaborate a bit more on the four basic themes upon which I touched during the previous narrative. It takes *time* for new dimensions of our personal and cultural lives to become visible, for ethical awareness to emerge (Manoussakis, 2009). *Monstrous* events occur at the crossroads of individual lives and cultures, and these two paths feel torn asunder, as if struggling to maintain a sense of unity and integrity amidst the upheavals (Grotstein, 1997). Unpleasant, sometimes horrifying, *truths* confront us, and our deep *shame* makes us want to flee, blame others, or find ready panaceas.

To speak more of time: Temporal awareness is uniquely human (Tulving, 2005). It is closely interconnected with ethics and consciousness (Hinton, 2019; Manoussakis, 2017). The primal shock and awareness of death, the future destiny of us all, plays a primordial role in bringing time fiercely into consciousness. The first intentional burial practices appeared in the Middle Palaeolithic Age. Cave art appeared around 40,000 BC, and there was clearly an expectation of a regular return, a future. The paintings themselves were likely the recollection of a collective past, real or mythic, a combination of which is also seen in the Sophocles trilogy. Culture stems from anticipating the future, as well as preserving memories. Laplanche asked, why does a poet poetise, except for the hope of an audience "scattered in the future"? One could also imagine the future audience, looking back toward the creative poet of the past (Laplanche, 1999, p. 224).

Jonathan Lear regards *Oedipus Rex* as the fundamental myth of 'knowingness,' and laments the tendency toward too much 'knowingness' in psychoanalysis. For example, from Lear's point of view every transference is a unique creation with its own qualities, not merely an inevitable triangle. He also points out that there was no evidence at all that Oedipus was driven by what have come to be known as classical 'Oedipal wishes' (Lear, 1998, pp. 39–53 & 140).

Speed, not taking time for reflection, is also a major 'dis-ease' of our own era. Oedipus was always a man in a hurry, analytic and rational but unreflective (Lear, 1998, p. 43). For instance, when asked about his deformed feet, he did not wonder about the question in regard to his past, and instead became

Originally published in IFPE's online journal, "Other/Wise," Issue 1: Spring 2020: "UNSILENCING" www.IFPE.org

angry. After receiving the prophecy that he would kill his father and marry his mother, he acted impulsively, rather than feeling or reflecting upon the ambiguity of all prophecies. When he met the Sphinx at the entry to Thebes, he gave a superficial, rational response, and didn't reflect on its ancient nature, or upon why the enigmatic monster was there in the first place. When he first entered Thebes, Oedipus entered his place of memories, and showed that he was a man lacking in dimension. As Hans Loewald described, we all have the ethical task of turning our ghosts into ancestors (Loewald, 1960). This requires full participation in the flow of time, and honorable reflection on the past. This perspective has great relevance for us today.

As mentioned earlier, Oedipus encountered the Sphinx, a monster with the body of a lion, the head and breast of a woman, an eagle's wings, and a serpent's tail. In the gigantic monuments of Egypt, it was male, and was a guardian of the secrets of another dimension of being. In regard to the concept of monstrousness, we tend to deem a person, a behavior or an event monstrous when they exceed our capacity to comprehend them. There is a strong sense of horror and possible transgression, an emotional excess that we cannot assimilate. 'Monsters' tend to appear at times when cultures or individuals approach a profound crossroads of good or evil (Grotstein, 1997). Oedipus did not reflect upon his encounter with, or meaning of, monstrousness, and his unexamined 'victory' eventuated in incest and plague.

To the 'rational' mind, with its privileging of mastery and unity, the excesses of being such often feels monstrous and terrifying. Kristeva has written of the 'Black Sun,' and the semiotic 'Chora,' describing a pluralistic view of psychic reality that values the abject and overlooked in their multiplicity (Hinton, 2007; Yuan, 2016, pp. 191–201). From that point of view, coming into being means coming into differences, rather than into a unified symbolic order. It implies that there are events in life that are just not possible to assimilate, although consciously acknowledging such a reality may foster a wise humility.

Truth, the next prism of exploration, is perhaps the core ethos of psychoanalysis. Immersed in our 'knowingness,' we tend to take such a basic thing for granted, forgetting its crucial significance. It has repeatedly struck me over the years that too much of analytic training emphasises conformity over creativity and new truth. Free association and free play have the intention to allow new dimensions of truth to emerge, but they are often taught as techniques or rules, rather than as means to foster openness to novel perspectives (Bitan, 2012).

In the sense of the Greek term, *aletheia*, truth is a process of uncovering or disclosing something that makes life worth living. However, when we see one

Originally published in IFPE's online journal, "Other/Wise," Issue 1: Spring 2020: "UNSILENCING" www.IFPE.org

dimension, we tend to close off others. It is a never-ending process. Truth is something we see, but only really know upon reflection. Its effects are often violent, we want to evade it, and it can tear us apart and even destroy us. How much truth can we bear, personally or in our social and organizational life?

Last but not least is *shame* (Hinton & Willemsen, 2018). Shame is an indicator of great or small disruption in our sense of a unified self. We cannot escape its inner and outer gaze, and that is what can make it so unbearable. As Levinas said, shame occurs when we cannot hide what we would like to hide (Levinas). 'Skin shame' stems from the shaping of culture and family life, and at the extreme can lead to a stale conformity. 'Deep shame' can evoke profound questions about who we are and can have ontological dimensions. For instance, Primo Levi described shame when he left Auschwitz: not shame at having been a prisoner, but a shame that human beings were capable of doing such things (Filipovic, 2017).

It is important to note that Greek culture was a shame culture, not a guilt culture.

Guilt is closer to morals, a perception of specific wrongs done to others, while shame occurs because we have contemptibly fallen short of what we, or others, might have hoped of ourselves. Shame can understand guilt, but guilt cannot understand itself (Williams, 1993). The emotion of shame slows down the temporal flow and forces us to reflect, but at the other extreme can freeze the process of life. Living now in an age of shamelessness, at least on the surface, we keenly experience a lack of tact, mutual respect, and humility – all shame-related virtues. We project our monsters onto others. There is a devaluation of the importance of shame, and a tendency to view it as a symptom to be medicated rather than seen as a teacher (Hinton, 1998). Unsilencing our lives, to deeply experience the truth of what we have experienced and who we are, always involves deep shame and traumatic memories.

The broader Oedipus myth has deep relevance for all times, very much including our own and a lesson to be learned. It is well worth Unsilencing. I hope this small introduction, or for many readers a re-introduction, provides useful food for future thought.

References

Bitan, S. (2012). "Winnicott and Derrida: Development of Logic-of-Play." *International Journal of Psychoanalysis*, 93, 29–51.

Caruth, C. (1996). *Unclaimed Experience: Trauma, Narrative, and History*. Baltimore: Johns Hopkins University Press.

Originally published in IFPE's online journal, "Other/Wise," Issue 1: Spring 2020: "UNSILENCING" www.IFPE.org

Civitarese, G. (2008). "'Caesura' as Bion's Discourse on Method." *International Journal of Psychoanalysis*, 89, 1123–1143.

Filipovic, Z. (2017). "Toward an Ethics of Shame." *Angeliki*, 22, 4, 99–114.

Fritsch, R. C. (2018). "Review of *Murdered Father, Dead Father: Revisiting the Oedipus Complex* by Rosine Jozef Perelberg." *The Psychoanalytic Quarterly*, 88, 1, 213–221.

Goux, J. J. (1993). *Oedipus, Philosopher*. Stanford: Stanford University Press.

Grotstein, J. (1997). "'Internal Objects' or 'Chimerical Monsters?': The Demonic 'Third Forms' of the Internal World." *Journal of Analytical Psychology*, 42, 47–80.

Hinton, L. (1998). "Shame as a Teacher: 'Lowly Wisdom' at the Millennium." In Mary Ann Matoon (Ed.), *Florence (1998): Creation and Destruction*. Zürich: Daimon Publications.

Hinton, L. (2007). "Black Holes, Uncanny Spaces, and Radical Shifts in Awareness." *Journal of Analytical Psychology*, 52, 433–447.

Hinton, L. (2019). "Jung, Time and Ethics." In Jon Mills (Ed.), *Philosophizing Jung*. London & New York: Routledge.

Hinton, L. & Willemsen, H. (2018). *Temporality and Shame: Perspectives from Psychoanalysis and Philosophy*. London & New York: Routledge.

LaCapra, D. (2000). *Writing History, Writing Trauma (Parallax: Re-Visions of Culture and Society)*. Baltimore: Johns Hopkins University Press.

Laplanche, J. (1999). *Essays on Otherness*. London & New York: Routledge.

Laplanche, J. & Pontalis, J.-B. (1973). *The Language of Psychoanalysis*. New York & London: W. W. Norton.

Lear, J. (1998). *Open Minded: Working Out the Logic of the Soul*. Cambridge: Harvard University Press.

Loewald, H. W. (1960). "On the Therapeutic Action of Psychoanalysis." In Peter Buckley (Ed.), *Essential Papers on Object Relations*. New York: New York University Press.

Manoussakis, J. P. (2009). "Thebes Revisited: Theodicy and the Temporality of Evil." *Research in Phenomenology*, 39, 292–306.

Manoussakis, J. P. (2017). *The Ethics of Time: A Phenomenology and Hermeneutics of Change*. New York: Bloomsbury Academic.

Perelberg, R. J. (2015). *Murdered Father, Dead Father: Revisiting the Oedipus Complex*. London & New York: Routledge, Taylor & Francis Group.

Priel, B. (2002). "Who Killed Laius?: On Sophocles' Enigmatic Message." *International Journal of Psychoanalysis*, 83, 433–443.

Scarfone, D. (2016). "Interpretation beyond Meaning: A Brief Discussion of Virginia Ungar's Keynote Presentation." *Zeitschrift für Psychoanalytische Theorie und Praxis*, 31, 1, 54–58.

Tulving, E. (2005). "Episodic Memory and Autonoesis: Uniquely Human?" In H. S. Terrace & J. Metcalf (Eds.), *The Missing Link in Cognition* (pp. 3–56). New York: Oxford University Press.

Vattimo, G. (2016). *Of Reality; the Purposes of Philosophy*. New York: Columbia University Press.

Originally published in IFPE's online journal, "Other/Wise," Issue 1: Spring 2020: "UNSILENCING" www.IFPE.org

Williams, B. (1993). *Shame and Necessity*. Berkeley: University of California Press.

Yuan, Yuan. (2016). *The Riddling between Oedipus and the Sphinx: Ontology, Hauntology, and Heterologies of the Grotesque*. Lanham, Boulder, New York, Toronto & Plymouth, UK: University Press of America.

Zupančič, A. (2000). *Ethics of the Real: Kant and Lacan*. London & New York: Verso.

Originally published in IFPE's online journal, "Other/Wise," Issue 1: Spring 2020: "UNSILENCING" www.IFPE.org

Chapter 15

Man and Machine*
Dilemmas of the Human[1]

Prelude

This chapter is composed as a reflection that unfolds its dimensions revealed in the process of reading. Layers of thought and memory, of present, past and future, unfold as life experience, as a texture, not in a linear and machine-like fashion.

The central focus is a random happening on the streets of Seattle that disrupted the flow of the everyday, the familiar, and opened multiple dimensions of thought and imagination, leading from immediate impacts and impressions to a reflection on the nature of the human, the vicissitudes of capitalism and the sad history of chattel slavery and its haunting aura.

The epilogue is a brief reflection on the appearance of the coronavirus.[2]

The Encounter

One afternoon I went to the pharmacy to pick up a prescription, and when I emerged from the store, there was tension in the air. Cars were lined up in all directions. There was an African American man at the centre of the nearby intersection, loudly and energetically singing gospel songs. His performance was stopping the traffic. His voice was loud and clear, and he threw his head back to give full-throated expression to his songs.

The drivers were confused, some clearly angry and impatient, honking at times, and others looked puzzled or curious. Clumps of people along the sidewalks were attentively watching the scene, and it quickly engaged my full attention. What was going on?

My Capitol Hill neighbourhood in Seattle is at the edge of the urban core of Seattle, and 15th Street is filled with shops, restaurants and coffee

* Hinton, L. (2021). Man and Machine: Dilemmas of the Human. In: Ladson Hinton & Hessel Willemsen (eds.). *Shame, Temporality and Social Change: Ominous Transitions*. London: Routledge. Reprinted by permission of the publisher (Taylor & Francis Ltd, http://www.tandfonline.com).

DOI: 10.4324/9781003641063-16

houses. To the south is a region of apartment houses and small dwellings, as well as halfway houses, whereas to the north is an upscale area of larger family dwellings. It is a varied neighbourhood of the modestly affluent and the affluent, and many residents are connected with technology industries. The area is mainly white but with a broad smattering of people from varied racial and ethnic backgrounds. The atmosphere is moderately avant-garde.

The presence of psychotic or 'disturbed' people on the street is not at all rare in the neighbourhood, but this man did not have an air of fragmenting anxiety or explosiveness. He felt present to me and connected to the *surround*.[3] There wasn't a hostile edge in his voice or manner, and his presence felt almost welcoming. I intended to cross the street to have a cup of coffee, and as I approached the intersection, I could see that he was nicely dressed, as if prepared for a performance. He was of average height and build and was well-trimmed.

The man suddenly stopped singing, left the middle of the street and walked to the street corner that I was approaching. His demeanour had become quiet and contained, and it felt as if he were leaving a stage, like a performer who had done his job. The traffic quickly began to move normally, settling back into its constant, *synchronous* pace.[4]

People faded back on the street corner as the man approached. I hesitated for a moment, unsure of what might then emerge, but shrugged it off and proceeded to the crossing to wait for the light alongside him. The now-contained world of stoplights, pedestrians, traffic and crosswalks was reassembling itself. In a moment, I was there beside him.

The man was half a head shorter than me, and as I came closer, I could see that he now looked depleted, emptied of energy and slightly anxious, his posture a bit slumped as he gazed downward. He glanced at me out of the corner of his eye, with a quick look of appraisal and a glimmer of fearful uncertainty, subtly cringing, probably feeling the gaze of an affluent white man.[5]

His songs and his proud, expressive voice were still alive in my mind, and I felt an urge to respond to him, something beyond good manners or protocol, perhaps like the call-and-response mode of gospel (Williams-Jones, 1975, p. 375). Feeling friendly, I looked at him directly and said, 'You have a pretty good voice!' His visage changed abruptly, and his face suddenly looked almost joyful. Our eyes met, and I felt a momentary mutuality, a respect, a reciprocity. He shed the hint of cringe, the trace of shame at his visible performance (Jay, 1994, p. 311). The crossing light changed, and he gave me a quick nod, straightened his posture with a renewed air of pride, looked me in the eye and said in a clear voice, 'Thank you, brother! Thank you, brother!'

I was subtly but profoundly moved by this special moment of meeting. He and I crossed the street together, then he turned and proceeded quietly down the sidewalk, returning to his own workaday world, apparently satisfied that his more special work was completed for now. I went into the corner coffee shop and reflected on this incident that had disrupted my intimate territory. The experience has lingered in my mind ever since, provoking many dimensions of reflection.

On my immediate level of thought, I was struck how the event highlighted the presence of affluence, technology and race in my intimate space, a space that I, for the most part, took for granted. However, in such territory, the boundary of 'interior' and 'exterior' can always shift, in ways that are not clear, fostering an undercurrent of the *uncanny*.[6] Disruptive and yet exciting, such openings can lend a sense of uncertainty as well as possibility to life.

At yet another level, one could also see the implicit presence of race and slavery as the shadow of capital accumulation, along with technology and the temporal landscapes and enclaves associated with it. The man, with his song, was disruptive, even haunting, to the comfortable surroundings on the 15th Street. There was also a hint of something different, an openness to new life. The presence of the man and his song, as well as the contrasting levels of experience that he invoked, provoked my mind into a whirl of reflection.

My Perspective

This experience has percolated in my mind for several months now. It was dreamlike in a way, but to call it dreamlike would diminish it, not quite honouring its stark realness. My memories are probably different, perhaps quite different, from the experiences of others on the scene. I mused to myself, 'Were those really gospel songs the man was singing? How exactly was he dressed?' The memory has its shifting shades of real and less real, but the core remains absolutely clear and influences my sense of those surroundings and my strong take on events. In 2020, a Black man stood in that intersection near my house, singing gospel songs in an engaging fashion, not apparently angry or psychotic, and for a short period of time, totally *stopped the flow of traffic* in my familiar world.

We tend to take our intimate surroundings for granted, but it is the everyday 'grammar' of our lives.[7] The unspoken surround of past history is always with us (Slaby, 2020, p. 174). When we are surprised by disruptions of the synchronous, customary flow of everyday life, we often slow down or stop and become more aware of how much we are woven, unconsciously entwined in a deep-woven network of history and culture. Disruptions of the everyday and customary can open up diachronic time, revealing hints of imaginative, creative threads that we usually overlook because they are inauspicious, unapparent, hidden in the flow of everyday consciousness (Alvis, 2018, pp. 211–238).

My experience on 15th Street was a prime example. What had caught my eye most immediately at that time, when I first left the pharmacy and engaged the outside world, was the locked parade of automobiles stretching in four directions. The machines seemed to exude a pent-up energy and growling impatience, and their drivers peered out, some honking impatiently, others looking puzzled or angry.[8] When I spotted the man singing gospel was the fulcrum of the action, performing loudly in the middle of the intersection, it indeed felt like a fundamental encounter of man and machine – 'machine' with all its implications – in the midst of my everyday world (see note 1).

The everyday world has interconnections with the whole of human history, if you can let them surface in your mind. It is always there. 'Details' are not isolated facts but rest upon pulsating human life over millions of years. Without such a vast temporal perspective, human beings become creatures of the moment, lacking any anchor in the vast flow of time and lacking the sense of debt to the endless generations of ancestors who enable us to be (Bloch, 2008, pp. 2055–2061). To broaden that perspective, and its connection to the basic scene in the street, I will explore some deep background perspectives in myth, palaeoanthropology, philosophy and psychoanalysis. These perspectives will highlight my experience on 15th Street, illustrating the ongoing, everyday presence of multiple dimensions of human history, from evolution to slavery and racism, capitalism and technology.

A Story About Origins

Such a moving encounter evokes profound questions about the nature of the human, including the origin of our species. We seek insight about what is always already there in our human world. Using a genealogical[9] approach, Barnard Stiegler often refers to the myth of Epimetheus and Prometheus to lend perspective for understanding human evolution and especially the meaning and use of tools (Stiegler, 1998, pp. 187–188).

This is a creation story that begins with the making of creatures to populate the new world. Before that, there were only gods and no mortal creatures. The gods delegated an important task to two brothers, Epimetheus and Prometheus, who were also gods. They were to allocate special powers of survival to each new species to compensate for any deficiencies in their makeup. For instance, rabbits would be given speed to compensate for their lack of strength to fight. Epimetheus persuaded his brother to allow him to carry out the distribution of the special attributes. However, he was not a good planner and had a poor memory. By the time he got to the human race, he had used up all the compensatory powers. On the day they were to emerge into the new world, Prometheus came to inspect the result, and he found humankind naked, barefooted and defenceless. Fearing for the survival of the human race, he stole the gifts of art and invention, along with fire, from Hephaestus and Athena, and gave them to the human species to compensate for their weakness.

From that time, therefore, humankind had a share of the powers of the gods and erected altars and created images to honour them. Soon, using their gifts, humans discovered words and speech; invented houses and clothes, and shoes and bedding and grew food from the earth. They had some powers like the gods, but they were still human in other respects, such as mortality. Due to their unique origins, they were caught between worlds.[10]

Humankind was born of a double fault, an act of forgetfulness by Epimetheus and an act of theft, the crime of Prometheus (Stiegler, 1998, p. 188). Due to the original theft and its sequelae, the human race was also born into a conflict between the gods. This view of human genealogy is not a fall from an earlier state, a Paradise Lost, as depicted in the Biblical story of Adam and Eve. In the Greek myth, the species required rescue from a fatal vulnerability; there was no *loss* at their origin but a *fault*. There is a *de-fault of origin* or *origin as default*. This lends an important, humbler perspective to human existence. There is no lost Paradise to regain but only the flow of existence.

The stolen gift of the arts became technology in all its dimensions, of all our large and small 'machines' driven by their fire. This conveys the distinctive tone of human existence, according to Stiegler (Stiegler, 1998,

p. 188). *Man is a prosthetic being* who must depend on special, acquired qualities to survive, haunted by a sense of being 'in default' at the core.

From that perspective, one can reimagine the gospel singer confronting mechanical fire chariots on 15th Street, Seattle, his presence highlighting the fragile prosthetic defensiveness of the daily processions of machines and affluence. Through arts stolen from the gods, human beings developed their fire chariots as an ultimate prosthesis of speed and power. Despite this dramatic creation of speed and seeming invulnerability, an ancient sense of default and shame persists, along with a haunting awareness of mortality. Human beings try to evade the shame of their underlying sense of default and fear of death. However, nothing can erase the primal default of origin. We earthly creatures remain mortal and prosthetic, unlike the gods!

The Tool as Brainmaker

This genealogical story sets the stage for reflection upon some empirical findings regarding human evolution. There was a slowly emerging bifurcation in human development around 1.75 million years ago, a simultaneous step forward in both stonecutting and cortical development.[11] The freeing of the human hand and bipedal locomotion (erect posture) had set the stage for this possibility (Leroi-Gourhans, 1993, p. 70; McHenry, 2009, p. 263). It is not possible to say which developed first, the brain or the tool, as per Leroi-Gourhans:

> *A tool is, before anything else, memory* (my italics) . . . the transformations provoked by the technical . . . [evolved] . . . on a timescale that spans countless millennia. . . . One can hardly imagine the human as its . . . inventor; rather, one more readily imagines the human as what is invented.
> (Leroi-Gourhans, 1993, pp. 134 & 254)

Henceforth, it became difficult, if not impossible, to separate the 'who' of the human and the 'what' of *technos* (see note 1).

Tools involved *speed* in accomplishment, of environmental mastery, of the increasing possibilities for finding food. Tools also involved *anticipation* – an emergence of a sense of the 'what might happen' by means of a tool and the emergence of a sense of *time* (Suddendorf et al., 2009, pp. 1317–1324). In Simondon's words, 'Every technical gesture implicates the future' (Nielsen, 2017, p. 66; Simondon, 1965, pp. 17–23). This is the same speed and temporality that we now experience with our *light-speed* technology. Evolution has become no longer genetic but *the pursuit of living by means of other than life*, that is by means of *technos*: tools and language. Henceforth, *epiphylogenesis* supersedes *phylogenesis*, supersedes that which stems from the genetic makeup of the individual human being (Stiegler, 1996, pp. 135 & 140).[12]

Social groups were of course present from the 'beginning', but memory in its *external* forms adds vastly to the complexities and dimensions of communal existence. Stiegler describes a form of memory, 'tertiary retention', or tertiary memory that is essential in this crucial shift. This involves cultural memories and structures, history both written and 'forgotten', language forms, music, as well as, regrettably, advertising that manipulates and endlessly influences our patterns of consumption on all levels (Stiegler, 2014, pp. 34–35, 52–56, 88, & 89).

It is difficult or impossible to discern what is 'inside' and what is 'outside'. This quality is similar to what Lacan called the 'extimate' (*extimité*), 'something strange to me although it is at the heart of me' (Zwart, 2017). Our memories and our language – *technos* in general – are both 'inside' and 'outside'. This makes subjectivity possible and yet can feel 'Other', alien, uncanny. We live at that fulcrum. The happening on 15th Street was certainly an example of that.

There was no singular creative act or set of acts at the core of human emergence. We must live as the prosthetic creatures we are, as human beings who are always incomplete, whose origins are ambiguous and who are dependent on our prosthetic devices, especially those we drive down the street.

Capitalism and Desire

As creatures 'in default', human history often seems like an enactment of the Prometheus/Epimetheus story. Capitalism is the form of default and desire that dominates our own era. Since the development of the Jacquard Loom in the early nineteenth century, the savoir faire of the worker has been more assumed by the machine.[13] Machine memory is far superior to human memory, and the machine is also more capable of repetitive tasks. As we sit before our computers, we have access to a seeming infinity of memories on the World Wide Web. It never forgets.

Increasing human dependence on memory technologies and automation, as well as endless, complex incitements of desire through algorithms and advertising, has resulted in a diminished capacity to form dreams of a meaningful future. Stiegler terms this process 'The Proletarianization of the Mind' (Vesco, 2015). According to McGowan (2016), we live lives substantially controlled by the wedding of desire and capitalism: a kind of 'black hole' capitalism that never creates final satisfaction (Wilson & Bayón, 2016). Capitalism sustains subjects in a state of desire that keeps the system in motion. We are constantly on the edge of having our desires realised, *but we never reach the point of realisation* (McGowan, 2016, p. 11). This is an inherently unstable structure because no object is ultimately fulfilling (McGowan, 2016, p. 24). There is no perfect commodity. The power of advertising in all its overt and covert forms keeps us consuming the plethora of objects our smart machines present to us, but we are never satisfied because we are mortal creatures always 'in default'. 'Black hole' capitalism depends on the impossibility of final satisfaction to sustain the chain of production and consumption. If consumption were to stop, the system would likely collapse. This machine-like pattern seems independent of the formal qualities of government, capitalist or communist (McGowan, 2016, p. 19).

The people on 15th Street that were brought to a halt by the singing man were behind the wheel of their computerised, metal-skinned fire chariots, mostly on unthinking quests for satisfaction to buy or sell. His songs stopped the inexorable parade for a brief time. It was in many ways an act of courage. He brought the surroundings into a brief awareness of addiction to speed, consumption and the pursuit of some unnamable thing of the future (Stiegler, 2013, pp. 38–39). To be halted is to realise at some level, for a few moments, that addiction and the void or default that lies underneath. Awareness of our finitude can evoke a deeper sense of shame and guilt for our plight and a sense of responsibility to our ancestors and future generations. This is the vision of a moral future. The appearance of the man singing gospel had somehow, for a brief time, placed the speedy world of commerce and consumption into question. There was a joy in his tones, like a proud African American preacher, 'forged in the fiery furnace' of slavery (Chandler, 2017, p. 159). That memory still inspires and intrigues me.

Reflections: The Singularity of Being

Who was this man who sang gospel in the middle of the street? Was his act an act of madness? The mind wants to capture and then dismiss what disrupts experience, have it 'wriggling on a pin', captured in a cliché. Was he on a drug high, perhaps someone with an addiction who had been in a local halfway house, rebelling against the constraints of a drug program, imbibing some of the cannabis products readily available on 15th Street? Did he have a 'mood disorder' and was out of meditated control? It was clear that he had a religious background. Might he be a frustrated preacher, looking for a place to express his calling? Was his behaviour merely a manifestation of the politics and the confrontational dynamic of race?

'Madness' resists definition (Hinton, 2007, 2009). To quote Derrida (Derrida, 1978, p. 60; Stiegler, 2019, p. 145), 'From its very first breath, speech, submitted to the temporal rhythm and reawakening, is able to open the space for speech only by enclosing madness'. That is *madness calls forth speech*; 'it creates a caesura and a wound that *open up life as historicity in general*' (Derrida, 1978, p. 54). Without 'madness', things stay the same.

In his 'madness', I strongly believe that this man expressed the best aspect of the human race. His appearance on the street of machines was a singular act of 'mad' imagination, and 'singularity expresses the individual's nonnegotiable distinctiveness, eccentricity, or idiosyncrasy. It opens to layers of rebelliousness that indicate that there are components of human life that exceed the realm of normative sociality' (Ruti, 2010, p. 1113; 2014, pp. 297–314).

Our situational reactions are heavily influenced by the past, but some people are able to visualise and enact, something that shines forth as unique, a thread of emergence of a new dimension of being. 'It is precisely human creative activity that makes the human being a creature oriented toward the future, creating the future and thus altering his own present' (Vygotsky, 2004, p. 9; Zittoun et al., 2020, p. 5). I am indebted to this courageous man whom I briefly encountered on the streets of my city. His imaginative act evoked an interlude in the course of time that was free of the sway of the 'machinic unconscious' (Stiegler, 2016, p. 127). He helped me glimpse a future to come.

Historical Unconscious/Chattel Slavery

My experiences with the man in the street evoke layers of what one might call the 'historical unconscious' (Frie, 2020, p. 5; Zeddies, 2002). Intertwined with these levels is the obvious fact that the gospel-singing man was an African American with all the sad, complex and heroic history that entails. His performance provoked not only an awareness of the prosthetic creatures we are, compensating with our speedy omnipotence, but also the shameful heritage of chattel slavery in North America. This primal shame was certainly a major reason why his presence was disruptive. His presence evoked many levels of historical truth as well as our tendency to flee from it. To write history is to write trauma and to begin to own unclaimed experience (Caruth, 1996; Hinton, 2006; LaCapra, 2014). That is a difficult, gut-wrenching task. I am a white man, and although I have been involved in racial equality activities since my teenage years, the shame of that history still jolts me.

The evolution of chattel slavery – the commodification of human beings – began in North America in the 17th century. It is important to remember that this perverse institution coincided in time with the evolution of modern capitalism and the invention of computer-like machines and automated technology (Autor et al., 2001, pp. 3–4; Kolchin, 2016). The slave was a cog in the machine.

'Joy Songs, Trumpet Blasts, and Hallelujah Shouts' have been essential elements of the African American preaching tradition (Stewart, 1997). That inspiration kept hope alive and nurtured a sense of self and future amidst the chronic terrors of racism. When a person is reduced to nothing, a mere thing of a master, it forces them to face the raw reality of the human condition (George, 2018, p. 281; 2016, p. 70). It is that proud tradition that the man on 15th Street conveyed.

Gospel music epitomises the enduring depth and creativity of a pertinent African American culture. Its African roots, combined with Christian themes, represent a continuity with a past before slavery as well as something new and unique. It is a social music that calls for responses from the listeners so that they feel actively engaged. That responsiveness, with its play with discourse and language, is also very much a part of the split of jazz and blues. It is a democratic wellspring, a togetherness of audience and preacher or performer, incarnating a vision of hope both in the present and into the future. In a broader sense, it is a community of joy and a celebration of the creative vitality of the human race.

The man who sung gospel in the street brought the mad rush of things to a stop for a moment, proudly yet humbly offering his own perspective, drawing attention to another possibility, a slowing down and a hint of the joy that could emerge if given a chance. He shared a gift of possibility and joy, created amidst the catastrophic losses and cruelties of enslavement. The event will stay in my mind the rest of my life, especially in light of what later ensued with COVID-19.

Epilogue: COVID-19 and Miasma

As I was writing this chapter, life in Seattle and in the world radically shifted. The parade of cars on 15th Street vanished. A few scattered pedestrians scurry about the sidewalk, mostly wearing masks, alert and fearful that anyone might come close. The lively shops are closed except for grocery stores and pharmacies. A mood of miasma, a sense of deadly pollution, has come upon the land in the form of a deadly viral pandemic: COVID-19.

Twenty-five hundred years ago, during a plague in Athens, Thucydides observed (Manoussakis, 2020, p. 2; Thucydides, 431 B.C./2019, p. 51):

> It was appalling how rapidly men caught the infection, dying like sheep if they attended on one another; and this was the principal cause of mortality.

At the present time we are living this reality, much like the ancient Greeks.

The virus is one of a huge phylum of entities, a thing so tiny that it can barely be imagined (Huerta-Cepas et al., 2019). There are more viruses than stars in the universe (Wu, 2020). Philosophers debate whether viruses are actually forms of life because they cannot replicate on their own but must use biological life for reproduction (Koonin & Starokadomsky, 2016). We give each one a number and create virtual depictions of its structure to provide a reassuring sense of a manageable reality. However, it persists in its aura of an unassimilable real. This unknown thing pervades and disrupts our land and, like our ruler, has great resistance to the science and truth.

In *Oedipus Rex*, Thebes was also in the grips of miasma because their King Oedipus avoided the truth, taking attempts to speak the truth as a personal insult. The citizens encouraged his denial, and he became extremely angry when the wise men spoke of truth. He believed only in his personal will. When Oedipus finally learnt the terrible truth, it resulted in a profound personal and collective anguish.

This mythic story is a striking parallel with the present times. In the United States, we have a president who has a violent and visceral disdain for the truth. The free press is denigrated or eliminated, and scapegoats are blamed for any problem. Immigrants are violently mistreated, sometimes kept in cages as if they were the disease causing the problems in the land. They are treated like 'vermin' and are scapegoated and denigrated. Another disturbing truth of the pandemic is its disproportionate effects on the poor around the world, including many African Americans (Eligon et al., 2020). It often feels like a continuation of the heritage of slavery.

Our land is polluted, and we are in a crisis of truth. The pandemic has struck us and the whole world. Scientific knowledge, an aspect of truth that might save the land, is disparaged like an enemy. Truth nourishes the soul but can also be painful and shattering; it is our only real hope in times when endless lies pollute the land (Grotstein, 2004).

Like the age of Oedipus, our age is in a crisis of truth, and the disruption of a man singing gospel in the street was a small, disruptive harbinger of such truth, the truth of the pollution and madness of our world, the truth of our blind pursuit of money and power and the terrible truth of slavery.

A Black man singing gospel brought conventional traffic to a halt for a time on 15th Street and also brought a new possibility. It is uncertain whether our leaders and our populace have the capacity to endure the suffering that the future might entail. Truth itself is not a peaceful companion and often evokes deep disturbances and violent perturbations (Grotstein, 2004).

In the future, we may see glorification of a 'lost' group unity that never was, with continued persecution of minorities accused of bringing 'impurity' to the land, and perhaps flight to a parental regime that will maintain a facade of unity by algorithmic government and suppression of dissent. The dire unknown of COVID-19, with its economic and psychosocial impacts, will likely foment an exaggeration of these tendencies (Sly, 2020).

The challenge will be to maintain the stance of critical thought and reflection amidst these illusions, that is to hold fast to a respect for truth. It is possible that the capacity for critical thought has so deteriorated that the centre cannot hold (Sly, 2020). It may swing widely and over an extended period of time. However, the man on 15th Street provided a fragment of hopeful counsel that a future with care, joy and meaning can emerge from the worst of ominous transitions. He was also a living reminder of neglected truth.

Notes

1 I am using 'machine' to describe an imaginal entity that conveys an embodied sense of technology (Krakauer, 2020). For instance, we get angry at our computer when it crashes. In a much broader way, when we think of the World

Wide Web, we think of a concrete web of energy or light encircling the Earth. In these times, it conveys more and more a computational capitalism in which everything is calculable; we are all cogs in an economic machine, the opposite of care. Such an invisible algorithmic governability gives rise to images of a 'deep state' running things. This eventuates in a sense of victimhood and a proneness to totalitarian rule by 'saviors' (Stiegler, 2016, p. 23). *A dream that thinks can* provide hints and shreds of new realisations for a future worth living (Stiegler, 2016, p. 72). That is the core topic of this chapter.

I will use *technos* to imply all the uses that the human species has developed to be involved creatively with the environment, endogenous and genetic, or the exogenous givens of existence. This contrasts with pure nature that comes into presence on its own (Doucet, 2017, p. 3), I reserve *technology* to signify the mushrooming developments in memory and calculation since the coming forth of the Jacquard Loom in the early 19th century.

2 This encounter took place a year before a Minneapolis policeman murdered George Floyd, an African-American, during an arrest on May 25, 2020. There were extensive national and international Black Lives Matter protests and demonstrations, including many in Seattle, and often centred on Capitol Hill. The present chapter was written two months before the death of George Floyd.

3 I had extensive experience with psychotic patients during my residency at Stanford and in my early years of practice. R. D. Laing was a visiting professor. What is 'psychotic' and what is 'normal' is a difficult question. My own take on it is based on a gut-level feeling of how much a person is prone to go so far off the rails as to be enable to minimally adapt to everyday life. I do not romanticise madness. We all have mad parts, and these can be generative of creative works (Hinton, 2007; Kristeva, 1987, p. 87). Someone who cannot sublimate significant dimensions of their madness into creative, eccentric adaptation is usually in a chronically unhappy state – not a romantic exponent of underground 'truth'.

4 Levinas described 'synchronous' time as the time of sameness, of just going on, of everyday being. The disruption of the 'in-synch' traffic on 15th Street was 'diachronic'. In diachronicity, 'the self [is] pierced . . . by time's transcendent dimensions, the irrecuperable past and the unforeseeable future' (Gant & Williams, 2002, p. 44; Severson, 2013).

5 Eric Santner mentions the 'cringe' as a posture of the human being as a *creature* who is regarded as outside the law (2006, p. 86). I take this as feeling 'caught' in a sort of anonymous, collective gaze, and that brings into doubt any hope of recourse to ordinary authority or justice. It is akin to the 'downcast eyes' of shame but with an extra twist of exposure without recourse (Jay, 1994). It is related to the experience of those who are seen as 'outside the law', such as racial minorities, scapegoated groups and others who are seen as outside the normal structures of the state.

6 I am referring here to Lacan's term *extimité*. It implies that what is 'exterior' is also, potentially, the most intimate. That is 'inside' and 'outside' are not so distinct. The enigmatic otherness of the 'inside' is equally the enigmatic otherness of the 'outside' (Miller, 1994). The lack of unity or certainty regarding the boundary between 'inside' and 'outside' is also related to Freud's concept of the *uncanny* (Barnaby, 2014). In the setting of my neighbourhood, my emotional response transcended the 'inner' or 'outer'. The unusual event was indeed a bit uncanny.

7 For Stiegler [this] refers to the broader analytical process by which temporal and perceptual flows of all kinds are rendered discrete and reproducible through being spatialized, to the grammatisation of the manual gestures of the worker or the craftsman that are spatialised [by] being programmed into the machinery of the industrial revolution, and finally to what is unfolding right now: the grammatisation of 'everything' made possible by the inscription of binary code into central processing units composed of silicon.

(Ross, 2018, pp. 20–21)

8 The automobile is a useful tool that has gotten out of control. We don't have to recreate its fire on our own; it does that for us and translates that released energy to the wheels. It always 'remembers' and incarnates the human history with fire and tools in many ways (how upset we get when it won't start!). We merge with our mighty tools and feel safe and powerful behind the wheel and within its metal armour. It becomes a question of how much we control our technologies or they control us.

The automobile is also a symbol of unthinking mass production, consumerism and the spectre of climate change. Our complex technological tools often seem to function as a kind of 'grammar of our minds' (Stiegler, 2013, p. 19ff).

In the everyday sense, most of us enjoy our cars and find them extremely useful! Stiegler often uses the *Pharmakon*, which refers to the idea that things are both poison and cure. This is the best way to view the automobile. Now the 'poison' side has become a threat to our survival as a species. It is a good metaphor for our ambivalent relation to *technos* or *technology* in the present era (see note 1). The question is, how much have we become subservient to the remarkable tools we have created? Has the tool become the master? Do we drive it, or does it drive us? (Stiegler, 2013, p. 37).

9 'Genealogy is a form of historical critique, designed to overturn our norms by revealing their origins' (Hill, 1998). It was pioneered by Nietzsche and Foucault.

To produce the shock and confusion that are needed to help subjects to disengage from [their customary contexts and presuppositions] techniques of estrangement and confrontation with the unfamiliar . . . have to be used.

(Saar, 2008)

10 Later on, the behaviour of the human race was so destructive and turbulent that Zeus feared the species would destroy itself. Hoping to preserve them, he sent

Hermes to impart to humans the qualities of respect for others (*aidos:* shame, modesty, respect; a sense of finitude and *dike*, a sense of justice; Stiegler, 1996, p. 200).

11 The Zinjanthropian was discovered in 1959: it is an Austrolanthropian, dating back 1.75 million years, whose oldest biped ascendants go back 3.6 million years. It weighs about 30 kilos. It is a true biped: it has an occipital hole exactly perpendicular to the top of its cranial box. It has by then freed its rear legs for motricity: they are henceforth essentially destined to make tools and to expression, that is to *exteriorisation*. Its skeleton was found with its tools in the Olduvai ravine. Based on these facts, Leroi-Gourhan showed that what constitutes the humanity of the human, and which is a break in the history of life, is *the process of the exteriorisation of the living*. That which up to then was a part of the living, namely, conditions of predation and defence, passes outside the domain of the living: the struggle for life – or rather for existence – can no longer be limited to the Darwinian scene. The human conducts this struggle that we could say is spiritual in nature, by nonbiological organs, that is by *artificial organs that are techniques* (http://arsindustrialis. org/anamnesis-and-hypomnesis).

12 George Hogenson has discussed a somewhat similar idea that influenced Jung's ideas on evolution (2001, pp. 591–611).

13 The substitution of machinery for repetitive human labour has of course been a central thrust of technological change since (at least) the industrial revolution . . . What computer capital uniquely contributes to this process is the capability to perform symbolic processing, that is to calculate, store, retrieve, sort and act upon information. Although symbolic processing depends on little more than Boolean algebra, the remarkable generality of this tool allows computers to supplant or augment human cognition in a vast range of information processing tasks that had historically been the mind's exclusive dominion. In economic terms, advances in information technology have sharply lowered the price of accomplishing procedural-cognitive tasks (i.e. rules-based reasoning). Accordingly, computers increasingly substitute for the routine information processing, communications and coordinating functions performed by clerks, cashiers, telephone operators, bank tellers, bookkeepers and other handlers of repetitive information-processing tasks.

References

Alvis, J. W. (2018). "Making Sense of Heidegger's 'Phenomenology of the Inconspicuous' or Napparent (*Phänomenologie des Unschelnbaren*)." *Continental Philosophy Review*, 42, 211–238.

Autor, D. H., Levy, F. & Mumane, R. (2001). "The Skill Content of Recent Technological Change: An Empirical Exploration." Massachusetts Institute of Technology, Department of Economics, Working Paper Series.

Barnaby, A. (2015). "'After the Event': Freud's Uncanny and The Anxiety of Origins." *The Psychoanalytic Quarterly*, 84, 4, 975–100.

Bloch, M. (2008). "Why Religion Is Nothing Special But Is Central." *Philosophical Transactions of the Royal Society B*, 363, 2055–2061. https://doi.org/10.1098/rstb.2008.0007.

Caruth, C. (1996). *Unclaimed Experience*. Baltimore: Johns Hopkins University Press.

Chandler, D. J. (2017). "African American Spirituality: Through Another Lens." *Journal of Spiritual Formation & Soul Care*, 10, 2, 159–181.

Derrida, J. (1967/1978). "Cogito and the History of Madness." In Alan Bass (Trans.), *Writing and Difference* (pp. 31–63). Chicago: University of Chicago Press.

Doucet, T. A. (2017). *Heidegger, Foucault & Taylor: A Phenomenology of Technology and Being*. Field Exam Question #3, The University of Texas at Dallas.

Eligon, J., Birch, A. D. S., Searcey, D. & Oppel Jr., R. A. (2020, April 7). "Black Americans Face Alarming Rates of Coronavirus Infections in Some States." *New York Times*. www.nytimes.com/2020/04/07/us/coronavims-race.html?smid=em-share.

Frie, R. (2020). "Facing the Nazi Past: Silence, Memory, and Inhabiting Responsibility." *Psychoanalysis, Self and Context*, 15, 1, 5–9. https://doi.org/10.1080/24720038.2019.1688331.

Gant, E. E. & Williams, R. N. (2002). *Psychology for the Other*. Pittsburgh: Duquesne University Press.

George, S. (2016). *Trauma and Race: A Lacanian Study of African-American Racial Identity*. Waco: Baylor University Press.

George, S. (2018). "*Jouissance* and Discontent: A Meeting of Psychoanalysis, Race and American Slavery." *Psychoanalysis, Culture & Society*, 23, 3, 267–289.

Grotstein, J. S. (2004). "The Seventh Servant: The Implications of a Truth Drive in Bion's Theory of 'O'." *International Journal of Psychoanalysis*, 85, 5, 1081–1101.

Hill, R. K. (1998). "Genealogy." In *Routledge Encyclopedia of Philosophy*. New York: Taylor and Francis. https://doi.org/10.4324/9780415249126-DE024-l.

Hinton, L. (2006). "The Sheltering Sky." *The San Francisco Jung Institute Library Journal*, 25, 4, 61–67. Berkeley: University of California Press.

Hinton, L. (2007). "Black Holes, Uncanny Spaces, and Radical Shifts in Awareness." *Journal of Analytical Psychology*, 52, 433–447.

Hinton, L. (2009). "The Enigmatic Signifier and the Decentred Subject." *Journal of Analytical Psychology*, 54(5), 637–657.

Hogenson, G. (2001). "The Baldwin Effect: A Neglected Influence on C. G. Jung's Evolutionary Theory." *Journal of Analytical Psychology*, 46, 591–611.

Huerta-Cepas, J., Szklarczk, D., Heller, D., Hernández-Plaza, A., Fborkorslund, S. K., Cook. Mende, D. R., Letunic, I., Rattel, T., Jensen, L. J., von Mering, C. &

Bork, P. (2019). "eggNOG 5.0: A Hierarchical, Functionally and Phylogeneti-cally Annotated Orthology Resource Based on 5090 Organisms and 2502 Viruses." *Nucleic Acids Research*, 27, Database Issue, D309–D314. https://doi.org/10.1093/nar/gky1085.

Jay, M. (1994). *Downcast Eyes: The Denigration of Vision in Twentieth Century French Thought*. Berkeley: University of California Press.

Kolchin, P. (2016). "Slavery, Commodification, and Capitalism." *American History*, 44, 217–226. Baltimore: Johns Hopkins University Press.

Koonin, E. V. & Starokadomsky, P. (2016). "Are Viruses Alive? The Replicator Paradigm Sheds Decisive Light on an Old But Misguided Question." *Studies in the History and Philosophy of Sciense Part C*, 59, 125–134.

Krakauer, D. C. (2020, April 20). "At the Limits of Thought." *Aeon*.

Kristeva, J. (1987). *Tales of Love*. NY: Columbia University Press.

LaCapra, D. (2014). *Writing History, Writing Trauma*. Baltimore: Johns Hopkins University Press.

Leroi-Gourhans, A. (1993). *Gesture and Speech*. Trans. Anna Bostock Berger. Cambridge, MA: MIT Press.

Manoussakis, J. P. (2020). "The City is Sick." *Church Life Journal*, 1–8. University of Notre Dame.

McGowan, T. (2016). *Capitalism and Desire: The Psychic Cost of Free Markets*. New York: Columbia University Press.

McHenry, H. M. (2009). "Human Evolution." In Michael Ruse & Joseph Travis (Eds.), *Evolution: The First Four Billion Years* (p. 263). Cambridge, MA: The Belknap Press of Harvard University Press.

Miller, J.-A. (1994). "Extimité." In Mark Brasher, Marshall Alcorn, Ronald Cor-thell & Françoise Massardier-Kenney (Eds.), *Lacanian Theory of Discourse* (pp. 74–87). New York: New York University Press.

Nielsen, M. A. (2017). *What Makes Us Who We Are: On the Relationship between Human Existence and Technics, Thinking and Technology, and the Philosopher and the Technician*. Unpublished Master's Thesis, University of Oslo, Oslo.

Ross, D. (2018). "Introduction." In B. Stiegler (Ed.), *The Neganthroprocene* (pp. 5–32). London: Open Humanities Press.

Ruti, M. (2010). "The Singularity of Being: Lacan and the Immortal Within." *Journal of the American Psychoanalytic Association*, 58, 1113. https://doi.org/10.1177/0003065110396083.

Ruti, M. (2014). "In Search of Defiant Subjects: Resistance, Rebellion, and Po-litical Agency in Lacan and Marcuse." *Psychoanalysis, Culture & Society*, 19, 297–314.

Saar, M. (2008). "Understanding Genealogy: History, Power, and the Self." *Journal of the Philosophy of History*, 2, 295–314. Leiden: Brill NV.

Santner, E. L. (2006). *On Creaturely Life*. Chicago and London: The University of Chicago Press.

Severson, E. (2013). *Levina's Philosophy of Time: Gift, Responsibility, Diachrony, Hope*. Pittsburgh: Duquesne University Press.

Simondon, G. (1965). "Culture and Technics." Translated by Olivia Lucca Fraser, Revised by Giovanni Menegalle in *Radical Philosophy*, 189, January–February 2015, 17–23.

Slaby, J. (2020). "The Weight of History: From Heidegger to Afro-Pessimism." In L. Guidi & T. Rentsch (Eds.), *Phenomenology as Performative Exercise*. Leiden & Boston: Brill NV.

Sly, L. (2020, April 19). "Stirrings of Unrest Around the World Could Portend Turmoil as Economies Collapse." *Washington Post*. www.washingtonpost.com/world/coronavirus-protests-lebanon-india-iraq/2020/04/19/1581dde4-7e5f-1-lea-84c2-0792d8591911-story.html.

Stewart, C. F. (1997). *Joy Songs, Trumpet Blasts, and Hallelujah Shouts*. Lima, OH: CS Publishing Company.

Stiegler, B. (1996/1998). *Technics and Time*. Vol. 1: *The Fault of Epimetheus*. Stanford: Stanford University Press.

Stiegler, B. (2013). *What Makes Life Worth Living: On Pharmacology*. Malden, MA: Polity Press.

Stiegler, B. (2014). *Symbolic Misery*. Book 1: *The Hyperindustrial Epoch*. Trans. Barnaby Norman. Malden, MA: Polity Press.

Stiegler, B. (2016). *Automatic Society*. Vol. 1: *The Future of Work*. Trans. Dan Ross. Malden, MA: Polity Press.

Stiegler, B. (2019). *The Age of Disruption: Technology and Madness in Computational Capitalism*. Malden, MA: Polity Press.

Suddendorf, T., Addis, D. R. & Corballis, M. C. (2009). "Mental Time Travel and the Shaping of the Human Mind." *Philosophical Transactions of the Royal Society B*, 364, 1317–1324. https://doi.org/10.1098/rstb.2008.0301.

Thucydides. (431 B.C./2019). *The History of the Peloponnesian War*. Trans. Richard Crawley. Compass Circle.

Vesco, S. (2015). "Collective Disindividuation and/or Barbarism: Technics and Proletarianization." *Boundary 2*, 42, 2. Duke University Press.

Vygotsky, L. S. (2004). "Imagination and Creativity in Childhood." *Journal of Russian & East European Psychology*, 42, 1, 7–97. https://doi.org/10.1080/106 10405.2004.11059210.

Williams-Jones, P. (1975). "A Crystallization of the Black Aesthetic." *Ethnomusicology*, 19, 3, 373–385.

Wilson, J. & Bayón, M. (2016). "Black Hole Capitalism." *City*, 20, 3, 350–367. London: Routledge.

Wu, K. J. (2020, April 15). "There Are More Viruses Than Stars in the Universe: Why Do Only Some Infect Us?" *National Geographic*. www.nationalgeographic.com/science/2020/04/factors-allow-viruses-infect-humans-coronaviius.html.

Zeddies, T. J. (2002). "Behind, beneath, above, and beyond: The Historical Unconscious." *Journal of the American Academy of Psychoanalysis*, 30, 2, 211–229.

Zittoun, T., Glåveanu, V. & Hawlina, H. (2020). "A Sociocultural Perspective on Imagination." In Anna Abraham (Ed.), *Cambridge Handbook of the Imagination*. Cambridge: Cambridge University Press.

Zwart, H. (2017). "'Extimate' Technologies and Techno-Cultural Discontent: A Lacanian Analysis of Pervasive Gadgets." *Techné: Research in Philosophy and Technology*, 21, 1, 24–55.

Bibliography

Hinton, L. (1960). *Husserl's Definition of the Term, Transcendent: A Study in the Use of a Concept.* Unpublished Thesis, University of Arkansas.

Hinton, L. (1978). *Humor and the Transcendent Function.* Fifth Annual Conference of the Societies of Jungian Analysts of Northern and Southern California, etc., 20–35.

Hinton, L. (1979). Jung's Approach to Therapy with Mid-Life Patients. *Journal of the American Academy of Psychoanalysis*, 7, 525–541.

Hinton, L. (1980). Fools, Foolery and Feeling Foolish. *Psychological Perspectives*, 12, 43–51.

Hinton, L. (1993). "The Goose Girl." In Murray Stein & Lionell Corbett (Eds.), *Psyche's Stories: Modern Jungian Interpretations of Fairy Tales.* Illinois: Chiron Publications.

Hinton, L. (1993). "A Return to the Animal Soul." *Psychological Perspectives*, 28, 47–60.

Hinton, L. (2001). *The Hunt for the Wild Unicorn; Containment, Sacrifice, and Evolution.* Paper Presented at the National Conference of Jungian Analysts. Santa Monica, California.

Hinton, L. (2007). "Black Holes, Uncanny Spaces and Radical Shifts in Awareness." *Journal of Analytical Psychology*, 52, 433–447.

Hinton, L. (2008). "Teaching 'Origins of Depth Psychology': Overview and Candidate-Members' Experience." *Journal of Analytical Psychology*, 53, 91–100.

Hinton, L. (2009). "The Enigmatic Signifier and the Decentred Subject." *Journal of Analytical Psychology*, 54, 637–657.

Hinton, L. (2015). "Temporality and the Torments of Time." *Journal of Analytical Psychology*, 60, 353–370.

Hinton, L. (2018). "Is Jung Existential or Not? Reflections on Temporality and Everydayness." *Journal of Humanistic Psychology*, 61, 5, 1–12.

Hinton, L. (2018). "Shame and Temporality in the Streets: Consumerism, Technology, Truth and Raw Life." In Ladson Hinton & Hessel Willemsen (Eds.), *Temporality and Shame.* London: Routledge.

Hinton, L. (2018). *Trauma, Shame & Shifts in Ethical Consciousness: Joseph Conrad's Lord Jim.* Paper Presented at the Annual Meeting of the New School of Analytical Psychology, Seattle.

Hinton, L. (2019). "Jung, Time and Ethics." In Jon Mils (Ed.), *Jung and Philosophy*. London: Routledge.

Hinton, L. (2021). "Man and Machine: Dilemmas of the Human." In Ladson Hinton & Hessel Willemsen (Eds.), *Shame, Temporality and Social Change: Ominous Transitions*. London: Routledge.

Hinton, L. (2021). "The Unsilencing of Oedipus: Time, Monstrousness, Truth, and Shame." *Internal Forum for Psychoanalytic Education*, 1, Spring 2020 (Online Other/Wise).

Hinton, L. (2025). "Love, Death and the Infernal Machine." In Lius Moris (Ed.), *Confronting Death*. Ashville: Chiron Publications.

Hinton, L., III, Hinton, L., IV, Hinton, D. & Hinton, A. (2011). "Panel: Unus Mundus Transcendent Truth or Comforting Fiction? Overwhelm and the Search for Meaning in a Fragmented World." *Journal of Analytical Psychology*, 56, 375–380.

Hinton, L. & Willemsen, H. (2018). *Temporality and Shame*. London: Routledge.

Hinton, L. & Willemsen, H. (2021). "An Interview with Ladson Hinton, Conducted by Hessel Willemsen on 5th April 2021." *Journal of Analytical Psychology*, 66, 1206–1220.

Hinton, L. & Willemsen, H. (2021). *Shame, Temporality and Social Change: Ominous Transitions*. London: Routledge.

Index

Note: page numbers followed by an 'n' indicate a note on the indicated page.

For Product Safety Concerns and Information please contact our EU
representative GPSR@taylorandfrancis.com
Taylor & Francis Verlag GmbH, Kaufingerstraße 24, 80331 München, Germany

www.ingramcontent.com/pod-product-compliance
Lightning Source LLC
Chambersburg PA
CBHW050637280326
41932CB00015B/2678